To my good friends
Clarence and Barbara -
What a joy it is to share
the Founder's experience
with you

Love,
Hyatt Carbon

Thinking Is the Best Way to Travel

Essays along the Journey

by

Hyatt Carter

authorHOUSE®

AuthorHouse™
1663 Liberty Drive, Suite 200
Bloomington, IN 47403
www.authorhouse.com
Phone: 1-800-839-8640

First published by AuthorHouse 1/31/2008

ISBN: 978-1-4343-5945-2 (sc)

Library of Congress Control Number: 2007910311

Cover Image: R. Stöckli, A. Nelson, F. Hasler
         NASA/GSFC/NOAA/USGS

Printed in the United States of America
Bloomington, Indiana

This book is printed on acid-free paper.

For Linda

Contents

Introduction

The American philosopher Charles Hartshorne once remarked, "The great adventures of my life have been books." By this I assume he meant both the *reading* of certain great books and also the adventures of *writing* more than twenty books of his own.

The adventures of ideas last for a lifetime, even for someone who enjoys exceptional longevity, as did Hartshorne, who lived to 103, and was especially active, intellectually, in his eighth and ninth decades. These essays express some of the adventures I've enjoyed with books, ideas, and the thinkers behind them. Many have already appeared in print, in periodicals, and three of the longer ones are papers I presented at national conventions.

The division into four sections, symbolized by the four elements— Air, Earth, Water, and Fire—is perhaps more intuitive than cerebral, but there is method nonetheless.

In Part One, the clear air of reason provides room, and ground, for adventurous flights of imagination and, especially in the Goethe piece, a cleansing, or better, a *transformation* of the windows of perception.

Part Two is more down-to-earth and invites participation in several practical adventures or techniques for cultivating mental and spiritual faculties and growing in consciousness.

Water is one of our richest metaphors that finds protean expression in the path of spirituality, explored in Part Three, as well as in all great literature and in the other arts.

Part Four concerns the liberating and refining fire of philosophy, namely the adventurous frontier of *process philosophy*, as first conceived and clearly formulated by Alfred North Whitehead, further developed by Charles Hartshorne, and now carried robustly forward by the worldwide community of process thinkers and scholars.

Traveling with Whitehead, understanding his *new* way of thinking, can be both a challenge and the best of fun, as two examples reveal:

In what may seem at first almost as baffling as a Zen koan, Whitehead invites us to wonder about this question: "Does the thinker create the thought, or the thought, the thinker?" You know how Descartes would answer, or at least I *think* you do; I am, therefore, confident that, even now, you are beginning to suspect that Whitehead's answer,* and thinking, is the exact opposite, and that he reverses, and thereby corrects, what was topsy-turvy in the thought of Descartes.

In yet another utterance to make you stop and wonder, Whitehead makes the assertion that "No thinker thinks twice." While we may easily agree with Heraclitus that no one steps twice into the same river . . . but more about this later.

Thinking *is* the best way to travel!

*Whitehead's answer can be found in his magnum opus, *Process and Reality*, in section 3 of chapter 6, pp. 147-51 (Corrected Edition).

As many of you will recognize, the title—*Thinking Is the Best Way to Travel*—is a line from The Moody Blues' song, "The Best Way to Travel."

Part One
Air

Butterflies:
Metaphors of Transformation

In all places and at all times, the whole world over, the butterfly has enchanted people who have beheld this flower that flutters by on wings. In France it's *papillon*, Spaniards call it *mariposa*, and in Portugal they say *borboleta*. The Irish, delving deep into the Celtic imagination, came up with a word for "butterfly" that tingles the spine. In their native Gaelic they call it *dealbhan-dé*, which means the "fire of God."

And not only in this world, but far beyond, in the deep distances of outer space, are what are called Butterfly Nebulae—late phases in the evolving life of stars when they begin to cool as "red giants" and eject huge clouds of gas and dust that form symmetrical patterns in the shape of butterflies. Some evolve so rapidly that astronomers speak of watching the heavenly butterflies as they emerge from a chrysalis of stellar dust.

From the dim recesses of antiquity up to the present moment, people have felt both inspiration and fascination for the process, called metamorphosis, whereby the humble caterpillar is transformed into the beauty of a butterfly. It so inspired the ancient Egyptians that they imitated the process with their practice of mummification. The mummy—an embalmed human body wrapped in strips of linen, layer upon layer, from head to toe—bears a striking resemblance to the chrysalis that hardens around a freshly molted caterpillar as it enters the pupal phase that will transform it into a butterfly. Whoever it was who first saw metamorphosis as a metaphor, pointing the way to possibilities of transcendence—whatever else he was, surely he, or she, was a poet.

This essay will explore what I see as two intertwining themes of the butterfly metaphor: one stemming from that branch of biology which studies insects, and the other deriving from meteorology, the study of weather patterns. The latter theme is called the Butterfly Effect.

The Butterfly Effect

In 1979, at a meeting of the American Association for the Advancement of Science, Edward Lorenz, a meteorologist from MIT, presented a paper on the dynamics of weather systems. The title of the paper posed an intriguing question: "Does the Flap of a Butterfly's Wings in Brazil Set Off a Tornado in Texas?" The principle he advanced in this seminal paper was that predictability on a global level was as uncertain as quantum theory had shown it to be in the micro-realm of subatomic particles.

This principle came to be called the "Butterfly Effect," and it exemplifies yet another of contemporary science's departures from the neat and tidy world of Newtonian physics. In Newton's scheme of things, equal and opposite reactions are the rule, but with the idea of the Butterfly Effect, small initial causes can produce momentous consequences.

The Butterfly Effect is thus a powerful metaphor suggesting that the same principle can work in our lives.

As a concrete example to illustrate this, consider the image of the civil rights pioneer, Rosa Parks, sitting quietly on a bus in Montgomery, Alabama. That was the first day of December, 1955, an otherwise ordinary day—but not for long. When ordered to yield her seat to a white man, Rosa quietly and steadfastly refused. This was a courageous act, true enough, but still, it was action on a small scale. And yet, as the many entailments began to unfold, it would trace the slow curve of an upward spiral that would ignite the career of Martin Luther King, Jr., and change forever the consciousness, and the conscience, of a nation.

Rosa's demonstration of the Butterfly Effect shows that even a modest beginning can have the potentiality to result in revolutionary change. This is a model for all of us to ponder in terms of personal and planetary transformation.

The Butterfly Metaphor

First, some basics on butterflies. The stages in the life cycle of a butterfly reveal an archetypal fourfold pattern:

1. egg
2. larva, or caterpillar
3. pupa
4. imago, the adult butterfly

Egg and Larval Stages:

The tiny butterfly egg is the size of a pinhead, and female butterflies lay their eggs on plants that will later serve as a source of food when the larva, or caterpillar, is hatched.

The defining characteristic of a caterpillar is its appetite. This voracious worm spends its time gobbling one leaf after another and grows so rapidly that it must shed its skin several times to accommodate growth. By way of comparison, if a human baby were to grow as fast as a caterpillar, in one month it would weigh several tons and be the size of a London double-decker bus. The purpose of this exponential growth is to supply a rich reservoir of energy for the next phase of metamorphosis.

Pupal Stage—Metamorphosis:

As the larval stage comes to an end, the caterpillar attaches itself to a twig, or some other vegetation, where it hangs upside down and sheds its skin for the last time. The soft and moist outer surface of the caterpillar's body begins to harden to form a shell (a chrysalis) that will serve as protection and camouflage during the stage of metamorphosis.

Within the chrysalis, amazing events begin to happen. First, by a process called histolysis, the body and internal organs of the caterpillar are liquefied and turned into a cellular soup.

And now the key players, hitherto dormant, make their presence felt. At strategic areas within the organic soup, special cells cluster together in small islands of pure potentiality. These tiny but robust centers of creativity are called imaginal cells (or imaginal discs) and they initiate and guide the developmental process that will generate the

5

organs and tissues that constitute the *imago*, the adult butterfly. There is also a holistic flow of information as the clusters communicate with one another so that, together, they form a constellation of coordinated creative activity. This is necessary because the many parts they fashion must become not merely an *assemblage of parts*, like an automobile, or a computer; they must become *one organic entity*, a living and breathing unity—a butterfly.

Imago Stage—the Adult Butterfly

When the metamorphosis is complete, the chrysalis splits open and the butterfly emerges, unfurls her colorful wings and readies them for flights of adventure the caterpillar could, perhaps, only dream about. For what is a butterfly but the realization of a caterpillar's dream?

The Fourfold Constant

Along with three and seven, four is a richly symbolic and mythic number that seems to turn up all over the place: four elements, four seasons, four directions, four dimensions (in our universe), DNA and RNA both have four bases . . . the list is long indeed, and you no doubt can think of many more.

The Scottish entomologist David Spooner has made a brilliant exploration of this, and a fourfold theme weaves a meandering path throughout his *four* books.[1] In an analogy to the many constants in science, such as Planck's constant, he calls this the Fourfold Constant[2] and his many examples show that it has cosmic scope.

In one of his many insightful "patterns that connect," he compares the movements of a symphony to the life cycle of a butterfly:

"In the first movement, themes are stated (the egg, or by some recent interpretations the proto-larva); the second movement proceeds slowly like a caterpillar; the third, such as the scherzo of the *Eroica*, tends to be febrile and anticipatory like a shimmering chrysalis trembling with incipient finality; while the fourth usually represents a summation, which as Berlioz analyzed in relation to Beethoven's composition, leads from tension to release, from compulsion to liberation, from the tragic to the joyous . . . As listeners or performers, we travel through these stages as the musical form unfolds. . . . [T]he four-movement symphony had already become dominant even by 1780, although three-movement ones continued to be composed. In other words, the very fabric of the great period of classical achievement is both an anthem to quaternity, and a reverberation of the insect connection. The great works of Haydn, Mozart and Beethoven, and those who followed them, are metaphysical to our consciousness, yet have a very real basis in the natural world."

For those who have ears to hear, the experience of listening to a symphony is thus "a passing through four major stages of intellectual and spiritual life corresponding to the four stages undergone by those insects that undergo complete metamorphosis. In other words, the key works of Beethoven, Mozart, Haydn, and Brahms, suggest an especially exact resemblance between music and our sense of time passing, of *growth*."

The emphasis that science has placed on our close "family" connection with the higher apes, a connection that becomes apparent when you visit the primate section of any zoo, can obscure the closer connection we have with insects on a developmental level or in terms of the evolution of consciousness. One of Spooner's main contentions is that "the indisputable primate connection has caused mainstream evolutionary theory to miss the all-round interrelationship of human development to entomology, and that this relation is enshrined in the greatest of the higher art forms and religion. There is a crucial oblique relationship between metamorphic insects and humans, a connection transmitted through the great works of music and literature, and through many of the paradigms of world religions."

Spooner traces variations of this fourfold theme as it flowers in the works of novelists Herman Melville, William Faulkner, Vladimir Nabokov, Joseph Conrad, Franz Kafka, and James Joyce; poets William Blake, Samuel Coleridge, William Butler Yeats, T. S. Eliot, and Dylan Thomas; twentieth-century Spanish literature; and the author of *Walden*, Henry David Thoreau.

I can't resist mentioning that Spooner finds significance in Eliot's last great work: *Four Quartets*, with four figuring not once, but twice in the title! For those unfamiliar with this work by Eliot, *Four Quartets* is a long poem divided into four parts, or four poems, each with its own title: Burnt Norton, East Coker, Dry Salvages, and Little Gidding. A basic symbolism that resonates within the poem are the four elements.

Although all four elements are present in each of the quartets, each quartet gives primary expression, or emphasis, to a single element, as follows:

Burnt Norton—air
East Coker—earth (dust)
Dry Salvages—water
Little Gidding—fire

One more example of the fourfold theme: the first four notes of Beethoven's *Fifth Symphony*. Spooner observes, "The overall structure of the symphony follows the general pattern of the fourfold quartet movement, the slower third movement running into the finale without a break. The first four notes of the piece are therefore an urgent microcosm of the whole symphony, not only the thematic basis of much of it, but a stamping out or imprinting of the total mathematical impact. In Beethoven's words, they are destiny knocking at the door."

In light of all this, it seems safe to say that there is something deeply archetypal about the number four and the fourfold pattern of growth expressed in the life cycle of a butterfly, and that the "fire of God" is a robust metaphor. And so, with a little foresight, let us now turn to:

A Man's Reach Should Exceed His Grasp, or What's a *Meta-* For?

George Lakoff and Mark Johnson, in their groundbreaking book, *Metaphors We Live By*, reveal how metaphors, far from being mere rhetorical embellishments, are so integral a part of language that they affect the way we perceive, experience, and act in the world. For example, let us suppose two people, A and B, who each live by different metaphors:

A: Love is war
B: Love is a collaborative work of art

Not only will their perceptions of love be different, but their experiences will differ, and, since the decisions and actions of each are structured by different metaphors, the realities they create will be different. Thus, the metaphors we choose to live by can make all the difference in the world.

While reflecting on the metamorphosis that transforms a caterpillar into a butterfly, it occurred to me that this is a living metaphor that can help us to understand what Jesus said to Nicodemus in their encounter as told in John 3: 1-5:

> There was a man of the Pharisees, named Nicodemus, a ruler of the Jews. The same came to Jesus by night, and said unto him, "Rabbi, we know that thou art a teacher come from God: for no man can do these miracles that thou doest, except God be with him." Jesus answered and said unto him, "Verily, verily I say unto thee, except a man be born again, he cannot see the Kingdom of God." Nicodemus saith unto him, "How can a man be born again when he is old? Can he enter the second time into his mother's womb, and be born?" Jesus answered, "Verily, verily, I say unto thee, except a man be born of water and of the Spirit, he cannot enter into the Kingdom of God."

Through the process of histolysis, the caterpillar must "die" before it can be reconstituted, or "born again," as a butterfly. And to be "born of water and of the Spirit" correlates well with organic soup and imaginal cells. It is also interesting to note that the Greek word for "soul" or "spirit" is *psyche*, a word which also means "butterfly."

The metamorphic process also perfectly illustrates the parable of the grain of wheat as told by Jesus in John 12:24—"Verily, verily, I say unto you, Except a grain of wheat fall into the ground and die, it abideth alone; but if it die, it bringeth forth much fruit."

The metaphor also sheds light on the Buddhist and Christian concepts of emptiness, as in the terms *sunyata* and *kenosis*, and the idea of the "death" or "letting go" of the old self to realize a transformation to the true self.

Aristotle clearly recognized the power of metaphor: "But the greatest thing by far is to be a master of metaphor . . . ordinary words convey only what we know already; it is from metaphor that we can best get hold of something fresh."

And the Mexican poet Octavio Paz said, "The highest form of imagination is analogy. Both the baroque and the modern poet believe that the metaphor—the image—is the center of the poem; its function is to create surprise, the 'marvel that suspends the soul,' through the discovery of unsuspected relationships among objects."

In his Foreword to *Metaphoric Process*,[3] Paul Ricoeur writes:

> . . . metaphor, far from being limited to a linguistic artifact, is characterized by its epistemological function of discovering new meanings. What is at stake is still knowing in process, but considered in its 'nascent moment.' In this sense metaphor is a thought process before being a language process.

Quoting *Metaphors We Live By*: "The reason we have focused so much on metaphor is that it unites reason and imagination. Reason, at the very least, involves categorization, entailment, and inference. Imagination, in one of its many aspects, involves seeing one kind of thing in terms of another kind of thing—what we have called metaphorical thought. Metaphor is thus *imaginative rationality*.

"New metaphors have the power to create a new reality. This can begin to happen when we start to comprehend our experience in terms of a metaphor, and it becomes a deeper reality when we begin to act in terms of it. If a new metaphor enters the conceptual system that we base our actions on, it will alter that conceptual system and the perceptions and actions that the system gives rise to. Much of cultural change arises from the introduction of new metaphorical concepts and the loss of old ones."

A first step on the path of "imaginative rationality" is simply to become enchanted by the metaphor of transformation the butterfly so beautifully expresses. Let it lead you into the still waters—the chrysalis of transformation.

Endnotes

1. Books by David Spooner:

    The Insect-Populated Mind: How Insects Have Influenced the Evolution of Consciousness (2005)

    Thoreau's Vision of Insects & the Origins of American Entomology (2002)

    The Poem and the Insect: Aspects of Twentieth Century Hispanic Culture (1999)

    The Metaphysics of Insects and Other Essays (1995)

2. My term for these variations on a fourfold theme is "Meta-Fours." My fascination with the number 4 began many years ago with the study of James Joyce's book of the dark, also known as *Finnegans Wake*, a tall tale—well, a *meanderthalltale*—wherein four plays a central role both structurally and thematically. Joyce would have been quick to notice a sexual innuendo in the previous sentence and, indeed, my continuing meditations on numinous and numerous epiphanies of the number four may be thought of as foreplay . . . or four-play!

    Four is the model of wholeness and completion. The examples from physics suggesting totality or completeness are most impressive: the four dimensions of space-time, the four basic forces underlying all interactions (gravitation, electromagnetism, and the strong and weak nuclear forces, which physicists of the 1970s and 1980s are striving to merge into one unified force), the four components needed for a complete quantum relativistic description of the electron, and from the primitive sciences, the four basic elements: air, earth, water, and fire. Roger S. Jones, a research physicist and author of *Physics as Metaphor*, points out that the major task of his book is to explore "the four foundation concepts of physics: space, time, matter, and number." He also refers to them as the four cardinal *metaphors*.

    At the same time, in the psyche, four is the symbol of unity and wholeness. Indeed, as Marie-Louise von Franz says, "Jung devoted practically the whole of his life's work to demonstrating the vast psychological significance of the number four. . . ." Quaternity is so fundamental to Jung that it is a primary archetype.

May the *fours* be with you!

3. *Metaphoric Process: The Creation of Scientific and Religious Understanding*, Mary Gerhart and Allan Russell.

The Way of Flow

Were you ever so absorbed in a good book that you lost all track of time? So caught up in the story that even your sense of self vanished? While playing some sport such as tennis or basketball, did you ever experience moments when the level of your skills so matched the challenges of the event that you excelled with almost effortless ease? That in each instant you felt such a sense of control that you knew exactly what to do and the next instant confirmed that your action had been exactly right? Were you so *carried away* that your very veins thrilled with exhilaration? And did you later feel that such an experience was so deeply enjoyable that the experience itself was its own reward?

Both of these are examples of what is known as the experience of *flow*. Flow probably goes back in history as far as the very beginnings of humanity. But a Hungarian with what looks like an unpronounceable name, Mihaly Csikszentmihalyi, was the first to formally name the experience *flow*, and he has been studying it now for more than thirty years.

Csikszentmihalyi (pronounced "cheek-sent-me-high") identifies eight elements that constitute the flow experience:

1. Clear goals and feedback
2. Balance between challenges and skills
3. Merging of action and awareness
4. Focusing on the present
5. Sense of control
6. Loss of self-consciousness
7. The sense of time is altered
8. The activity becomes autotelic

The word *autotelic* derives from two Greek roots, *auto* and *telos*, meaning "self" and "goal." Therefore, when an activity is autotelic, this simply means that it is intrinsically rewarding, or worth doing for its own sake.

During episodes of flow, people function on a higher level, display more creativity, feel a deeper sense of involvement, enjoy what they are doing, and emerge from the experience with more self-esteem and confidence. And, since it feels so good, there is a deep desire to recapture the experience again and again.

Csikszentmihalyi's book, *Flow: The Psychology of Optimal Experience*, was published in 1990 and the possibilities for the practical application of flow first aroused interest in athletics and leisure activities. Jimmy Johnson, coach of the Dallas Cowboys, announced after the 1993 Super Bowl that *Flow* helped the team prepare for and win the big game. In the past few years, perhaps in light of such success, the idea is catching on within the business community. Some major companies, such as Microsoft and Toyota, are introducing the concept of flow into the workplace with impressive results.

Although flow is so positive that it accounts for many of the best moments of our lives, there are negative forces that can undermine flow, such as parasitic memes.

Memes and Minds

A meme is 1) a cultural artifact, or 2) a unit of cultural information or instruction, and a simple example of each would be: 1) a shoe lace, and 2) how to tie a shoelace. Children learn how to tie shoelaces from their parents and, with practice, it becomes second nature.

Csikszentmihalyi suggests this definition of a meme: "any permanent pattern of matter or information produced by an act of human intentionality. Thus a brick is a meme, and so is Mozart's *Requiem*."

Richard Dawkins coined the word *meme* on an analogy with *genes* and, like genes that transmit information from one generation to the next on the physical level, memes pass on their instructions on the level of consciousness. Whereas genes leap from body to body via sperm and egg, memes leap from mind to mind via example and imitation. Dawkins gives the example of a scientist who hears or reads about a good idea and then passes it on to his colleagues. He may write about it in articles and discuss it in his lectures and, if the idea catches on, a new meme will begin to propagate as it spreads from mind to mind. Unfortunately, the same thing can happen with bad ideas, such as the meme that spread throughout Germany before World War II and led to the extermination of millions of Jews in the Nazi Holocaust. This means that memes can be either parasitic or symbiotic.

Memes are said to be *parasitic* when, like actual parasites, they infect and exploit the energy of their hosts. The result is a lack of flow, and this lies behind the cause of many social problems. What is addiction but the attempt to recapture the flow of optimal experience by artificial means? With too little flow to engage them, people can become dependent on passive entertainment such as recorded music, TV, movies, pulp fiction, spectator sports, and sleazy magazines. Watching television is one of the least flowlike activities—it presents virtually no challenges and requires minimal skills—and yet many people spend most of their free time in front of a television set. TV thus has the dubious distinction of being one of the most parasitic memes on the planet. Lest you think I exaggerate, Csikszentmihalyi has researched this for decades and here's what he has to say:

"Television is a dramatic example of a meme that invades the mind and reproduces there without concern for the well-being of its host. Like drugs, watching TV initially provides a positive experience. But after the viewer is hooked, the medium uses consciousness without providing further benefits. . . . All television does is replicate itself—screens get bigger, pixels multiply, sitcoms beget other sitcoms, talk shows generate further talk shows, all the while using our psychic energy as their medium of growth."

The Rockies May Crumble

In opposition to flow, there is a counter-force, powerful and primordial, at work in the universe. It is the force behind the second law of thermodynamics which states that any system free of external influences becomes more disordered with time.

Cars end up in junkyards where they rust away; dropping dirt on the coffin, the pastor officiating at a burial solemnly says, "Dust to dust, ashes to ashes." Or, as the Gershwin song puts it: "In time the Rockies may crumble, Gibraltar may tumble . . ." This steady deterioration is the process of *entropy*, from whose inexorable workings no finite entity ultimately escapes.

Although entropy is a technical term used in physics, Csikszentmihalyi borrows the word to describe a similar process that occurs in consciousness. He calls this *psychic entropy*. Psychic entropy is characterized by disorder in consciousness. Some examples are: bad moods, passive feelings of incompetence, lack of motivation, and the inability to focus attention. Psychic entropy is a downward spiral that feels bad. Some activities, such as watching TV, should be limited because they produce psychic entropy. It is not without reason that the term "couch potato" entered our vocabulary to designate someone who vegetates in front of a television set.

But it should be pointed out that psychic entropy also has a positive side. We are genetically hard-wired to feel pleasure when we get comfortable, relax, and wind down after any strenuous activity. Without this conservative urge, this "built-in mechanism," we could, as Csikszentmihalyi points out, easily self-destruct by running ourselves ragged. An optimal balance must be found between conserving energy and using it constructively.

Left unchecked, however, entropy can take over consciousness. When the mind makes the shift to entropy, it can continue to idle, in neutral, unless interrupted by the counter force of flow. Flow activities move the mind in the opposite direction. When, instead of running down, order increases in a system, *negentropy* is busy at work. And so, in contrast to psychic entropy, flow is psychic negentropy. One is the direction of death and decay; the other, the direction of creation and growth.

Some examples of psychic negentropy: positive feelings toward self and others, an active sense of competence, identification with intentions and goals, and effective concentration. Psychic negentropy spirals upward and feels good, very good!

Csikszentmihalyi points out some practical implications of this: "Negative emotions like sadness, fear, anxiety, or boredom produce *psychic entropy* in the mind, that is, a state in which we cannot use attention effectively to deal with external tasks, because we need it to restore an inner subjective order. Positive emotions like happiness, strength, or alertness are states of *psychic negentropy* because we don't need attention to ruminate and feel sorry for ourselves, and psychic energy can flow freely into whatever thought or task we choose to invest it in."

With negentropy, mind and body are moving in measure, so harmoniously ordered that thoughts, feelings, and desires come together, mutually consistent, mutually supportive, intertwining in a seamless flow of unified action.

The Flow of Evolution

Is flow built into human nature just for our enjoyment and satisfaction, and as a counter force to entropy, or is there a purpose over and above this?

Let us look at the inner dynamics of the flow experience. First, flow is autotelic: that is, worth doing for its own sake. Because flow produces such positive feelings, people desire "repeat performances" to experience the satisfaction over and over. One way Nature gets us to do important things, such as reproduce, is to make it enjoyable. Would humans get all hot and bothered about sex if it didn't feel so good? However, what constitutes flow on Monday may not do so on Thursday. Any experience that remains on the same level will eventually lead not to flow, but to boredom. To slightly rephrase the famous saying of the philosopher Heraclitus—you cannot, without some measure of diminishment, step twice into the same stream of flow.

A tennis player, for example, whose skills match those of his opponent will enjoy the contest, and the closer they match, the better! However, when his skills improve and surpass those of his opponent, the play will lose its zest. To recapture flow, or the feeling of optimal experience, he must seek stronger opposition.

Thus, for the flow experience to be sustained, new challenges must be taken on, and skills improved to meet those challenges. The direction or curve of flow is an *upward spiral* of increasing complexity. There is a close correlation here with process thought which holds that the essence of all reality is not just process, but *self-surpassing* process.

Flow is one way we go beyond the status quo, established patterns of human behavior, and the routines of everyday life. It is a way of transcendence. What is being described here is *evolution*. Flow is built into the very nature of reality to encourage both personal and cultural evolution.

With the flow of evolution, whole new vistas of experience become available for our enjoyment and satisfaction. The discovery of the oxygen tank made possible underwater adventures where one could explore beautiful coral reefs and the mysteries deep down in the sea.

On a summer day in June in 1783, when the Montgolfier brothers exhilarated the Parisian public with their first demonstration of a hot-air balloon, the meme for human flight took one small step. From this would follow airplanes, helicopters, and NASA spacecraft that would take us up, up, and away . . . from a giant leap to the moon to ever so far beyond! And thus by *flow* do we expand the horizons of our human adventure.

Ken Wilber's
Mandalic Model of Reality

This is an introduction to one of Ken Wilber's most versatile ideas: his model of what he calls the Four Quadrants. As a formal structure, the four quadrants display a striking resemblance to a mandala. Wilber also speaks of his philosophy as "weaving a mandala of the many faces of Spirit." My approach, therefore, will use the mandala as a way to approach Wilber's model, and I will then explore its significance and some of the many insights it can help you discern as well as some of the oversights it can help you avoid.

Mandala is a Sanskrit word meaning "circle," and it denotes the circular, concentric pattern of images used in spiritual practices, such as meditation, as an object of concentration. Most mandalas express a fourfold pattern. Simply place a cross within a circle, dividing it into four equal facets, and you have the basic formal structure of a mandala.

The figure below is a template for the construction of a mandala. Note how the theme of "4" appears *four* times in this figure: 1) four circles, 2) a cross that makes a fourfold division, 3) the square, 4) a "flower" of four blossoms made by the intersecting arcs of the four circles.

Figure 1

This fourfold aspect of a mandala, this "squaring of the circle," is one example of what the great psychologist C. G. Jung calls a *quaternity*: a symbolic expression containing four elements. This variation on a fourfold theme is so pervasive in myth and other sacred writings, that Jung calls it "the principle of four."

Circles and quaternities: both are symbols of wholeness. Together, integrated into one figure—the mandala—they become an even deeper symbol: an *archetype* of wholeness.

Holons and Holarchies

First, notice the pattern in the following three series:

1) particles, atoms, molecules
2) cells, tissues, organs
3) letters, words, sentences

Each series is a natural *hierarchy*, that is, an arrangement of increasing complexity of order. The next thing to notice is how the members of each series are related in terms of part to whole. An atom, for example, is a part of a molecule; but it is also a whole that is made of parts: subatomic particles such as electrons and protons. Seen in this light, the atom, as a member of a natural hierarchy, is not a whole *or* a part, but both at the same time: an irreducible whole-part.

Arthur Koestler was the first to draw this distinction, and to designate this "whole-part" he coined the word *holon*. As Koestler wittily put it, holons "behave partly as wholes and wholly as parts." Koestler showed true artistry and precision in the coining of this word. The prefix "*hol-*" derives from a Greek word *holus* that means "whole," while the suffix "*-on*" means "part" or "particle," as in words like electron or proton. The word itself exemplifies its meaning: whole-part.

In his book *Janus: A Summing Up*, Koestler describes why he felt a need to coin the word: "A good terminology, someone has said, is half the game. To get away from the traditional misuse of the words *whole* and *part*, one is compelled to operate with such awkward terms as *sub-whole*, or *part-whole, sub-structures, sub-assemblies*, and so forth. To avoid these jarring expressions, I proposed, some years ago, a new term to designate those Janus-faced entities on the intermediate levels of any hierarchy, which can be described either as wholes or as parts, depending on the way you look at them from 'below' or from 'above'. The term I proposed was *holon*, which seems to have filled a genuine need, for it is gradually finding its way into the terminology of various branches of science, from biology to communication theory."

There are many kinds of holons: behavioral, linguistic, social . . . Humans, along with every other critter in the animal kingdom, are biological holons.

Koestler also coined one other related word: *holarchy*. A *holarchy* is simply a hierarchy of holons. Most natural hierarchies, such as the three series listed above, are holarchies. These are called *actualization* holarchies because they show a pattern of growth: each higher level transcends but includes its predecessors. Molecules go beyond atoms, yes, but they are made of atoms. Holarchies are a basic formal pattern that is pervasive on all levels of reality.

The Four Quadrants

The idea of the Four Quadrants came to Wilber while he was researching and writing his 851-page magnum opus, *Sex, Ecology, Spirituality*. For the purpose of contrast and comparison, he had summarized the hierarchies representing over 200 systems of thought. And then one day, as he was wondering how to fit them together, he suddenly saw that they all fell into four major categories. Those four categories he christened the Four Quadrants. These quadrants represent four fundamental features of every entity in the universe. Following the fourfold structure of Figure 1, I will introduce the Four Quadrants with four tables of increasing complexity. [Note: the tables in this essay are based on schematic figures that Wilber has presented in his writings, both online and in books.]

The first table is simplicity itself:

I UL	It UR
LL We	LR Its

Do you see the familiar fourfold or *mandalic* structure?

Four quadrants: Upper Left, Upper Right, Lower Left, Lower Right. In human terms, they represent:

I: individual consciousness, mind, the inner reality

It: the outer physical reality of body and brain

We: culture or the inner realm of shared beliefs, values, language

Its: social systems and external environment

These are four basic aspects of all holons, and thus, all humans. Adding more detail, the table looks like this:

Interior	*Exterior*
I Intentional **UL**	**It** Behavioral **UR**
LL Cultural **We**	**LR** Social **Its**

This simply shows that you have an *inside* and an *outside*, and you are, at the same time, both *individual* and *communal*. These are simple distinctions, but they are fundamental and important. Another way to put this is to say that you, like all holons, have intentional, behavioral, cultural, and social aspects.

With this in mind, let's add some more detail to the table:

I Intentional **The Beautiful** (self and consciousness) **UL**	**IT** Behavioral **The True** (brain and organism) **UR**
LL Cultural **The Good** (worldview) **WE**	**LR** Social **The True** (system and environment) **ITS**

In Wilber's system, holons are the basic units of reality, and the universe is a vast holonic network: holons within holons within holons—all the way down, all the way up—to the ultimate Holon: God, or Spirit.

The four-quadrant model may be seen as an abstract "anatomy" of a holon. Take a few moments to observe this model and note the different elements in each of the four quadrants and how they correlate. Note once again the primary distinctions of the *interior* and *exterior* of the *individual* and the *collective*, and consider how *minds* (consciousness) actualize inner intentions, *bodies* display observable behaviors, *cultures* share interior worldviews, *social systems* display physical realities. Each quadrant has a distinctive language, and *beauty* is in the eye or "I" of the beholder, *goodness* is reflected by the ethics of the community, *truth* (objective truth) is ascertained by the empirical sciences.

The two Right-Hand quadrants can be thought of as the physical correlates of the two Left-Hand quadrants. Mental operations—no matter how high the level—are grounded in the physiology of the brain. Cultural life has its correlates in museums, libraries, universities, sports arenas . . .

Human reality is moment-to-moment: we *are* our experiences. If you stop for a moment and do a careful analysis of your own experience, you will find that all four quadrants play a fundamental part in making you what you are. To give some examples:

UL: In the domain of mind or spirit, Saint Paul's experience on the road to Damascus (Acts 9: 1-22) is a dramatic example of how an event in the UL quadrant can cause a profound transformation.

UR: The power of the brain, body, and the physical world is revealed by the central practice of the Native American Church: ingestion of their "Medicine," peyote, produces transformational mystical experiences. In this sacred context, peyote is not a drug, but an *entheogen*: a psychoactive sacramental taken to generate a primary religious experience.

LL: If we are of a religious persuasion, the system of beliefs we share is a part, indeed an essential part, of what makes us who we are. But beliefs can make for good or ill—as 9/11 has made clear, even "religious" beliefs can turn some people into cold-blooded murderers.

LR: Religious temples that we cherish, and the many concrete symbolic motifs that we absorb by simply being inside: this is a part of our individual identities. Ritual and liturgy—such as the Eucharist (or the Lord's Supper)—this too contributes to what we are. And, as mentioned previously: museums, libraries.

The influence of the four quadrants, or rather the emphasis on one quadrant, can also be seen as shaping the lives, and the minds, of some theorists who displayed a tendency to work in only one quadrant—Sigmund Freud: UL, B. F. Skinner: UR, Max Weber: LL, Karl Marx: LR.

To summarize: the *whole* of any momentary experience, or of any holon, is made of *parts* contributed by all four quadrants. Even the most simple thought is complexly *quadratic*. This is an intrinsic feature of the cosmos and any comprehensive model of reality, or any knowledge quest, will require that all quadrants be honored.

Why Is the Model Important?

One reason is that, by its integral perspective, it allows one to see how things can go wrong, or express only *partial* truths, when one or more of the quadrants is neglected.

Science has rightly and robustly staked its claim in the Right-Hand quadrants. And how can we but applaud the many accomplishments of science and technology? But when science becomes "scientism"—the claim is made that the *only* truths are the truths revealed by science, the *only* realities are the realities revealed by science. This leads to the rejection of the very existence of the Left-Hand quadrants and reality is thereby sliced in half and reduced to what Wilber calls Flatland: "the collapse of the richly textured Cosmos into a flat and faded one-dimensional world . . . a flat and faded world of drab and dreary surfaces." Flatland is the reigning paradigm in contemporary science. This is not to say that science is *totally* wrong—far from it! Each of the four quadrants has important and essential truths to contribute, but, taken in isolation, or in exclusion of the other quadrants, these are *partial* truths. To get the *whole* picture, none of the intrinsic *parts* can be left out, that is, none of the four quadrants.

It is easy to find one quadrant so very cozy that you neglect the others. New Agers, for instance, have a tendency to cluster in the UL quadrant, resulting in an approach to life that can become "top-heavy." An integral spiritual practice will involve work and development in all four quadrants.

Traditional medical practice in the United States operates largely in the UR quadrant. A more integral approach to the healing arts—a truly *mandalic* medicine—would discover, develop, and utilize resources in all four quadrants.

Dr. Andrew Weil, a leader in the field of health and healing who uses a blend of both conventional and alternative medicine, is one physician who employs a more holistic approach in his medical practice.

Although spiritual experiences are immediately given, they must always be interpreted, and those interpretations can be good or bad, balanced or lopsided. Let's say that someone experiences a truly profound spiritual experience or spiritual intuition, but he interprets this exclusively as a UL event—as finding his Higher Self. There is a tendency, then, to assume that this somehow solves everything and, as a result, all other problems will not only take care of themselves but will work themselves out in a most wonderful way. This allows one to conveniently ignore the other quadrants, that is, the behavioral, cultural, and social aspects. This is, as Wilber puts it, "a very narcissistic orientation—find your True Self, and the rest of the world will take care of itself." Those in the "Higher Self" camp, Wilber adds, "are thus notoriously immune to social concerns. This is the totally disengaged Ego gone horribly amuck in omnipotent self-only fantasies."

This can lead to nutty exaggerations of the notion that *You create your own reality.* "You don't create your own reality," Wilber says, "psychotics create their own reality." What he means is that, although there is some truth in the idea that you (in consciousness) create your own reality—again, it is a *partial* truth. Reality is *mandalic* in the making: a four-quadrant process.

Wilber, in a stirring image, says that each quadrant has a voice, whispering quietly its truth, and together they form a harmonious chorus that calls us home to unity. As compound individuals, we also have different levels—and each level manifests in all four quadrants. This is his AQAL perspective (all-quadrant, all level) with an aim toward balance, fullness, and integrity.

It is also important to notice that the model represents "Spirit in Action" or a mandalic image of the Great Chain of Being. God, or Spirit, expresses in and as all four quadrants. No single quadrant is privileged above any of the others—all four taken together, as a unity-in-quaternity, are "the radiant glory of Spirit's manifestation."

The Great Chain of Being is, in Wilber's words, the "nearly universal view, [that] reality is a rich tapestry of interwoven levels, reaching from matter to body to mind to soul to spirit." Some early thinkers, such as Plotinus, saw the Chain of Being as having been given all at once. But, in one of the seminal insights of modernity, Leibniz was perhaps the first to see that the Great Chain was temporal and unfolded over vast stretches of time. As Wilber puts it, "Plotinus temporalized equals evolution."

The Spirit of Evolution

Finally, here's the fourth and final table, and a very impressive table it is, that Wilber offers for our contemplation. And now seems the time to point out that mandalas are not only circular but are also like wheels, and wheels are not static—they *turn*. So let us now imagine the mandala below in motion so that it turns, or *unfolds*, in four ways from the center, and we can then behold the Spirit of evolution:

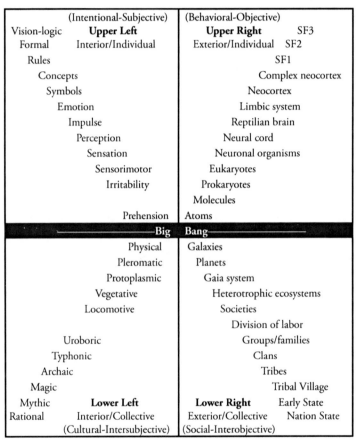

(Intentional-Subjective)		(Behavioral-Objective)	
Vision-logic	**Upper Left**	**Upper Right**	SF3
Formal	Interior/Individual	Exterior/Individual	SF2
Rules			SF1
	Concepts	Complex neocortex	
	Symbols	Neocortex	
	Emotion	Limbic system	
	Impulse	Reptilian brain	
	Perception	Neural cord	
	Sensation	Neuronal organisms	
	Sensorimotor	Eukaryotes	
	Irritability	Prokaryotes	
		Molecules	
	Prehension	Atoms	
—————————Big		Bang—————————	
	Physical	Galaxies	
	Pleromatic	Planets	
	Protoplasmic	Gaia system	
	Vegetative	Heterotrophic ecosystems	
	Locomotive	Societies	
		Division of labor	
	Uroboric	Groups/families	
	Typhonic	Clans	
	Archaic	Tribes	
	Magic	Tribal Village	
Mythic	**Lower Left**	**Lower Right**	Early State
Rational	Interior/Collective	Exterior/Collective	Nation State
	(Cultural-Intersubjective)	(Social-Interobjective)	

The Four Quadrants

That's just what this table does—it adds evolution to the picture, but that's quite an addition: 15 billion years, and still counting! It is not necessary to understand all the technical terms, only to notice the general contours, and that evolution has unfolded across all four quadrants.

The center of the table represents the Big Bang: the beginning of our universe.

The four lines of development proceed outward from this center; for example, in the UR quadrant, the order of development is atoms, molecules, living cells (prokaryotes)—all the way to SF1, SF2, SF3, terms that refer to structural functions of the human brain that correlate with advances in cognitive powers of the mind. For each step of development in one quadrant, there is a corresponding step in the other three. Evolution is thus a fourfold process, a *mandalic* process, with correlative advances in all four quadrants.

As the UR quadrant perhaps most clearly indicates, each developmental sequence is a *holarchy*: the journey outward is through holons that display ever increasing orders of complexity, organization, and autonomy. Holons evolve through *holarchic* advance: a process that builds on what has been achieved thus far. The first molecules didn't just float in out of the blue from nowhere; rather, they emerged as higher-order entities through a synthesis of atoms. Each creative advance lays the foundation for what will come after. And so molecules would pave the way for their transcendence, and inclusion, by simple living cells. There is economy in this, but also elegance, and the beauty of ever increasing depth in each newly emerging holon.

The Way of Evolution is through a creative process that is both *mandalic* and *holarchic*, creating ever more depth with each advance. As Wilber has nicely put it, we humans, along with all other holons, have not only the *horizontal* history of our day-by-day existence, but also a *vertical* developmental archeology. This "developmental archeology" refers to our astonishing depths. Digging down we find:

Our bodies are an integration of all the basic physical and biological units that nature has evolved this far: subatomic particles, atoms, molecules, living cells . . . Underlying and potentiating the human mind is the entire spectrum of consciousness, as shown in the upper-left quadrant of the table. Compounded with this are the many centuries of contributions from the cultural and social spheres.

These four great holarchies constitute the vast infrastructure of the human self. In a very real sense, to look at this table is like looking in a mirror. It has taken *all this*—over a period of 15 billion years—to make you what you are. But these four are not separate streams; they mutually arise, interacting, intermeshing—they shape and are shaped by one another. They are a dynamic unity-in-quaternity: a mandala. The self is *mandalic*.

There are many ways to state our inner depth and spaciousness. Mystics have long told us that microcosm mirrors macrocosm: as above, so below. Freud wrote of our unconscious archaic heritage, and Jung, excavating even deeper, uncovered the inner realm of archetypes and the collective unconscious. Biological science says that "ontogeny recapitulates phylogeny"—the development of a human embryo retraces the general contours of the evolution of life itself.

The microworld of quantum physics—the downward spiral of ever finer particles—is proving to be as vast as the universe explored by astronomy. In developmental psychology, the term "microgenesis" refers to the split-second developmental steps that lead to a single thought, feeling, or perception within the individual.

Each microgenesis recapitulates, in miniature and in milliseconds, the general contours of countless stages, innumerable steps, over eons of time and light-years of space, of an evolutionary process that has been 15 billion years in the making.

And so—turn within to explore light-years of inner space over eons of time. To designate this temporal dimension within, I'll add an "-ic" suffix to "eon" to make the adjective *eonic*. Holonic, holarchic, mandalic, and eonic—the human self stands tall, casting a spatio-temporal *fourfold* shadow that stretches back all the way to the Big Bang.

If Wilber's model is mandalic, and if mandalas embody both a fourfold and a *circular* theme—some of you may be wondering where the circles are in this final model of the Four Quadrants. As Wilber points out, the holarchies in each quadrant are to be thought of not as a linear sequence of stair steps, but as concentric circles or, better, as nested spheres with each successive sphere transcending but including its predecessors. As each new level *unfolds*, it also *enfolds* the preceding levels. To glimpse the dynamics of this, imagine a stone dropped in the center of a still pond and the waves rippling out in ever-widening concentric circles . . . (((((( )))))) . . .

Wilber believes that we are poised on the very edge of a profound transformation of the human species, and that this will involve changes in all four quadrants. As Wilber says, "It will involve a new worldview [LL], set in a new techno-economic base [LR], with a new mode of self-sense [UL], possessing new behavioral patterns [UR]." Wilber's model can be of use in helping us to understand and attune with this.

Like the four points of a compass, the four quadrants can help us get our bearings, make us more aware of the creative currents flowing around and through us, and thus enable us to more ably navigate these transformational streams. Merely making a big splash in our favorite quadrant will no longer work; we must take an integral, a *mandalic*, approach and find ways to sail forward in all four. If we do not take this fourfold approach, we risk, as Wilber says, being left behind as driftwood on the shore as the great adventure sails on without us.

As the title of this section suggests (The *Spirit* of Evolution), Wilber sees God, or Spirit, as intimately involved in evolution. God is Alpha and Omega, both our source and our destiny. For those with eyes to see, the universe itself is transparent to Spirit. The workings of the universe, and the long saga of evolution—these are, as Wilber says, Spirit in Action.

Wilber's model reveals that *the way of creation* proceeds, simultaneously and in unity, by a fourfold process: weaving everlastingly one Cosmic Mandala, inclusive of myriad upon myriad of holonic mandalas—mandalas within mandalas within mandalas—radiant, all of them, with truth, beauty, and goodness—shimmering, all of them, with the many faces of Spirit.

Addenda

Four Quadrants Upgrade

Ken Wilber's recent book, *Integral Spirituality* (2006), has some new insights to offer, including an upgrade of his four-quadrant model. Taking into account that a holon in any of the four quadrants can be seen from the outside, or experienced as, or as if, from within, this gives a total of eight perspectives or zones.

The Four Quadrants with eight primordial perspectives, or hori-zones of arising, and their respective methodologies:

Upper Left	Upper Right
"I" inside: zone 1	"it" inside: zone 5
phenomenology	**autopoiesis**
outside: zone 2	outside: zone 6
structuralism	**empiricism**
subjective	objective
Lower Left	**Lower Right**
"we" inside: zone 3	"its" inside: zone 7
hermeneutics	**social autopoiesis**
outside: zone 4	outside: zone 8
ethnomethodology	**systems theory**
intersubjective	interobjective

Although there is some overlap in these zones, a point to notice is what all this reveals. Eight zones, each with its own methodology, yield eight supplementary perspectives which, when integrated, give a more comprehensive revelation about the complexity of human nature and the nature of all holons. A parallel could be drawn with quantum physics as it delves within the atom to discover the beauty and the complexities of the particulate subatomic realm.

Wilber also points out that, as we tetra-evolve, Enlightenment has both vertical and horizontal components. This means that the Buddha's Enlightenment was a complete Enlightenment at that time, but it is only partial in comparison with what is possible now, for there are structures of consciousness now that were just not available then. The world moves on, continuously.

A Precursor to the Four Quadrants?

In his book *A Guide for the Perplexed* (1977), E. F. Schumacher recognizes Four Great Truths that should be on any map, or guidebook, about how to live in the world:

1. The Great Truth about the world is that it is a hierarchic structure of at least four great "Levels of Being."
2. The Great Truth about man's ability to meet the world is the principle of adequateness.
3. The Great Truth about man's learning concerns the "Four Fields of Knowledge."
4. The Great Truth about living in this life, living in this world, relates to the distinction between two types of problem, "convergent" and "divergent."

Drawing on the ancient tradition of the Great Chain of Being, he then goes on to identify a hierarchy of four levels of being: 1) mineral, 2) plant, 3) animal, 4)human.

That which distinguishes plant from mineral, or the organic from the inorganic world, is *life*; *consciousness* distinguishes animals from plants; and the feature that distinguishes humans from animals is *self-awareness*. If mineral be designated as "m," life as "x," consciousness as "y," and self-awareness as "z," the four levels of being can be summed up as:

Human can be written	$m + x + y + z$
Animal can be written	$m + x + y$
Plant can be written	$m + x$
Mineral can be written	m

Schumacher next observes that the world, for us humans, is divided into *inner experience* and *outer appearance*. *Here* I am, a living center of consciousness and self-awareness, and *out there* is everything else, including other humans. A notable aspect of this is that inner experiences are *invisible* whereas outer appearances are visible and, as we ascend the Great Chain of Being, it is the *invisibilities*, or intangibles, that will begin to play an increasingly important role. These four combinations can be stated as:

1. I—inner
2. The world (you)—inner
3. I—outer
4. The world (you)—outer

These, for Schumacher, are the Four Fields of Knowledge and there are four questions which lead to these fields:

1. What is really going on in my own inner world?
2. What is going on in the inner world of other beings?
3. What do I look like in the eyes of other beings?
4. What do I actually observe in the world around me?

Or, to simplify further, they can be put this way:

1. What do I feel like?
2. What do you feel like?
3. What do I look like?
4. What do you look like?

The importance of these four fields to Schumacher can be seen in that he devotes an entire chapter to the analysis of each field.

In conclusion, it is interesting to note, as Frank Visser was the first to point out in his insightful book on Ken Wilber,* that Schumacher's Four Fields seem to be a precursor to Wilber's Four Quadrants model. As the above discussion clearly shows, there can be little doubt, if any, that Schumacher was a serious *quadratic* thinker!

*Frank Visser, *Ken Wilber: Thought as Passion* (2003)

Let There Be — Levity!

Webster's dictionary gives one definition of the word "levity" as "lightness or gaiety of disposition, conduct, or speech." Another meaning is defined as "lightness in weight" or "buoyancy." This definition of *levity*, as lightness in weight, especially as the action of a counter-force that is the opposite of *gravity*, will be the main concern of this essay.

Gravity is a "down" force—a force that causes, when the time is ripe, the fall of such things as apples, and also keeps our feet planted firmly on the ground. Gravity is what makes a bushel of apples hard to lift. Gravity makes things *heavy*.

Blow on a dandelion puffball and watch the gossamer seed puffs sail away in the breeze. Inflate a yellow balloon with helium, release it, and behold as it floats up, up, and away. This is levity. Levity makes things *light*.

Frown, which rhymes with "down," is a word of obvious gravity, just as its opposite, a sunny smile, fairly shines with levity. Levity was once a scientific term, and the *Oxford English Dictionary* defines it thus: ". . . a positive property inherent in bodies in different degrees, in virtue of which they tend to rise, as bodies possessing gravity tend to sink."

In Scotland, at Glasgow University, there's a scientific experiment still up and running that was begun over a century ago by William Thomson, also known as Lord Kelvin. Imagine a large glass jar filled with water and, situated at the mid-point in the water, a thick slice of wax, equally dividing the upper and lower regions of the jar. Small corks have been placed underneath the wax and metal bullets above.

Over the course of a year, the bullets will have sunk down through the wax to drop to the bottom of the jar, while the corks, buoyant with levity, will have migrated up through the wax to rise and float on the water's surface. Does this not beautifully illustrate the contrasts of gravity and levity?

So associated is his name with his discovery that the very mention of Newton brings to mind the Law of Gravity, suddenly intuited by Sir Isaac when he chanced to glimpse a falling apple, and saw in its fall the same force that impels the moon in its orbit round the earth. John Ruskin points out that Newton's law of gravity explains the fall of an apple from a tree, but doesn't even begin to explain the infinitely more complex process by which the apple got *up there* in the first place.

Natural examples of levity abound: water evaporating and rising up to form clouds, waterspouts at sea, dust devils, radioactive elements such as uranium, phosphorous, the fermentation of wine, the bubbly effervescence of champagne, flowers growing upward, heliotropic plants that follow the sun, the lusty spring sap rising in an apple tree, or all the way to the top of a giant redwood.

The same capillary action that moves sap up a tree is used by a burning candle to draw the melted wax up the wick where it vaporizes, mixes with air, and fuels the flame. And, as Arthur Zajonc points out in his book *Catching the Light*, "If this were all, as it is for some flames, a candle would shed little light. The bright yellow cone that spreads its gentle radiance, however, is due to tiny glowing embers of unburned carbon, the same that turn up as soot when the wick is too long. Cold, it is the blackest of substances, but when hot, soot becomes beautifully luminous."

Levity is centrifugal; gravity, centripetal. The centrifugal lure of levity can be seen in merry-go-rounds, carousels, Ferris wheels, and dancing round the maypole. All light-winged creatures—birds and bees and butterflies—beautifully express the self-surpassing spirit of levity. The "four elements"—earth, air, fire, and water—align with levity and gravity as follows: levity: fire (lightest) and air (lighter) . . . gravity: water (heavier) and earth (heaviest).

This "lightness" of levity also expresses as the lightheartedness of laughter, good humor, playfulness, frolic, and smiles on a summer night. This is light in both senses, for have you not seen the light that sparkles in her eyes when she, the apple of your eye, is aglow with laughter. Love songs, such as "On the Street Where You Live," from the musical *My Fair Lady*, lift you up with levity. Does not Freddy seem to walk on air when he sings:

> I have often walked down this street before,
> But the pavement always stayed beneath my feet before.
> All at once am I several stories high,
> Knowing I'm on the street where you live.

In fire we find one of the purest expressions of levity. What is lighter than a dancing flame of fire? Fire is "light" in both senses of the word. The nighttime sky is wonderfully aflame with billions of galaxies, each with its billions upon billions of stars, every star expressing beautifully the levity of flames of fire. The sun is an exaltation, an exultation, of levity. When young children draw a picture of the sun, they put a smile on its face.

Children know all about levity. Think back. Remember the times as a young child when, with your playmates, you would hold out both arms and spin in circles so fast that you soon felt light-headed and dizzy and reeled round and round in peals of laughter? The Whirling Dervishes take this up at least one level to experience religious ecstasy.

David Tasker, an English architect, describes how both gravity and levity have found expression in the great cathedrals:

> In architecture there are clear examples of the dynamic between gravity and levity; an historical example would be the development of cathedral architecture from the heavy early Romanesque, characterized by gravity forms of thick pierced walls with small openings and horizontal timber roof tie-beams, to the light, slender fluted columns and delicate curved soaring vaulting giving the upward levity forms of the late Gothic.

Geometry plays a central role in Tasker's work as an architect and engineer. He argues that the polarity of levity and gravity can be found even in the beautiful abstractions of mathematics. Euclidean geometry, which he characterizes as point-centered with forms expanding outward from a center, is based on measure and is more connected to the material realm and thus with gravity.

By way of contrast, one of the newer geometries, projective geometry, "is formed from the outside in, with lines streaming from the plane at infinity, taking its form primarily from the plane and is not structured on measure but relationships." Projective geometry is thus more an expression of levity.

Hugh Kenner, one of the most influential literary critics of the twentieth century, writes of another, almost transcendental, expression of levity in architecture:

> In 1917 Buckminster Fuller was watching the bubbles boiled up in the wake of a Navy ship, and concluding from those millions of changing spheres that nature did not use pi. For pi will only describe a sphere once formed, and a sphere moreover idealized because static. But the generation of forms is described by vectors ('Vectors represent energy events, and they are discrete'), and Fuller proposed to make it his business to find nature's energetic geometry. Just 50 years later the bubble behind the ship had become in Montreal a geodesic dome 20 stories high, enclosing seven million cubic feet of air, as free as a water bubble of internal supports, and weighing a hundredth of what former technology dictated that such a structure should weigh. The load on its foundations was less than the weight of its materials, and had it been a mile wide it would have floated away.

The word *levity* derives from a root "lev-" that is also found in words such as levitation, and in virtually all the world's religions there are stories not only about the levitation of saints, but also about feats of flying. And this brings to mind Superman, Mary Poppins, Peter Pan, and the flying escapades in the wildly popular Harry Potter novels and films.

Along these lines, we can state a basic polarity: for those people, such as atheists, who believe that human life ends in the grave (period!), this is the ultimate grab of gravity; whereas, for those who believe in the resurrection of the body, this is the ultimate lift of levity.

Indeed, levity is about "getting high," and one way to get high is simply to go high. Some astronauts who have soared up into orbit and, while there, experienced the weightlessness of space, have come back down to earth as mystics. Flotation tanks, which simulate the weightless state, produce similar results. Some ocean divers report "rapture of the deep." To such "psi" experiences as out-of-body and near-death, perhaps we should add another: the O.G.E, or out-of-gravity experience.

The force of levity is not directed solely up, but also outward. Whereas gravity has to do with contraction, cohesion, and density, levity is the force that expresses as growth, extension, and expansion. Mix flour with water and leaven with yeast and, as the dough begins to rise, this is levity in action as is, later, the aroma of the freshly baked bread. In our own lives, we can sense levity as the innate urge to become more, the inner impulse to stretch, to move beyond boundaries.

Robert Sardello, in his book *Facing the World with Soul*, observes how levity "forms the basis for the preparation of medicinal substances in homeopathy. A homeopathic remedy is prepared by taking a substance from the world and successively diluting it more and more with water until not a single molecule of the original substance remains; at this point of dilution, what was substance becomes a healing remedy. In the practice of homeopathy the quality of levity belonging to substances is transferred to the medium of water. Homeopathy is a process of removing the levity of a substance from its gravity, and thus is curative because it produces a like movement within the body, the movement from the gravity of disease to the levity of soul. The point of learning to give attention to things is similarly homeopathic: to free them from the deadening force of gravity through the perception of their levity, that is to say, their qualities—to see things as qualities rather than quantities."

The quantum of gravitational energy, a hypothetical particle called the *graviton*, is said to carry the forces of gravity between bodies such as the earth and moon, or the apple that may or may not have fallen on Sir Isaac Newton's head. Levity figures in this hypothesis, and the particle of levity, known as the *leviton*, plays a counter, or balancing, role to that of the graviton. It is crucial that things, such as molecules, be held together, but equally important that the components be held apart—so that there is not a complete collapse or implosion. This suggests that specific gravity is balanced by specific levity; gravitational fields, by levitational fields.

A solid, such as lead, tends to be heavy with gravity whereas helium, a gas, is buoyant with levity. In the change from solid to liquid to gas, such as ice-water-steam, an increase in levity can be clearly observed. It is interesting to note that the radioactive metal radium disintegrates into two other elements: lead and helium—one that sinks, such as the lead sinkers that fishermen use, and the other that spontaneously rises!

And the plot thickens—or does it lighten?—to learn that the word "helium" derives from the Greek word *helios*, meaning "sun," and was first discovered not on earth but in the atmosphere of the sun.

Light itself shines forth as the very paragon of levity. Like fire, light is "light" in both senses of the word. One of the paradoxes about light is that a photon, as a particle of light, has no mass and therefore no weight, thus making it the lightest thing there is. Black holes, I suppose, are the heaviest things there are; even light, moving at 186,000 miles per second cannot escape from a black hole.

As tiny, as diminutive, as micro-minute as it is, a photon has inexhaustible energy in that it can propagate everlastingly—witness the photons that make up the cosmic background radiation that has been around ever since the Big Bang, and is it not amazing that these particles of light wave to us all the way from the very birth of the universe: fifteen billion years ago.

Since to be a photon is to be never at rest but always on the move, at the speed of light, the universe has to keep expanding to make room for light, and in this expansion we see an expression of levity as vast as the universe itself.

During the initial moments of the Big Bang, the only elements present were light and the "light" elements—light in terms of weight, such as hydrogen and helium—so, in a very real sense, light itself, the light of the original incandescence, and levity were the precursors of all that evolved afterward. "Omnia quia sunt, lumina sunt," said the Irish philosopher John Scotus Erigena. "Everything that is, is light." In *both* senses of the word, I would add.

And so, to slightly retell Genesis 1:3-4, God said, Let there be light, yes, and let there be lightness. Let there be . . . levity! And God saw that it was good.

Addendum

In his book *Man or Matter*, Ernst Lehrs provides a comprehensive exploration of the concept of "levity" chiefly in terms of the thought of Rudolf Steiner. I did not come across this book until after I had written this essay and so I add here, as I understand Lehrs, the role that levity plays in Nature's creative process.

Levity presides, as a formative power, over a fourfold creative process that Rudolf Steiner names as, in descending order: life, chemical, light, and warmth. Allowing that Steiner equates *chemical* with *sound*, these four constitute the upper tier of a hierarchy with the traditional four elements:

Life

Sound

Light

Fire　　　　Warmth

Air

Water

Earth

Warmth

Just as fire brings about a melting of solids or the evaporation of liquids, so does warmth bring about *chaos*: a melting or divestiture of physical form that enables the physical level to become open and receptive to the workings of the higher levels.

This *chaos* brings to mind the creation story in Genesis where "the earth was without form, and void, and darkness was upon the face of the deep. And the spirit of God moved on the face of the waters."

It also accords well with the metamorphosis that takes place in the life cycle of the butterfly. Inside the chrysalis, the first step is a virtual liquefaction of the caterpillar's body whereupon the imaginal cells then fashion the butterfly's body from the *chaos* of cellular soup.

Warmth, therefore, works by way of *chaoticizing*.

Light

One clue as to the influence of light can be clearly seen by comparing two types of the same unicellular organism: green algae live in light and have highly differentiated forms whereas, by way of contrast, those algae that live in the dark are relatively formless.

The same contrast can be observed in the leaves of green plants. Those plants that favor low damp places, or that grow underwater, have less intricately structured leaves than do those that grow in the open air of higher regions.

The web of veins in the pattern of a green leaf suggests that the development of a leaf can be likened to the process of weaving. The wisdom of language supports this—the word for organic substance, "tissue," derives from the Latin word *texere*, meaning "to weave." George Adams, in his book *Space and the Light of Creation*, shows how this weaving can be done in terms of projective geometry.

The work of light is, therefore, by way of *weaving*.

Sound

It is said of *kiai*, the loud shout used in Japanese martial arts, that the vibration of the *kiai* carries so much power that it can paralyze an adversary for a brief instant. Is this not fascinating?

Equally fascinating is Hans Jenny, a Swiss engineer and doctor, and his work, which he named Cymatics: the study of the relationship between wave-forms and matter. Using sand, metal filings, powders, plastic particles, Jenny would scatter one of these on a metal plate, and then, using sound controlled by an oscillating crystal, vibrate the plate to various frequencies and pitches.

Energized by the vibrations, the particles on the metal plate seemed to "come to life" as they began to move and undulate, and then to assume beautiful and symmetrical shapes. Some of the shapes were those that Sacred Geometry sees as underlying the generation and preservation of all physical forms. With the right vibrations, the particles even assume organic shapes: the hexagonal cells of a honeycomb, concentric rings of tree growth, tortoise shell patterns, radiating wheel spokes, like in the canals of a jellyfish.

Dr. Jenny later built an instrument he called a "tonoscope" which transformed sound spoken into a microphone into a visual representation on a monitor screen. "Om," the sacred Hindu syllable, when spoken correctly, produces first a circle, then, within the circle, an array of interlocking triangles forming a "yantra," an archetypal pattern expressive of sacred vibration. David Tame, in his book, *The Secret Power of Music*, in a chapter called "The Physics of Om," writes:

> Other photographs have been taken of liquids such as water, by means of a stroboscope. They capture intricate yet beautifully symmetrical interactions of various amplitudes of waves passing through the substances. The viewer has the impression of seeing the Creation itself as when the Word went forth into the Celestial Waters. The figures produced are in a constant state of flow. Rotary waves often emerge and set the pattern turning. One experiment resulted in the perfect and dynamic shape of the *T'ai chi*, which symbolizes the interplay of cosmic forces, or the *yang-yin* polarities underlying all manifestation.
>
> Complex and meaningful patterns are even more apparent in Jenny's sound-affected substances when viewed at the *microscopic* level. Then are revealed beautiful and mathematically-precise mandala-structures looking like groupings of microscopically-viewed snowflakes. The stress-interactions created in substances by their exposure to sound frequencies always result in formations replete with meaningful numerological, proportional and symmetrical qualities.

This is, therefore, the way of *sounding*.

Life

Musical tones, or a language with only vowels, make possible a wonderful fluidity and flow for the expression of emotion, but it is with the use of consonants that the word arises as constructive units of thought.

As Lehrs writes:

> The emergence of the sense-bearing word from the merely ringing sound is an exact counterpart to what takes place in nature when the play of organic liquids, regulated by the sound-element, is caused by the life-element to solidify into outwardly perceptible form. By reading in this way the special

function of the life-element among the other three, we are led to the term Word as an appropriate name.

Chaoticising, Weaving, Sounding, and, lastly, Speaking the form-creative Word into the realm of Gravity—these are the four activities through which the dynamic realm which we first designated comprehensively as Levity brings forth nature's manifold entities of which we finally become aware through our corporeal senses.

The Life element works, therefore, by *Speaking* the form-creative Word. We thus have the following correlation:

Air	Light	Weaving
Earth	Life	Word
Water	Chemical	Sounding
Fire	Warmth	Chaoticizing

Reason It Through:
A Guide to Critical Thinking

A basic understanding of logic, and its formal operations, is central to critical thinking. In the elegant formalisms and insights of logic we find powerful analytical tools, the rules of inference, how to distinguish between (and thus recognize) deductive and inductive reasoning, how to evaluate our own thinking, what constitutes good as opposed to poor reasoning, the art of formal argumentation . . .

For those of you who are fans of the TV series, *Star Trek*, the character of Mr. Spock may come to mind here. The unflappable Vulcan is surely worthy of high esteem for founding his life on logic, but Socrates is perhaps a better and more balanced model for our emulation.[1]

Donald Wayne Viney, a philosopher who teaches logic and has written a textbook thereon, tells us that in the study of logic "one is introduced to the principles that make for valid and strong arguments. Since *validity* is a *formal* property of arguments, an introduction to formal principles is indispensable to a full understanding of what it means to think critically. In addition, formal logic provides numerous examples of *reducing problems to their simplest elements*. On its informal side logic invites one to *consider alternative points of view*, to *examine the larger context of isolated arguments*, and generally to *play fair and to demand fair play from others* when it comes to reasoning." And writing of logic's aesthetic appeal:

"Finally, an aspect of logic that is too little appreciated is its sublimity. . . . the abstract structures of the logicians are, in their own ways, every bit as beautiful as a Grecian urn. Quite apart from their usefulness, logic's truths are beautiful." (LN xvi, 35)

And we are reminded by philosopher Charles Hartshorne, who made original and significant contributions to the field of logic, that "logic as a normative science is a branch of ethics." (CSPM, 303) This suggests that the good life clearly entails good thinking.

Just as we smile at some of the beliefs held by people long ago, so too must we realize that some of the ideas that we believe to be firmly established may, some centuries hence, seem merely quaint anachronisms. The "logical" lesson to learn from this is not one of despair, but of humility.

Through the study and practice of logic we can learn:

Not to leap at the first explanation that comes to mind. On the old TV series *Cannon*, William Conrad, as the inimitable logician Frank Cannon, was once heard to utter: "Jumping to conclusions can cause some serious bruises."

That to determine whether or not you are a logical thinker is a matter of not *what* you think, but of *how* you think.

To become aware of the patriarchal bias in our very language, the presuppositions of received thought, and our culture, and thus come to an understanding of why so many feminists are active in the critical thinking movement.

The importance of logical implication:

"Implication is what makes our system of beliefs cohere. If we see that a sentence is implied by sentences that we believe true, we are obliged to believe it true as well, or else change our minds about one or another of the sentences that jointly implied it. If we see that the negation of some sentence is implied by sentences that we believe true, we are obliged to disbelieve that sentence or else change our minds about one of the others. Implication is thus the very texture of our web of belief, and logic is the theory that traces it." (WB, 41)

Although the basic procedures of logic are essential, critical thinking is not reducible to these procedures, but also includes creative imagination, aesthetic sensibility, affective evaluation, intuition . . . As Bernard Meland has suggested, reason is not a single faculty among many, but an activity involving the whole person.

To be a critical thinker is also to cultivate what are called—

The Intellectual Virtues:

- Intellectual autonomy: not captive to the ideas you hold, or "bound and determined" by your own belief system
- Intellectual confidence in reason: faith in your ability to think for yourself, trust in the process of reason and persuasion by reason
- Intellectual courage: to be true to your own thinking, but also to give a fair hearing to ideas you may strongly oppose
- Intellectual empathy: to imagine and feel how it would be to be inside someone else's point of view
- Intellectual fair-mindedness: guided by evidence, not by bias or vested interest
- Intellectual integrity: applying the same standards of reasoning to your arguments and those of your opponent
- Intellectual humility: knowing the limits of your own knowledge
- Intellectual perseverance: to continue to struggle with difficult problems and not look for the easy way out or the quick fix
- Intellectual sense of justice: impartiality and a sense of fair play

Richard Paul has pointed out how these intellectual virtues intertwine, and that to cultivate one entails cultivating the others: "Consider intellectual humility. To become aware of the limits of our knowledge we need the *courage* to face our own prejudices and ignorance. To discover our own prejudices in turn, we must often *empathize* with and reason within points of view toward which we are hostile. To do this, we must typically *persevere* over a period of time, for learning to . . . enter a point of view against which we are biased takes time and significant effort. That effort will not seem justified unless we have the *faith in reason* to believe we will not be 'tainted' or 'taken in' by whatever is false or misleading in the opposing viewpoint. Furthermore, merely believing we can survive serious consideration of an 'alien' point of view is not enough to motivate most of us to consider them seriously. We must also be motivated by an *intellectual sense of justice*. We must recognize an intellectual *responsibility* to be fair to views we oppose. We must feel *obliged* to hear them in their strongest form to ensure that we do not condemn them out of our own ignorance or bias. At this point, we come full circle back to where we began: the need for *intellectual humility*." (CT 327)

Practicing the intellectual virtues of critical thinking does not require that we be coldly objective, unfeeling, and without passion. On the contrary, to actualize our intentions and beliefs, they must be energized by passion.

To be a critical thinker in what Paul calls "the strong sense," we must feel a "passionate drive for clarity, accuracy, and fair-mindedness, a fervor for getting to the bottom of things . . . for listening sympathetically to opposition points of view, a compelling drive to seek out evidence, an intensive aversion to contradiction, sloppy thinking, inconsistent application of standards, a devotion to truth as against self-interest— these are essential commitments of the rational person. They enable us to assent rationally to a belief even when it is ridiculed by others, to question what is passionately believed and socially sanctioned, to conquer the fear of abandoning a long and deeply held belief. There is nothing passive, bland, or complacent about such a person." (CT 348-49)

A "Definition" of Critical Thinking

The word "critic" derives from a Greek word, *kriterion*, which means "a standard, rule, or test by which something can be judged." One of the dictionary definitions of critic is: "a person who indulges in faultfinding, nitpicking, and censure." That's not what we are concerned with here but rather with this: "a person who forms and expresses judgments of people and things according to certain standards or values."

Rather than subscribing to one definition, by looking at many, and also at what may be called the elements of critical thinking, perhaps we can come to a better understanding of what this activity means and what it can accomplish.

There are many helpful definitions of critical thinking that highlight different facets, and here are three:

"thinking appropriately moved by reasons." (Harvey Siegel)

"rational reflective thinking concerned with what to do or believe." (Robert Ennis)

"skillful, responsible, thinking that is conducive to judgment because it relies on criteria, is self-correcting, and is sensitive to context." (Matthew Lipman)

Critical thinking involves:

The careful consideration of opposing points of view, especially as those views are expressed in their strongest forms, and how our own ideas stand up to these opposing points of view . . .

A critical analysis of our own experience and the underlying assumptions we bring to any argument, and an understanding of the implications and consequences of the ideas and beliefs we strongly hold . . .

An increasing awareness of inconsistency, incoherence, and contradiction . . . and an acquaintance with the basic rules of inference as developed in logic, as well as common fallacies to be avoided . . .

Open-mindedness balanced by a healthy skepticism to protect against what seems to be a natural human tendency to gullibility . . .

Eternal vigilance to ensure that we are not stubbornly holding onto beliefs that no longer serve us, and to avoid letting doctrine ossify into dogma: "The desire to be right and the desire to have been right are two desires, and the sooner we separate them the better off we are. The desire to be right is the thirst for truth. On all counts, both practical and theoretical, there is nothing but good to be said for it. The desire to have been right, on the other hand, is the pride that goeth before a fall. It stands in the way of our seeing we were wrong, and thus blocks the progress of our knowledge. Incidentally it plays hob with our credibility rating." (WB133)

Why Is Critical Thinking Important—Especially Now?

The future we face in the new millennium is a post-industrial world of accelerating change and increasing complexity. Technology will continue to proliferate. Microsoft, and all the other software developers, will be presenting us with frequent upgrades.

The skills learned in Critical Thinking can help us keep pace with, and adapt to, this unrelenting technological advance. Critical thinking can help us not to be swept away by the tide of self-serving messages coming at us from all directions: public relations firms, advertising agencies, political campaigns, lobbyists . . .

P. T. Barnum is famous (notorious?) for saying, "There's a sucker born every minute." Just stop for a moment and think about how well the following have fared in human society: con artists, snake oil drummers, political spin doctors, demagogues, charlatans, swindlers, and sharks of corporate crime who enjoy feeding frenzies on other people's money. To counter this we must learn to critically examine rather than thoughtlessly accept.

What is it about recent times that seems to be an open invitation to the formation of cults? "And so it is that vast cults spring up around tissues of distorted description, inveigling innuendo, and concocted hypothesis—carefully woven webs, we might say, of misbelief." (WB121)

Critical thought is liberating and can free us from self-deception, vested interest, bias, prejudice, wishful and fearful thinking, delusion, defense mechanisms, and from our natural ego-, socio-, and ethno-centric tendencies. By applying the critical standard of open-mindedness in all activities where reasoning is involved, we can become better citizens, for, as someone has said, "An open society requires open minds."

Beyond these practical advantages of critical thinking, Raymond S. Nickerson speaks of an even more compelling reason:

"We call ourselves Homo sapiens, in our conceit some would say. Whether we deserve this appellation or not, there can be no question about the importance of cognition to our lives. No other species relies less on instinct and more on its ability to learn, and to think in the broadest sense. We want students to become good thinkers because thinking is at the heart of what it means to be human; to fail to develop one's potential in this regard is to preclude the full expression of one's humanity. Thinking well is a means to many ends, but it is also an end in itself." (TTS 32)

What do Socrates, Jesus, Voltaire, Mark Twain, and James Thurber have in common? How about the knack of using

Humor

as a powerful conceptual tool?

What better weapon than the rapier of wit to puncture pomposity, to skewer superstitions, or to humble hubris? After the notorious shoe-thumping incident by Nikita Khrushchev, we were delivered from this buffoonery with an incisive observation by James Thurber: "Great oafs from little icons grow."

Mark Twain writes of humor's illuminative power:

"Ours is a useful trade, a worthy calling: with all its lightness and frivolity it has one serious purpose, one aim, one specialty, and it is constant to it—the deriding of shams, the exposure of pretentious falsities, the laughing of stupid superstitions out of existence; and that whoso is by instinct engaged in this sort of warfare is the natural enemy of royalties, nobilities, privileges and all kindred swindles, and the natural friend of human rights and human liberties."

Voltaire, whose motto for a time was *Rire et faire rire* ("To laugh and to make laugh"), was hailed by Catherine of Russia as "a god of gaiety." Many of the superstitions and ecclesiastical corruptions prevalent in his age he "annihilated with laughter." Everyone has experienced the visceral pleasure of a good belly laugh but Frederick the Great said of Voltaire that he could make the "mind laugh." And whose mind does not laugh after reading this by Voltaire: "I have never made but one prayer to God, a very short one: 'O Lord, make my enemies ridiculous.' And God granted it."

In Matthew 7:3-5 Jesus tells the parable of the man aware of the mote in another's eye but unaware of the beam in his own. When the writer Elton Trueblood was somberly reading this to his four-year-old son, he was surprised to hear his son suddenly burst out laughing. "He laughed because he saw how preposterous it would be for a man to be so deeply concerned about a speck in another person's eye, that he was unconscious of the fact his own eye had a beam in it. Because the child understood perfectly that the human eye is not large enough to have a beam in it, the very idea struck him as ludicrous. His gay laughter was a rebuke to his parents for their failure to respond to humor in an unexpected place." This event proved to be a fruitful one, for it eventuated in Trueblood writing an excellent book called *The Humor of Christ.*

As for humor being a weapon against hubris, Don Viney tells us that "Socratic irony is itself quite humorous. In the dialogue called *Euthyphro* Socrates plays on Euthyphro's hubris by suggesting that he be Euthyphro's student, and Euthyphro takes the bait! Of course, by the end of the dialogue Euthyphro is trying to escape from Socrates' net of rational argument. It is a lesson in humility that Euthyphro is not eager to learn."

And, at his trial, Socrates surely had the last laugh on the jury when they asked him to come up with some alternative to the death penalty to which they were about to sentence him. Socrates' ironic suggestion was that they give him room and board for the rest of his life at the finest hotel in Athens.

A common saying has it that *in vino veritas*, but the great Irish writer James Joyce has suggested that there is more truth in the phrase *in risu veritas*, "in laughter there is truth." And Johan Huizinga, in his book *Homo Ludens*, makes a thought-provoking observation: "It is worth noting that the purely physiological act of laughing is exclusive to man . . . The Aristotelian *animal ridens* ('laughing animal') characterizes man as distinct from the other animals almost more absolutely than *homo sapiens*." (HL 6)

Last But Not Least

Human history may be read as a long litany of one atrocity after another: unceasing warfare, inquisitions, pogroms, slavery, murder, rape, molestation, genocide, the European witch-craze that has been called a female holocaust, and, in our enlightened age, the Holocaust wherein Hitler's goal was the extermination of an entire people and culture: to make the world *Judenrein*—"clean of Jews." Lest we feel too comfortable under our haloes, let us remember that we share a collective culpability, through our pollution of the planet, in the rapid extinction of thousands of species of plants and animals.

History reveals a human obsession with the development of more "sophisticated" and ever more deadly weapons of war: culminating in "smart" bombs and the apocalyptic nightmare of prolific nuclear arsenals whose crowning glory is Hiroshima and Nagasaki.

Human "hystery" as we are now leaving it behind us is a tale of terrorism: from our own Timothy McVeigh and the Oklahoma City bombing, to Osama bin Laden and the zombie fanatics, the living dead, who mindlessly follow him. The American consciousness will always hereafter be haunted by the image of American Airlines jets crashing into the World Trade Center, people leaping to their death from its windows, and the panic of stampeding people during the collapse of the Twin Towers into a heap of flaming and smoking rubble.

I invite you to stop for a moment and wonder about all this. And ask yourself whether this constitutes almost a divine cry in our time for Critical Thinking?

Alfred North Whitehead on Critical Thinking

Philosophy begins in wonder. And, at the end, when philosophic thought has done its best, the wonder remains. There have been added, however, some grasp of the immensity of things, some purification of emotion by understanding. (MT 168-69)

A clash of doctrines is not a disaster—it is an opportunity. (SMW 186)

In formal logic, a contradiction is the signal of a defeat: but in the evolution of real knowledge it marks the first step in progress towards a victory. This is one great reason for the utmost toleration of variety of opinion. Once and forever, this duty of toleration has been summed up in the words, 'Let both grow together until the harvest.' The failure of Christians to act up to this precept, of the highest authority, is one of the curiosities of religious history. (SMW 187)

Consider this contrast: when Darwin or Einstein proclaim theories which modify our ideas, it is a triumph for science. We do not go about saying that there is another defeat for science, because its old ideas have been abandoned. We know that another step of scientific insight has been gained. (SMW 188)

Religion will not regain its old power until it can face change in the same spirit as does science. Its principles may be eternal, but the expression of those principles requires continual development. (SMW 189)

Endnote

1. See "Awaken Your Inner Socrates" in the next section.

Key to Abbreviations

TTS   Baron, Joan, and Robert Sternberg (Editors). *Teaching Thinking Skills: Theory and Practice*

CSPM Hartshorne, Charles. *Creative Synthesis and Philosophic Method*

HL   Huizinga, Johan. *Homo Ludens: A Study of the Play Element in Culture*

CT   Paul, Richard. *Critical Thinking*

WB   Quine, W. V., and J. S. Ullian. *The Web of Belief*

LN   Viney, Donald Wayne. *Logic for NonVulcans: An Introduction to Logic*

MT   Whitehead, Alfred North. *Modes of Thought*

SMW Whitehead, Alfred North. *Science and the Modern World*

Intuition:
Language of the Soul

Carl Jung said that intuition is "perception via the unconscious,"[1] and Sharon Franquemont, waxing more poetic, says that intuition is "the language of the soul."[2] Though some gifted few such as Shakespeare and Mozart seem to be born with a knowledge of this soul language, most will find that they are not, and, like any other language, it must be slowly learned, and fluency requires much cultivation and much practice. We are assured that it is well worth the effort.

In light of all this, and if Charles Hartshorne is correct in claiming that "Intuition or feeling is richer than thought,"[3] then the importance that intuition plays in life can hardly be overstated.

We learn of the importance of the conscious and frequent use of our intuitive powers when Franquemont tells us that "as with any other skill, intuition is strengthened by use, stays dormant with disuse, and varies with expertise."[4] Many excellent ways to improve intuition may be found in her book, *You Already Know What To Do*. Designed around ten basic "invitations of the soul"—Just Say "Yes," Open Your Senses, Cultivate Silence, Nurture Joy, Set Time Free, Shift Space, Discover Your Purpose, Mate With Soul, Partner Exponentially, and Connect The Dots—the practice of these invitations promises to raise what she calls your "InQ" (Intuition Quotient). Franquemont also offers four models for understanding intuition:

1. The Science Centered Model: The Left/Right Brain Theory
2. The Psychologically Centered Model: Carl Jung's Four Functions
3. The Religious Centered Model: The Chakra System
4. The Earth-centered Model: The Wisdom of Indigenous People

She emphasizes the power of silence: "Because I believe that silence equals power, I've used the phrase 'the power of silence' throughout this chapter. Sige [the Roman goddess of silence], a powerful teacher of mysterious silence, gives birth to wisdom. The intuition which fosters powerful human encounters with creativity, peak performance, telepathic connections, and profound insights is recognized by experts to arise out of silence. In silence, you hear intuition's voice."[5]

Intuition and Theta

Creative intuitions often come not as words or voice, but as imagery. It was an image, an image of the uroborus, the snake swallowing its own tail, presented to him while he was in a light doze, that gave Friedrich Kekulé the key to the hitherto elusive structure of the benzene molecule. Einstein, who said, "I very rarely think in words at all," apparently intuited in the same manner via imagery emerging up from the creative unconscious. Archimedes had his famous "Eureka" experience while soaking in a tub of hot water. Almost twenty-five centuries ago Democritus flashed on the atomic structure of matter upon smelling the aroma of freshly baked bread.

Not verbal thought but an image from a nightmare gave Elias Howe the insight that enabled him to invent the sewing machine. It was not while racking his brain in the lab, but as he was walking down a *spiral* staircase at Oxford that James Watson intuitively glimpsed the *spiral* shape of DNA. In his book *The Quark and the Jaguar* (262-63), Murray Gell-Mann, winner of the Nobel Prize in Physics, describes how through a slip of the tongue he "immediately stopped dead" and had a sudden intuitive understanding of how "strange" particles differ from the more familiar ones such as protons and neutrons, an understanding to which he had formerly been blind because of intellectual baggage that, in the twinkling of an eye, he now saw to be mere superstition.

All these examples, I believe, show aspects of the subtle power of the intuitive mode for creative breakthrough. Note that many of these examples occurred when the person was probably in the brain-wave states known as Theta.

Until the age of around six, children spend most of their time in Theta. Is it mere coincidence that, during this time, they demonstrate their remarkable ability to so easily learn a language? And does not this Theta state, so natural to a child, shed new light on Jesus' saying that we should become as little children?

Consider the internationally acclaimed healer and medicine woman, Rosalyn Bruyere, who has been called "a healer's healer." In the July 1999 issue of *Intuition* magazine, Diane Goldner writes, "Stories of Bruyere's healing prowess are legion. I myself have seen her separate the fused spinal vertebrae of a young minister when doctors urged surgery . . ."

Is it not interesting that, when Bruyere is working with a patient, her brain wave state is typically Theta?

Intuition and Reason

There are intuitions and then there are "intuitions"—the ones that cause eyes of the wary to roll. This requires some method to distinguish between spiritual illumination and psychic hallucination. This is the function of reason and of sensibility. Franquemont offers this: "One simple criterion for distinguishing authentic intuition from ego projections or wishful thinking is that the real stuff is delivered as invitations, not demands. The words 'You should do . . .' or 'You must do . . .' are not part of intuition. Rather, intuition is your soul saying, 'Please consider . . .' or 'Will you . . . ?'"[6]

Also, even though some formulations may reflect intuitions of eternally valid truths, such formulations can always be improved, made clearer, more elegant, of a higher degree of generality so as to apply to a broader range of phenomena.

Another function of reason is to abandon those formulations when they become obsolete or antiquated, and come up with what Alfred North Whitehead calls "transitions to new fruitfulness of understanding . . . by recurrence to the utmost depths of intuition for the refreshment of imagination."[7] This is surely where *new* thinking comes into play: not only to update, but also to see to it that doctrine does not ossify into dogma.

In the adventure of ideas, reason and intuition, like yin and yang, mutually inform and augment one another in the creative advance into novelty. Think of the evolution of science and mathematics—Leibniz, for example, had to first intuit and then invent the calculus to further advance his understanding, and it was through the modality of the calculus that he advanced his understanding, his vision.

Intuition and Water

It's intriguing to learn that Buckminster Fuller had two of his major intuitions while gazing at water. One example:

"In 1917, while Ezra Pound in London was extracting *virtù* from *The Seafarer* to make what would be *Canto* I, a seafarer ten years his junior, great-nephew of Emerson's collaborator Margaret Fuller, was watching the bubbles boiled up in the wake of a Navy ship, and concluding from those millions of changing spheres that nature did not use pi. For pi will only describe a sphere once formed, and a sphere moreover idealized because static. But the generation of forms is described by vectors ("Vectors represent energy events, and they are discrete"), and Buckminster Fuller proposed to make it his business to find nature's energetic geometry. Just 50 years later the bubble behind the ship had become in Montreal a geodesic skybreak bubble 20 stories high, enclosing 7 million cubic feet of air, as free as a water bubble of internal supports, and weighing a hundredth of what former technology dictated that such a structure should weigh. The load on its foundations was less than the weight of its materials, and had it been a mile wide it would have floated away. Outlining the first principles of the universe whose differentiation by mind can yield such a marvel, its designer spoke of knots."[8]

In religious imagery, water is often a symbol for Spirit. Think of "the face of the waters" in the creation story in "Genesis." In the *Tao Te Ching*, the Tao is described as "a river flowing home to the sea" and Meister Eckhart likened God to "a great underground river that no one can dam up and no one can stop."

Alan Watts, in his de*lightful* and lucid book, *The Way of Zen* (p. 99), talks about *yun shui* (雲水 "cloud" & "water") "the common and revealingly picturesque term for the Zen student, who drifts like a cloud and flows like water."

It was a rainbow, that mystical mirage of sunlight and mist, that God chose as symbol to establish his covenant with humankind. Baptism, ablutions and rituals of pouring, sacred rivers such as the Ganges and the Jordan, rain dances, sweat lodges, water spirits in mythology such as nymphs and naiads, the still pool as metaphor for the enlightened mind, the living water that Jesus talks about in John's Gospel that keeps you from ever thirsting again—Jesus, whose ministry began with his baptism in the river Jordan, whose first disciples were fishermen, whose first miracle was turning water to wine, Jesus, who calms the tempestuous sea and walks on water, who tells us we must be born again, of water and Spirit, who washes the disciples' feet with water, and whose next to last utterance on the cross is, "I thirst."

Water, water, *everywhere!* . . . as Coleridge says in his poem, "Rime of the Ancient Mariner." "Life is an aquatic phenomenon," my old biology Prof told us again and again.

We humans are drawn to water for refreshment of body and spirit—just look at how people flock to lakes, rivers, waterfalls, geysers, beaches, the open sea. And the sound of water—how refreshing and soothing: the ocean surf, a babbling mountain stream, gentle rain, a quiet fountain in a peaceful garden . . . is this not music for the soul?

God's Spirit gives life, and also sustains it, and how God's Spirit refreshes and cleanses! But so does water! Life on this planet began in water, just as each one of us, with bodies over 70% water, began life in the amniotic fluids of our mother's womb. Water symbolizes not only the presence of Spirit, but also the activity of Spirit, and, in its many splendid forms, what a beautiful, rich, and endlessly suggestive symbol it is. As Bucky Fuller's example shows, the contemplation of water can cause revolutionary intuitive ideas to bubble up from our own watery depths.

Since water has the power of evoking the Presence, we would do well to often dwell in the evocative presence of water in all its myriad forms, water in stillness, water in flow, the "living water" shining through the real, sustaining, refreshing, cleansing: leading us by the still waters into the very water of Life itself.

Endnotes

1. C. G. Jung, *The Archetypes of the Collective Unconscious*, p. 282.

2. Sharon Franquemont, *You Already Know What To Do*, p. 2, *passim.*

3. Charles Hartshorne, *Insights and Oversights of Great Thinkers*, p. 104.

4. Franquemont, pp. 11-12.

5. Franquemont, p. 125.

6. Franquemont, p. 5.

7. Alfred North Whitehead, *Adventures of Ideas*, p. 159.

8. Hugh Kenner, *The Pound Era*, pp. 161-62.

Goethe's Way of Seeing:
The Science and the
Poetics of Perception

Norwood Russell Hanson, a philosopher of science, offers for our consideration this tantalizing thought: "There is more to seeing than meets the eye."[1] The truth of this was vividly brought home to me when I discovered that Goethe, the great German writer, developed a way of seeing that can be a powerful addition to everyone's perceptual experience.

Most people know that Goethe was a consummate poet and dramatist, but not so many know that he also accomplished significant work in science, and that he rivaled da Vinci in the versatility of his accomplishments.[2] While some of Goethe's discoveries have always attracted and continue to attract interest, there is perhaps even more interest in his Method of doing science, or his way of seeing.[3]

In his scientific studies, Goethe developed a way of observing nature that is so subtle and innovative that it amounts to creating new perceptive powers. As he put it, "Every new object, well contemplated, opens up a new organ of perception within us."[4]

In his essay "Elements and Ethers: Modes of Observing the World," the German biologist Jochen Bockemühl brings a new dimension to Goethe's Method by seeing it as a fourfold process that he interprets in terms of the four traditional elements: earth, water, air, and fire. Nigel Hoffmann, a philosopher who teaches at the University of Newcastle in

Australia, builds on the work of Bockemühl by putting it into practical application, and by bringing to light the link between art and science that is always present in Goethe's scientific studies.

This article will draw heavily on the thought of these two men as we explore Goethe's way of seeing. But first, to show the power of Goethe's Method, I will present a brief sketch of three of Goethe's scientific discoveries.

Goethe's Discoveries

Fossils

Goethe was the first to see that fossils bear a crucial relationship to the strata of earth where they are discovered, and that the organisms, of which the fossils are remains, lived during the geological periods when those strata were formed. He prophetically concluded from his studies that "the time will soon come when one will no longer just throw fossils all together but will classify them according to the world epochs."[5]

Bone of Contention

The scientific community in Goethe's day was in agreement about one of the physical characteristics that distinguish humans from apes and other mammals: a small bone in the upper jaw called the intermaxillary. Humans were the only mammal in which this bone was not present. Goethe's way of seeing enabled him to discern this bone in the skulls of human anatomical specimens. Although some scientists came around to Goethe's way of seeing when they read his argument and looked at the evidence he presented, many stubbornly refused to validate his discovery. There's a lesson here: when opinion ossifies into dogma, vision can ossify into blindness.

To his lasting honor, and as a tribute to his power of observation, the intermaxillary bone, or *os intermaxillare*, is also called the "Goethe bone."

The Metamorphosis of Plants

Goethe was a natural born holistic thinker and he coined a word for this kind of thought: *Ganzheitsdenken*—thinking your way into the wholeness of things. Thinking his way into what constitutes the wholeness of a living plant, Goethe came to see a rhythm of creative *movement* pulsating in the plant.

The unity of the plant is one complete formative *movement*—and the one form presiding throughout this movement is no static form, but a dynamic form that is mobile, temporal, and, while invisible to the senses, can become visible to the imagination. This formative movement is *metamorphosis*, which means "transformation."

But metamorphosis, as Goethe used the word, is not simply transformation, but an *upward* transformation. Goethe saw in the developmental sequence of an annual flowering plant a progressive enhancement of expression. In his words: "Regular metamorphosis may also be called *progressive* metamorphosis: it can be seen to work step by step from the first seed leaves to the last formation of the fruit. By changing one form into another, it ascends—as on a spiritual ladder—to the pinnacle of nature: propagation through two genders."[6]

This *movement* of metamorphosis will be discussed in more detail later in this article, in the section about the Water Element.

At this point I will also mention that the content of this section will suggest to some that Goethe has affinities with process thought. Indeed, some aspects of Goethe's thought are so suggestive of this that I have traced, in an endnote,[7] substantial links between Goethe and the premier process philosopher of the twentieth century, Alfred North Whitehead. With all this in place, I will now turn to Goethe's Fourfold Method and its first element: Earth.

Earth Element

The mode of observation used by science is empiricism—using the senses, especially sight, to see reality as it really is, objectively, and not guided by subjective bias. But whereas materialistic science tends to employ an *assertive* empiricism that stands completely apart from the object of investigation, Goethe called his method "a *gentle* empiricism" (*eine zarte Empirie*) that is so receptive to the object, and so participates in the life or being of the object, that it "makes itself utterly identical with the object."

As an object of study in this exercise, I suggest a small annual plant that flowers and bears fruit. In the Earth Element phase, the focus is on the external aspects of the plant. To begin: let it be *as if* you are seeing this plant for the first time, and open yourself to a fresh *first impression* of the plant. Linger with that impression for a while, release it, and let it meander into memory.

Now, simply look at the plant, but with the eyes of an artist. With an active gaze, take in the various contours, the colors, the surfaces, the shapes. What does the outer appearance really look like? In terms of external appearance alone, what is the plant expressing to the world, to you?

Run your fingertips lightly along the surfaces of the plant. What do they feel like? What is the scent of the stem, the leaves, the flowers? If you wish, you can taste a leaf, a petal of a flower, or, if present, the pollen.

Relax your eyes, allow your eyelids to almost but not quite close, and gaze at the plant in soft focus. Close your eyes and form an idea, or a mental image, of what the plant looks like. Do you see the image so clearly that you could draw a picture of the plant, but *without looking at it?*

As perception in this mode deepens, we begin to see that what is lacking is the temporal dimension of the plant. We can, of course, talk about the organic processes of a plant, but Bockemühl reminds us that descriptions of the temporal qualities of a plant (such as "it blossoms in May") easily become *established*—the German word he uses is *festgestellt*, which literally means "made solid."

He goes on to say, "It slowly becomes clear to us that we come to *firm* conclusions, that we are always *limited to the surface* of things and see them as *separate*, exactly because the qualities of *solidity*, *impenetrability* and *separateness* are rooted in our cognitional attitude itself. This attitude can be characterized . . . as having the quality of the earth element."[8]

And so we turn now to the second phase, or Water, the time dimension of the plant, and its inner dimension, where Goethe will help us to see with the eyes of imagination.

Water Element

To observe a living plant, even on a number of successive occasions, is to see only a series of "snapshots" of what is really a seamless flow, a metamorphic process of continuous change. As they unfold in temporal sequence, the various parts of a plant—stem, leaves, flowers—are the expressions of what Hoffmann calls _one generative movement_.

It is this _one generative movement_ that is the fundamental and dynamic nature of the plant. Just as the invisible energy of a whirlpool is made visible by the water wherein it swirls, so is the _one generative movement_ made visible by the external form of the plant itself. Although we can see the plant, the _movement_ itself cannot be perceived by the senses; however, we can directly experience it by re-creating, in imagination, the whole life of the plant.

This, too, is a mode of observation, but it is a _new_ way of seeing and Goethe calls it "exact sensorial imagination" (_exakte sinnliche Phantasie_). This kind of imagination, far from being a flight of fancy, is _exact_ and _sensorial_ because it is based on the precise observations of the Earth phase.

An exercise that will help you see this movement is to cut the leaves from a plant and then place them in sequence, for comparison, as in the illustration below. By following the sequence of changes, you become aware, as Bockemühl puts it, "of a sequential change in the forms—a _movement_ which is not present for the senses as movement in the normal sense."[9]

Figure 1

Leaves arranged from bottom of stem (lowest left) to top (bottom right).

And so, beginning with the sprouting seed, we create, in imagination, a moving picture of the development of the plant through stem, branches, leaves, flower, fruit, and new seeds within the fruit. As we run this moving picture over and over, and, as Goethe suggests, both forward and backward, we begin to see it as one flowing process: the *movement* of metamorphosis.

And this brings us to why this is called the Water phase. To experience the *movement* itself, the mind must become so fluid that it can flow like water and, also like water, conform to whatever it touches. As Hoffmann says, "Exact sensorial imagination does this by molding itself to one form and then 'flowing' to the next so that the particulars are 'dissolved' into one fluid movement."[10]

Air Element

Like water, air is a fluid, but it is lighter and more insubstantial than water—you cannot see it or touch it. The purer the air, the more transparent it is. The lightness or buoyancy of air supports beautiful cloud formations and the flow of air can be felt in every breeze. In the airy mode of observation we welcome these qualities of air into consciousness.

We have progressed from a mental image, a snapshot or a still life of the plant, to moving pictures from which we learned to glimpse the essence of *movement* itself. Each successive phase represents a higher "distillation" of whatever phenomenon it is that we are observing. The images we perceive reflect an increasing lightness, in both senses of the word, and intensification.

Now, with the element of air, we begin to perceive *meaning* in the images, to see them as what Goethe called "gestures." A gesture is a movement that expresses meaning. To give you an idea of the gestures to be perceived in plants, consider the following by George Trevelyan:

"In the workings of nature there seems to be a lifting of inert substance towards greater lightness and a more etherealized state. The living plant makes its gesture of opening its chalice towards the light, lifting dark substance towards a realm of higher frequency and offering a point where ethereal formative forces can stream down into the earth plane."[11]

We enjoy a natural intimacy with the air element through the breathing of air—our breath—and the rhythms of breathing, inhalation and exhalation, mirror the rhythms of expansion and contraction that, as we will see in the next section, Goethe saw as active in the growth of a plant. The mode of cognition in this phase, according to Hoffmann, is "inspiration," and when we look at the etymology of this word we find that it derives from two Latin roots that mean "to breathe into."

Fire Element

Imagine a candle flame and note how the flame rises in the air. Seemingly free from gravity, the flow of fire is always up, up, and away . . . and, like church steeples, fire reaches with fingers of flame for the heavens above. Imparting both warmth and light, fire burns with sheer intensity concentrated in the still point of the rising flame.

Observation in this phase will be in the intuitive mode, what Goethe called *anschauende Urteilskraft* or "intuitive judgment" or, as one writer translates it, the "perceptive power of thought." The object here is to perceive archetypal patterns, primal phenomena—*Urphänomen*, to use Goethe's word—and to experience what fundamentally constitutes the wholeness of the plant. But, as Hoffmann says, "The whole is nothing substantial or nothing actualized. It is pure potentiality or potency."[12] To perceive this is to see the *movement* discerned in the water stage at an even higher level of distillation.

As an example of primal phenomena, one gesture in the growth patterns of plants that Goethe was the first to see was a dynamic polarity that he saw as an archetypal creative principle. Writer Ernst Lehrs describes it thus:

"Goethe recognized a certain rhythm of expansion and contraction, and he found that the plant passes through it three times during any one cycle of its life. In the foliage the plant expands, in the calyx it contracts; it expands again in the flower and contracts in the pistil and stamens; finally, it expands in the fruit and contracts in the seed."[13]

Among the many variations on this theme of expansion and contraction, I'll mention only one: the rise and fall of barometric pressure, which Goethe saw as the "breathing" of our planet, thus linking the two elements, earth and air. As we experience the four elements one after the other—earth, water, air, and fire—we not only come to see the plant in a new way, but we also achieve a new way of seeing.

To sum up this section, Henri Bortoft, a physicist and philosopher of science, puts it as felicitously as it can be put:

"When we try to think concretely with the plant we participate in the doing of the plant. This doing, which *is* the plant, is the very being of the plant, as we can discover for ourselves when we think *with* the plant, instead of looking *at* it and thinking *about* it. In this way the movement of our thinking participates in the formative movement of the plant, so that the plant 'coins itself into thought' instead of into material form as in outer nature."[14]

The Metamorphosis of the Scientist

Frederick Amrine, a university professor who has published extensively on Goethe's scientific works, makes what seems at first a startling observation but, once understood, it seems as obvious as a Zen koan: whenever there is progress in science, "It is not the *data* that change in a 'Gestalt switch.' Rather, it is *we* who change."[15] And *what* changes is that we develop *new ways of seeing.*

An example provided by Ronald Brady will help to clarify this. When you observe the following figure, what do you see?

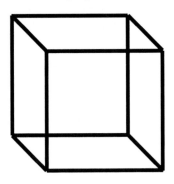

Figure 2

There is a deliberate ambiguity built into this figure. Looked at in one way, it appears as a cube slanting down to the right. But, if you gaze at it for a while, it will suddenly do a flip and appear as a cube slanting up to the left. With sufficient practice you can make the "two" cubes oscillate back and forth every few seconds and, with further practice, and patience, you can even come to see the figure not as a box, but merely as lines all on the same flat plane.

The point to notice here is that the figure itself does not change. What, then, does change? As Brady, in his essay "The Idea in Nature," explains:

"These differing configurations are not added by thought after the object is perceived but are intended by the perceiver in the act of perceiving. The observer who attempts to make the choice of cubes voluntary will find that to exchange one cube for another no further change is required than thinking (intending) the other cube. Simply look at the cube presently seen and think or imagine the alternate cube until it appears. The shift should take place in a few seconds. Only an intentional change is required to produce the difference, for the alternate cube represents an alternate set of relations rather than a new sensible report.

"The viewer makes these shifts by assigning the spatial relations to the elements in the diagram—particularly those of depth. After all, we must take the elements of the perceptual field to be at specific depths to reach this or that figure. Even the flat pattern presents no exception, for we can come to it only by seeing all elements on the same plane. Since, to see a figure, one must grasp the spatial relations of the same, seeing is also cognizing. Cognition in this sense is not a proposition about what is perceived but an activity that actualizes the perception. *Each act of seeing is necessarily an act of understanding.* The grasp of geometric relations that we use to understand the cube, once seen, is the same one that we use to see it in the first place. We do not perceive and then bring forward a concept to understand. We focus our understanding to bring forth a perception."[16]

Now, in your mind's eye, hold for a while, and compare, Figure 1 (the buttercup leaves) and the cube in Figure 2. Do you now see that both represent a series of transformations, or the movement of metamorphosis? With cultivation and practice, and through active participation in these movements of metamorphosis, Goethe found that he was himself transformed, because the observation of metamorphosis *gives rise to* metamorphosis of the observer. Indeed, this is the whole point!

"For Goethe," as Amrine says, "the experiment is not like a single, practical syllogism but rather like artistic practice directed towards the refinement of one's perception over time. Again we see that the primary aim of science, as Goethe understands it, must be self-development, *the metamorphosis of the scientist.*"[17]

There is an *enhancement* of understanding, an *intensification*, a *heightening*, what Goethe calls *Steigerung.* The verb form of this German word is *steigen* which means "to climb, increase, ascend,"—that is one reason I used, and italicized, the expression "gives rise to" two paragraphs above. We have seen this same heightening, or *Steigerung*, before, in the developmental process of a plant and its many metamorphoses from first sprouting, then stem, leaves, and to its fulfillment in flowers that blossom in beauty.

Imagine someone who has never seen a flowering plant who closely follows the process of growth for the very first time. From what he sees in the plant up until the time just before a flower blooms, must it not seem like a miracle when he goes out one morning to find something utterly new that the plant has given rise to during the night: the splendor of an open blossom. Ah!—would not wonder thrill in his veins at such a marvel!

As the blossom is to the plant, so is the moment of epiphany to the modes of observation that have preceded and prepared the way for it. *Steigerung!*

The Varieties of Perceptual Experience

Goethe's holistic thinking is reflected in his searching for not just one way of seeing a particular object, but many different ways. These modes of observation, or ways of conceiving things, are, to use the term that Goethe coined, *Vorstellungsarten.*[18] Together, these different modes of observation insure balance, do justice to the plurality, depth, richness, and complexity of nature, and give rise to a wholeness in perception that would otherwise be missed.

To give you some examples of *Vorstellungsarten*, Dennis L. Sepper notes that Goethe's magnum opus, *Zur Farbenlehre*, "is suffused with their presence. As we read through it we see the continual emergence, interplay, adaptation, ebb, and reemergence of—to name some of the chief ones—the genetic and the atomistic, the dynamic and the mechanical, the concrete and the abstract, the mathematical and the physical, the material and the spiritual ways of thinking and conceiving things."[19]

In contrast to Newton, and the scientific community of his day, whose *Vorstellungsarten* he saw as atomistic, mechanical, and mathematical, Goethe characterized his own way of conceiving as genetic, dynamic, and concrete. This method can be seen at work in how Goethe described, in a letter to a friend, how he went about his optical studies:

"The material is, as you know, extremely interesting and the elaboration a mental exercise of a sort that I perhaps would not have gained in any other way. To grasp the phenomena, to fixate them into experiments, to order one's experiences, and to come to know all the ways in which one might view them; to be as attentive as possible in the *first* case, as exact as possible in the *second*, to be as complete as possible in the *third*, and to remain many-sided enough in the *fourth*, requires that one work through one's poor ego in a way I had else hardly thought possible."[20]

Working with a method such as this, more comprehensive truth about something may be revealed by looking at it from various perspectives, and enhancements of understanding can sometimes be achieved by seeing as if through the eyes of someone whose mode of observation, or way of conceiving may differ from you, even to the point of being exactly opposite.

To be comprehensive, the truth, as Sepper points out, "must be approached from all its many sides. *A priori* there is no single, authoritative way to approach a given phenomenon; and a single human being, plagued by many kinds of one-sidedness, would scarcely be able to produce a science on his own. Thus pluralism is not just one among many desiderata but an absolute prerequisite for a constructive and progressive science, whose goal is less to produce a set of true propositions and indoctrinate scientists into their intention than to amplify the human experience of nature. . . . Goethe frequently pointed out to friends that his scientific work had made him many-sided by compelling him to entertain different points of view, some of which he was able to incorporate into his own; and by practicing sciences he gradually developed 'organs' for experiencing and understanding that originally he had not possessed."[21]

And so Goethe here exemplifies once again the movement of metamorphosis that results in a heightening or enhancement of his perceptual powers. The idea of metamorphosis is central to Goethe's thought and finds its fullest expression in a work he titled *The Metamorphosis of Plants*. In light of what we have seen, he could just as well have called it *The Metamorphosis of Goethe*.

Endnotes

1. Norwood Russell Hanson, *Perception and Discovery*, p. 61.

2. From the back cover of Goethe's book, *Maxims and Reflections*:

    Throughout his long, hectic, and astonishingly varied life, Johann Wolfgang von Goethe (1749–1832) would jot down his passing thoughts on theatre programs, visiting cards, draft manuscripts, and even bills. Goethe was probably the last true "Renaissance Man." Although employed as a Privy Councilor at the Duke of Weimar's court, where he helped oversee major mining, road-building, and irrigation projects, he also painted, directed plays, carried out research in anatomy, botany, and optics—and still found time to produce masterpieces in every literary genre.

    His fourteen hundred Maxims and Reflections reveal some of his deepest thought on art, ethics, literature, and natural science, but also his immediate reactions to books, chance encounters, or his administrative work.

And this from *The Columbia Encyclopedia*:

    Increasingly aloof from national, political, or even literary partisanship, Goethe became more and more the Olympian divinity, to whose shrine at Weimar all Europe flocked. The variety and extent of his accomplishments and activities were monumental. Goethe knew French, English, Italian, Latin, Greek, and Hebrew and translated works by Diderot, Voltaire, Cellini, Byron, and others. His approach to science was one of sensuous experience and poetic intuition.

    An accomplished amateur musician, Goethe conducted instrumental and vocal ensembles and directed opera performances in Weimar. Goethe's exquisite lyrical poems, often inspired by existing songs, challenged contemporary composers to give their best in music.

3. Frederick Amrine and Francis J. Zucker, in their Introduction to *Goethe and the Sciences: A Reappraisal*, have this to say about the stature of Goethe's scientific studies:

    In his scientific work, Goethe simultaneously stands within modern science, seeks to expand it, and stands opposed. This complex relationship is perhaps one reason why Goethe's scientific writings have remained a subject of perennial interest, while the work of so many of his contemporaries has been saved from oblivion only by the curiosity of historians.

    Goethe certainly considered himself a scientist in the fullest sense of the word: late in life, he even claimed that he hoped and expected to be remembered more as a scientist than as a poet. He participated actively in many of the important scientific debates of his day, performed and promoted research, corresponded with his great contemporaries in science, and published voluminously in numerous fields, including the history and philosophy of science. While some parts of his work (notably his meteorological and geological studies) have never found favor, others, such as his work in physiological optics, animal morphology, and botany were widely accepted—even hailed—by the scientific "establishment" of his day, and led directly or indirectly to further advances. A number of important scientific works were dedicated to him. For these reasons alone, Goethe the scientist would be worthy of continuing historical study.

    Yet surely Goethe's role in the history of "mainstream" science is not sufficiently large or important to account for the small mountain of secondary literature that his work has called forth. Granted that his stature as a literary figure has played a part, even this cannot account fully for the unbroken attraction of his scientific writings. After all, Newton's theological speculations (a roughly analogous case) have not elicited anything like the number of studies inspired by this aspect of Goethe—perhaps 10,000 in all. The reason for the attraction lies elsewhere: it is that Goethe sought to do science in a different way.

4. "Every new object, well contemplated, opens up a new organ of perception within us." In German: "Jeder Gegenstand, wohl

beschaut, schliesst ein neues Organ in uns auf." —this is from Goethe's "Significant Help Given by an Ingenious Turn of Phrase," a short essay in his book, *Scientific Studies*.

5. Goethe in a letter to Johann Heinrich Merck on October 27, 1782.

6. J. W. von Goethe, *Scientific Studies*, Edited and translated by Douglas Miller, p. 76. (This is Volume 12 of Goethe's Collected Works published by Princeton University Press.)

7. Morphology, the science of organic form, was founded and named by Goethe. In "The Purpose Set Forth," a short essay about this new science, he makes a distinction between two ways of conceiving the living forms of nature. The following quotation from the essay will show that Goethe articulates a "process" view of nature that clearly anticipates some elements in the thought of Alfred North Whitehead (1861-1947), the founder of process philosophy:

Thus the history of art, knowledge, and science has produced many attempts to establish and develop a theory which we will call "morphology." The historical part of our discourse will deal with the different forms in which these attempts have appeared.

The Germans have a word for the complex of existence presented by a physical organism: *Gestalt* [structured form]. With this expression they exclude what is changeable and assume that an interrelated whole is identified, defined, and fixed in character.

But if we look at all these *Gestalten*, especially the organic ones, we will discover that nothing in them is permanent, nothing is at rest or defined—everything is in a flux of continual motion. This is why German frequently and fittingly makes use of the word *Bildung* [formation] to describe the end product and what is in process of production as well.

Thus in setting forth a morphology we should not speak of *Gestalt*, or if we use the term we should at least do so only in reference to the idea, the concept, or to an empirical element held fast for a mere moment of time.

When something has acquired a form it metamorphoses immediately to a new one. If we wish to arrive at some living perception of nature we ourselves must remain as quick and flexible as nature and follow the example she gives.

In anatomy, when we dissect a body into its parts, and further separate these parts into their parts, we will at last arrive at elementary constituents called "similar parts." These will not concern us here. Instead we will concentrate on a higher principle of the organism, a principle we will characterize as follows.

No living thing is unitary in nature; every such thing is a plurality. Even the organism which appears to us as individual exists as a collection of independent living entities. Although alike in idea and predisposition, these entities, as they materialize, grow to become alike or similar, unalike or dissimilar. In part these entities are joined from the outset, in part they find their way together to form a union. They diverge and then seek each other again; everywhere and in every way they thus work to produce a chain of creation without end. [Douglas Miller, translator]

Like Whitehead, who called his thought the philosophy of organism, Goethe's focus was on the organic processes of nature and his work has been characterized by one writer as a "new organics." So impressed was Rudolf Steiner, who was called upon to oversee and edit the publication of a new edition of Goethe's scientific writings, that he hailed Goethe as "the Galileo of the organic sciences."

Goethe saw the natural world not as a finished product, but as an always or ever creating nature (*einer immer schaffenden Natur*). The essence or true nature of all natural entities can be apprehended, not by scrutiny of static forms, but only by bringing attention to the coming-to-be or the becoming of the entity. Instead of asking, What *is* it?—the crucial question for Goethe was, How does it *become*?

This is not to exclude permanence, or something that abides, for Goethe saw an essential polarity dynamically present throughout the universe (as did Whitehead), with one polar term serving as a necessary complement to the other. Thus, in making a distinction between reason and understanding, two modes of conceiving the world, he writes:

"Reason is directed to things in the course of becoming; understanding, to things that have become." (*Die Vernunft ist auf das Werdende, der Verstand auf das Gewordene angewiesen.*)

Again, like Whitehead, and unlike scientific materialism, Goethe found reason to seek explanations of phenomena in terms of a top-down approach rather than starting at the bottom. The highest expressions of nature may suggest what is also present, if only nascently, in the lowest forms. Speaking of this aspect of Goethe, Ernst Lehrs says, "He was in actual fact deeply interested in the lower plants, but . . . to understand the plant [in general] he found himself obliged to pay special attention to examples in which it came to its most perfect expression. For what was hidden in the alga was made manifest in the rose. To demand of Goethe that in accordance with ordinary science he should have explained nature 'from below upwards' is to misunderstand the methodological basis of all his investigations."

Yet another of Goethe's ideas, _Steigerung_, meaning, as discussed above, a heightening, intensification, or enhancement of experience—this, too, resonates with Whitehead's thought. One of Whitehead's deepest convictions was that value pervades the natural world and that the thrust of the evolutionary process is toward creatures who can enjoy ever higher harmonies and intensities of feeling.

To use a musical analogy, the heightening, or _Steigerung_, seen in the series from cicada to songbird to Mozart reveals a rising scale of such aesthetic enjoyments. "The teleology of the Universe," says Whitehead, "is directed to the production of Beauty." And, to give a concrete example, Goethe would say that the teleology of a plant is directed to the blossoming of a flower. For what is the flower but a masterpiece of _Steigerung_, as actualized by the plant itself.

Goethe's extensive studies and experiments in chromatics, the science of color, taught him also to be alert to the becoming, or coming-into-being, of colors in nature.

Again, as a variation on the above theme, for Goethe, the question is not: What _is_ color, but: How does color _arise_? How does color _come to be_?

For example, if you go outside early one morning, before daylight, and gaze up at the sky, you will see all the stars against a background of darkness. But as you continue to gaze, when dawn breaks and the day begins to lighten, you will then see the coming-into-being of the color blue as it suffuses the sky overhead. The color blue, as seen in the sky, is never a finished product, but is always in a process of becoming, of coming into presence.

As physicist Arthur G. Zajonc points out, Goethe agrees with Whitehead regarding the Fallacy of Misplaced Concreteness:

The mistaken ascription of reality to primary qualities and to the hypothetical schemes of the seventeenth century Whitehead calls the error of 'misplaced concreteness.' As a result of the ensuing confusion, he declares, "modern philosophy has been ruined" (SMW, 55).

Goethe fully shares Whitehead's concern regarding the error of misplaced concreteness. He writes in his Theory of Colors: "The investigator of nature should take heed not to reduce observation to mere notion, to substitute words for this notion, and to use and deal with these words as if they were things. . . . Yet how difficult it is not to put the sign in the place of the thing; how difficult to keep the being [*Wesen*] always livingly before one and not to slay it with the word."

The full sensual experience of nature which Goethe embraces can only suffer at the hands of an abstractive science. Nor will Goethe rest satisfied with a purely "descriptive" or "instrumentalist" rendering of natural phenomena. His is a search for the True, an attempt to catch nature showing an Idea in a pure archetypal phenomenon. Goethe's critique of hypothetical entities may sound like Mach or Duhem, but we must not confuse his view of nature or the scientific enterprise with theirs. Goethe was certainly no positivist born ahead of his time. He was remarkably perceptive as to the hidden assumptions of science as he knew it in his own lifetime. But his response was to develop a method of inquiry different in nearly every respect from the positivist school which would follow him.

Arthur G. Zajonc, "Facts as Theory: Aspects of Goethe's Philosophy of Science," 227-28, *Goethe and the Sciences: A Reappraisal* — Editors: Frederick Amrine, Francis J. Zucker, and Harvey Wheeler.

Martin Luther's translation of the Bible, which first appeared in 1534, renders Job 9:11 as follows:

Siehe, er geht an mir vorüber,
ehe ich's gewahr werde,

und wandelt vorbei,
ehe ich's merke.

Lo, He passes by me
before I am aware of it,
and is transformed
before I can take note of it.

The German verb *wandelt*, meaning "to change," or "to transform," expresses a nuance of meaning not found in the King James version:

Lo, He goeth by me,
And I see Him not;
He passeth on also,
But I perceive Him not.

Goethe quotes Luther's rendition of this verse as a thematic statement at the beginning of "Formation and Transformation," the first section of his book *On Morphology*. Bertha Mueller, translator of *Goethe's Botanical Writings*, observes: "Luther's version contains the core of Goethe's morphological thinking, namely, that each organic formation is a chain of transformations . . . In the passage from Job, Goethe interprets the 'He' as the active God-Nature as revealed in the development of organic life." (p. 21)

"Formation and Transformation," Mueller's translation of *Bildung und Umbildung*, suggests an ongoing process of making and remaking, creating and re-creating, which is at least a first approximation of Whitehead's idea of concrescence.

Parabase, a prefatory poem on the frontispiece of *On Morphology*, also resonates with this theme:

Freudig war, vor vielen Jahren,
Eifrig so der Geist bestrebt,
Zu erforschen, zu erfahren,
Wie Natur im Schaffen lebt.
Und es ist das ewig Eine,
Das sich vielfach offenbart:
Klein das Große, groß das Kleine,
Alles nach der eignen Art;

Immer wechselnd, fest sich haltend,
Nah und fern und fern und nah,
So gestaltend, umgestaltend —
Zum Erstaunen bin ich da.

Prose translation by David Luke:
"Many years ago, as now, my mind strove with eager delight to study and discover the creative life of Nature. It is eternal Unity in manifold manifestation: the great is little, the little is great, and everything after its kind; ever changing and yet preserving itself, near and far and far and near, and so shaping and reshaping itself—I am here to wonder at it."

Note the gestalt (shape or form) in *gestaltend* and *umgestaltend* and how these two words repeat the pattern of *Bildung* and *Umbildung*. A polar rhythm pulsates throughout the poem . . .

Zu erforschen, zu erfahren
Klein das Große, groß das Kleine
Immer wechselnd, fest sich haltend
Nah und fern und fern und nah
So gestaltend, umgestaltend

. . . pulsing with a rhythm—the oscillation between two phases—that finds pervasive expression throughout the universe and operates at every level of reality, whether it be the ebb and flow of tides, the rhythms of heartbeat and breath, or atoms that vibrate many billion times per second.

This little poem is big with process themes, such as creativity as the very life of Nature:

Zu erforschen, zu erfahren,
Wie Natur im Schaffen lebt
To discover, to experience,
How Nature in creativity lives

The many and the one find expression in:

Und es ist das ewig Eine,

Das sich vielfach offenbart
And it is the eternal One
That in multiplicity is revealed.

In this line we hear the Whiteheadian theme of permanence and change:

Immer wechselnd, fest sich haltend
Ever changing, ever constant

The penultimate line reverberates again with the theme of creativity:

So gestaltend, umgestaltend —
Shaping, re-shaping
(or)
Creating, re-creating
forming, transforming

The poem begins in joy (*Freudig war*) and ends where Plato says philosophy begins, in wonder (*Erstaunen*). Whitehead concurs: "Philosophy begins in wonder. And, at the end, when philosophic thought has done its best, the wonder remains. There have been added, however, some grasp of the immensity of things, some purification of emotion by understanding." (*Modes of Thought* 168-69)

Finally, since panentheism is a doctrine of process theology, I will mention that there is reason to suppose that Goethe was a panentheist before his countryman and his contemporary, the philosopher Krause, coined the term. The following quote, by Goethe, sheds light not only on his panentheism, but also on the way of seeing that revealed this:

A pure, profound, inborn, and practiced way of viewing things— this has taught me unfailingly to see God in nature, nature in God, and it is this way of thinking that has formed the foundation of my existence.

[. . . bei meiner reinen, tiefen, angeborenen und geübten Anschauungsweise, die mich Gott in der Natur, die Natur in Gott zu sehen unverbrüchlich gelehrt hatte, so daß diese Vorstellungsart den Grund meiner ganzen Existenz machte . . .]

8. Jochen Bockemühl, "Elements and Ethers: Modes of Observing the World," in *Toward a Phenomenology of the Etheric World*, Edited by Jochen Bockemühl, p. 9.

9. Ibid., p. 10.

10. Nigel Hoffmann, "The Unity of Science and Art: Goethean Phenomenology as a New Ecological Discipline," in *Goethe's Way of Science: A Phenomenology of Nature*, Editors: David Seamon and Arthur Zajonc, p. 134.

11. George Trevelyan, "Interlude on Metamorphosis in Plants," online at: http://www.sirgeorgetrevelyan.org.uk/books/thtbk-arch04.html

12. Nigel Hoffmann, "The Unity of Science and Art," pp. 135-36.

13. Ernst Lehrs, *Man or Matter*, pp. 83-84.

14. Henri Bortoft, *The Wholeness of Nature*, p. 289.

15. Frederick Amrine, "The Metamorphosis of the Scientist," p. 36.

16. Ronald H. Brady, "The Idea in Nature: Reading Goethe's Organics," in *Goethe's Way of Science: A Phenomenology of Nature*, Editors: David Seamon and Arthur Zajonc, pp. 87-88.

17. Frederick Amrine, "The Metamorphosis of the Scientist," p. 42.

18. As it may help to clarify the meaning of Vorstellungsarten to see the word used by various writers, here is a selection I culled from my recent reading:

from *Goethe's Way of Science*:
Here is the ground from which all our Vorstellungsarten—all scientific "paradigms"—arise. 47

from *The Wholeness of Nature*:
What Goethe discovered as a result of his encounter with Schiller, with his Kantian background, was the active role in all acts of cogni-

tive perception of what he called a Vorstellungsart [singular form of the word], a way of conceiving, or a mode of illumination, whereby the world becomes visible in a particular way. He realized that different Vorstellungsarten would result in the world being illuminated differently, and hence being disclosed in different modes. 120

from *Goethe and the Sciences*:

The history of the sciences, Goethe says, reflects the succession of "hypotheses, theories, systems and whatever other sorts of 'modes of conception' [types or 'modes of representation,' Vorstellungsarten] by which we strive to grasp the infinite." This notion of Vorstellungsarten is to become central to Goethe's theory of knowledge. If we are able to apply our knowledge in action, we have a certain control on our notions, "for life corrects us [*weist uns zurecht*] at every step." But when the observer is concerned with natural phenomena in themselves, and not as they affect us and are used in our actions, he enters a world in which he is in a sense alone. Then it becomes important to communicate his findings to others from the beginning and to take account of their responses. 51

from *Goethe contra Newton*:

Among the latter he included the Vorstellungsarten, the ways of conceiving things, which he had characterized as the attempt to bring many objects into a relationship that, strictly speaking, they did not have with one another. 91

19. Dennis L. Sepper, "Goethe against Newton: Towards Saving the Phenomenon," in *Goethe and the Sciences: A Reappraisal*, Editors: Frederick Amrine, Francis J. Zucker, and Harvey Wheeler, p. 185.

20. Note how the fourfold theme finds expression in this paragraph. It also finds expression in this excerpt from Goethe's *Theory of Colors*:

An extremely odd demand is often set forth but never met, even by those who make it: i.e., that empirical data should be presented without any theoretical context, leaving the reader, the student, to his own devices in judging it. This demand seems odd because it is useless simply to look at something.

Every act of *looking* turns into *observation*, every act of observation into *reflection*, every act of reflection into the *making of associations*; thus it is evident that we theorize every time we look carefully at the world.

The ability to do this with *clarity of mind*, with *self-knowledge*, in a *free way*, and (if I may venture to put it so) with *irony*, is a skill we will need in order to avoid the pitfalls of abstraction and attain the results we desire, results which can find a living and practical application.

21. Dennis L. Sepper, "Goethe against Newton: Towards Saving the Phenomenon," pp. 185-86.

References

About Formative Forces in the Plant World
   Dick van Romunde
Catching the Light:
The Entwined History of Light and Mind
   Arthur Zajonc
Goethe and the Sciences: A Reappraisal
   Editors: Frederick Amrine, Francis J. Zucker, and Harvey Wheeler
Goethe as Scientist
   Rudolf Magnus
Goethe the Scientist
   Rudolf Steiner
Goethe contra Newton
   Dennis L. Sepper
Goethe's Way of Science:
A Phenomenology of Nature
   Editors: David Seamon and Arthur Zajonc
Man or Matter:
Introduction to a Spiritual Understanding of Nature on the Basis of
Goethe's Method of Training Observation and Thought
   Ernst Lehrs
Toward a Phenomenology of the Etheric World:
Investigations into the Life of Nature and Man
   Editor: Jochen Bockemühl
The Wholeness of Nature:
Goethe's Way Toward a Science of Conscious Participation in Nature
   Henri Bortoft

BOOKS BY GOETHE:

Autobiography
(*Aus meinem Leben: Dichtung und Wahrheit*)
   Translated by John Oxenford
Maxims and Reflections
(*Maximen und Reflektionen*)
   Translated by Elisabeth Stopp

The Metamorphosis of Plants
(*Die Metamorphose der Pflanzen*)
Scientific Studies
(*Wissenschaftliche Schriften*)
     Edited and translated by Douglas Miller
Theory of Colors
(*Zur Farbenlehre*)
     Translated by Charles Eastlake

Part Two
Earth

Rhythms of Rest
and Rejuvenation

Some of you may be surprised to learn that we are all natural-born hypnotists and that we mesmerize ourselves, for the most part unconsciously, several times each day. It all has to do with a natural rhythm—of activity followed by rest—that recurs throughout the day.

This rhythm undulates on all levels, from cellular to conscious experience, where there is a natural oscillation of these two contrasting states of consciousness. Although these periodic fluctuations were glimpsed by Charcot, Freud, and Jung with increasing clarity, it was Milton Erickson, one of the most innovative and influential psychologists of the twentieth century, who first clearly saw the therapeutic potential for healing. Observing how clients during the rest phase showed behavior similar to that of someone under hypnosis, he called it "the common everyday trance." Erickson found it to be so powerful that he made it the fulcrum of his practice.

Whereas most therapists hold a 50-minute session, Erickson worked with patients for an hour and a half or more. He had observed that, during a 90-minute interval, people almost always drift into the common everyday trance, and that during these intervals, which he learned how to facilitate and deepen, a therapeutic window opened, and stayed open for 15 or 20 minutes. While the window was open, a natural healing response was activated.

Erickson became something of a legend because of his "magical" success with patients whose problems had completely baffled other therapists. This "magic" so mystified some of the media who reported on Erickson that an article about him in *Time* magazine was headlined as "The Sorcerer of Phoenix."

Ernest Rossi, a psychologist who studied under Erickson for eight years and who calls himself the Sorcerer's Apprentice, has continued to research and refine this therapeutic approach. It was he who traced how the idea developed via Charcot, Freud, and Jung, and he noted correlations with the many biological rhythms that had already been detected and were being studied by scientists, especially ultradian rhythms such as the *basic rest-activity cycle* (BRAC). (Circadian rhythms are those, such as wakefulness and sleep, that happen once a day. Ultradian rhythms repeat several times a day.) And speaking of sleep, it was in the study of sleep and dreams that the basic rest-activity cycle was discovered. Scientists observed a period of rapid eye movement that occurred every 90 minutes or so in subjects who were sleeping and, when awakened during this REM sleep, the subjects reported that they had been dreaming. Thus, cycles of REM sleep alternated with deep dreamless sleep throughout the night. As above, so below—as by night, so by day!

During the day, the 20-minute rest phase that recurs roughly every 90 minutes—Rossi designates this as the Ultradian Healing Response. This is nature's way of providing a pause that refreshes, so that body and mind can recover from previous exertions, and be recharged and rejuvenated.

According to Rossi, the UHR progresses through four stages of an upward spiral:

1. Recognition Signals
   (sensing signs or cues of nature's call to rest)
2. Accessing the Deeper Breath
   (leading to deeper states of relaxation and healing)
3. Mind-Body Healing
   ("letting go" as a natural process takes over to revive and restore)
4. Rejuvenation and Awakening
   (emerging calm, alert, and refreshed)

To help you notice the beginning of the UHR, here are some of the Recognition Signals that Rossi identifies:

- feeling a need to stretch or move about
- yawning or sighing
- feeling "spaced out"
- being distracted by fantasies
- sharp drop in performance and output

The UHR does not recur with automatic regularity. You can override the process by ignoring it, or by giving your focus to whatever in our sometimes hectic modern world is clamoring for your attention. But if you consistently override it, you are paving the way for what Rossi calls the Ultradian Stress Syndrome. This can lead to a downward spiral where you may find yourself experiencing such malfunctions as accident proneness, errors in judgment, memory problems, slips of the tongue, flashes of irritation, and social gaffes. And if, at this stage, you persist in ignoring the cues for rest and recovery, you can spiral down even further into stress-related illnesses such as ulcers, migraines, impaired immune systems, strokes, and heart problems.

After much research, experimentation, and thought about this, Rossi has come to believe that "the healing traditions of many cultures—medicine man, shaman, faith healer, and hypnotherapist—all tap into our natural Ultradian Healing Response without realizing it," and that the UHR is "the common core of all the holistic mind-body approaches to healing." He has also broadened its application as a source for problem solving, personal growth, creative insights, and the evolution of consciousness.

A practice I suggest we explore is to consciously synchronize our healing prayers with these 20-minute windows of access to our creative unconscious.

Give us this day our daily . . . rhythms!

If you wish to learn more about this, I recommend the following two books by Ernest L. Rossi: *The 20-Minute Break* and *The Psychobiology of Mind-Body Healing.*

Awaken Your Inner Socrates

Socrates is deservedly famous for the art of questioning he discovered and put to good use. Many who came to Socrates with confident beliefs soon came to see, under the light of his incisive questioning, that these beliefs were built upon the sands of confusion, self-contradiction, and superficial misunderstandings. This way of questioning has become known as the Socratic Method.

For Socrates, "the unexamined life is not worth living," and, as the gadfly of Athens, he was committed to autonomy of thought guided by critical reason. He has been called "the ideal thinker." But not only was he cerebral, he was also passionate in his pursuit of both the rational and the virtuous life. With plenty of "backbone" to spare, he was a skewerer of sacred cows; never one to set himself up as an authority, he was sharply critical of beliefs based solely on authority.

As a teacher, as a "midwife" of knowledge, he nurtured among those who came to him an attitude of healthy skepticism and doubt in regard to received opinion, while, at the same time, helping them to become aware of, and bring forth from within, their own original ideas. His method of teaching was not didactic, but the way of skillful questioning, how to reason things through and think one's own way into new insights, and the willingness to change or abandon beliefs when they are clearly shown to be in error.

Unlike the wily Sophists who would stoop to specious reasoning to win an argument, Socrates clearly stated that he would rather lose than win an argument if the truth was found to be on the opposing side:

"Now if you are one of my sort, I should like to cross-examine you, but if not I will let you alone. And what is my sort? you will ask. I am one of those who are very willing to be refuted if I say anything which is not true, and very willing to refute any one else who says what is not true, and quite as ready to be refuted as to refute—for I hold that this is the greater gain of the two, just as the gain is greater of being cured of a very great evil than of curing another." (Plato, *Gorgias*)

Socrates' claim was that he had no knowledge to teach to others, nor is it something that can be memorized from a book; rather, it is something that issues out of the dialogic give-and-take of a process of rational argumentation, whether with oneself or another.

This claim that he had no knowledge to impart to others is a good example of what is called Socratic irony: Webster defines irony as "the use of words to express something other than, and especially the opposite of, their literal meaning." Why "teach" in this roundabout way? In the words of philosopher Gregory Vlastos: "Not, surely, that he does not care that you should know the truth, but that he cares more for something else: that if you are to come to the truth, it must be by yourself, for yourself."[1]

And so this was yet another way of gently persuading others to think for themselves, and it worked like a Zen koan[2] to liberate the mind of some of his students. Irony so used was an original discovery by Socrates, and, as a contribution to the sensibility of the Western mind, Vlastos hails this as one of his chief titles to fame.

The depths of his passion for reason was dramatically shown, at his trial, when he was given the choice, in essence, of abandoning it or his very life. Later, drinking the cup of poison hemlock with complete equanimity among his friends, he chose to die rather than abandon the rational ideal.

For 25 centuries many people in every epoch have looked to Socrates with the greatest admiration. The historian Arnold Toynbee said, "The finest flower of Athens during this half century was not a statue, building, or play, but a soul: Socrates." And Montaigne, the French essayist, regarded Socrates as "the wisest one who ever was." Benjamin Franklin set for himself the goal to "imitate Jesus and Socrates."

If your inner Socrates is not already fully awakened, you may enjoy reading a book by Ronald Gross called *Socrates' Way* wherein he presents seven master keys, derived from Socrates, for using your mind to the utmost:

1. Know Thyself
2. Ask Great Questions
3. Think for Yourself
4. Challenge Convention
5. Grow with Friends
6. Speak the Truth
7. Strengthen Your Soul

Gross devotes a chapter to each of these keys and in each chapter also discusses what he calls "carriers of the flame," people who exemplify these keys in the modern era, such as Richard Feynman, Jean Houston, Dalai Lama, Barbara McClintock, Desmond Tutu, Gloria Steinem, and Carl Jung.

As a final observation on Socrates' enduring appeal, Professor Alexander Nehamas, of Princeton University, suggests a reason for this: "Socrates shows by example the way toward establishing an individual mode of life. His way does not force his followers to repeat his life, but compels them to search for their own."[3]

Endnotes

1. Gregory Vlastos, *Socrates: Ironist and Moral Philosopher*, p. 44.

2. Of the many ingenuities and subtleties in the Zen tradition, one of my favorites is the koan (Chi. kung-an [公案], pronounced in Japanese as two syllables: ko-an). A koan is a Zen "problem" or a Zen "story" or a theme of zazen to be made clear, and may be thought of as an ideal of bafflement. Logical reasoning will get you not closer but only ever more distant from the "solution" of a koan. Zen master Robert Aitken:

   "Koans are the folk stories of Zen Buddhism, metaphorical narratives that particularize essential nature. Each koan is a window that shows the whole truth but just from a single vantage. It is limited in perspective. One hundred koans give one hundred vantages. When they are enriched with insightful comments and poems, then you have ten thousand vantages. There is no end to this process of enrichment."

   One of the most famous and widely used koans is the Mu Koan, or Joshu's Dog:

   A monk asked Joshu in all earnestness, "Has a dog Buddha nature or not?"
   Joshu said, "Mu!"

   The Japanese word *mu* [無] means "no," "not," or "nothingness." As Aitken observes, "Forty generations of Zen students have breathed the word Mu, evoking the living presence of the Old Buddha himself. Thus Mu is an arcanum, an ancient word or phrase that successive seekers down through the centuries have focused upon and found to be an opening into spiritual understanding. In everyday usage the word 'Mu' means 'does not have'—but if that were Joshu's entire meaning, there wouldn't be any Zen."

   As a thought experiment that you may find to be a Western variation on the theme of the koan, I invite you to turn over in your mind the following question and the example that follows: How or why is it that people, even very smart people, even people of genius, can come to hold radically contrasting worldviews? Alfred North Whitehead and Bertrand Russell, two pivotal intellectual figures of the 20th century whose fundamental views were as different as night and day, present an illustrative case. In their younger days, Whitehead and Russell collaborated for ten years on *Principia Mathematica*. But when Russell began the William James Lectures at Harvard in 1940, Whitehead, who did the formal introduction, made this revealing remark: "Bertie thinks I am muddleheaded; but then I think he is simpleminded."

3. From his book, *The Art of Living: Socratic Reflections*, quoted in Ronald Gross, *Socrates' Way*, p. 17.

Fully Present
in the Present Moment

It would surely enrich our practice, as well as our lives, to stay fully present in every moment in all phases of life, especially some of the more unwelcome: washing dishes, the in-your-face homeless person who gruffly asks for some spare change, the reckless driver who cuts in front of us, the surly store clerk, the guest who drops in at the wrong time, the noisy neighbor who "disturbs" our meditation. I put "disturb" in quotes because I remember my sense of amazement upon reading many years ago about a Zen master who lived in a Chicago apartment over which an "L" train frequently rumbled and clambered—and this without disturbing his meditation!

To be fully present is an occasion for aesthetic appreciation and enrichment. To pause, to be quiet and still, and to be attentive to the beauty, say, of a lofty eucalyptus tree, a spray of colorful bougainvillea, a pelican diving for fish in the ocean, clouds drifting high up in a blue sky, the laughter of children, or just a momentary drop of experience itself, which brings to mind Goethe's famous saying in *Faust*: "Then, to the present moment I might say, Abide, you are so fair!"

While fully present we can optimize the moments when we choose and decide—the open moments when we exercise our wonderful power to live a life of freedom and choice. (The great Yiddish writer, Isaac Beshevis Singer, when asked if we have free will, said, "Of course, we don't have any other choice!")

In the spirit of unity, knowing that God is in us and that we are in God, we see the love and light of God's Presence in other persons. There is a Zen saying: "Be very clear about this. A fool sees himself as another, but a wise man sees others as himself."

Speaking of Zen, the notion of being fully present brings to mind the Buddhist idea of mindfulness, one-pointedness, and the emphasis placed on doing one thing at a time. To concentrate single-mindedly and whole-heartedly on one thing or activity—this is the spirit behind Dogen's *shikantaza* (just sitting). When sitting in zazen, you are just to sit; when working in the kitchen, you are to do just that; when chopping wood, you are just to chop wood. As Mozart might have said, we are to *be* natural and not *be* flat. Or, as Alan Watts writes in his book *The Way of Zen*: "Such contradictory 'naturalness' seems most mysterious, but perhaps the clue lies in the saying of Yün-men: 'In walking, just walk. In sitting, just sit. Above all, don't wobble.' For the essential quality of naturalness is the sincerity of the undivided mind which does not dither between alternatives."

This state of consciousness—of being fully absorbed in an activity yet, at the same time, to have one's feet solidly on the ground—has been the occasion for enlightenment for many Zen monks. In *The Gateless Barrier*, in his discussion of Case 5 of this famous koan collection, Robert Aitken describes such an occasion:

"One day while sweeping up fallen leaves, [Hsiang-yen's] bamboo broom caught a stone and it sailed through the air and hit a stalk of bamboo with a little sound. Tock! With that tock! he was awakened. Hurrying to his hut, he bathed and then offered incense and bowed in the direction of [his Master's] temple, crying out aloud, "Your kindness is greater than that of my parents. If you had explained it to me, I would never have known this joy."

The Zen monk Hsiang-yen was fully present in the present moment when he heard the sound of the stone hitting bamboo, thus allowing this unexpected event to accomplish its work, breaking once and for all the spell of space and time. Tock!

Inner Tech:
The Way of Conscious Evolution

How would you like to learn half the working vocabulary of a foreign language in a single day, learn in a few hours what formerly took a whole semester of training, read 68,000 words per minute with 74% comprehension (this translates into reading a book of around 500 pages in only two or three minutes)? How would you like to paint like Picasso or think like Einstein? Read on.

Einstein: Exception or Example?

Albert Einstein showed little intellectual brilliance in either high school or college. In those early days the future maestro of light certainly didn't shine. In fact, he did so poorly that one of his teachers said, "Albert, you'll never amount to anything." After graduation from college, failing to secure the academic post he desired, he settled for the routine job of a clerk in a patent office.

However, young Albert had begun "thinking" in a very special manner. Not so much thinking as *imaging*, for his process of thought was non-verbal, more like a daydream. Imagine, he whispered to himself, what it would be like to ride on a light beam, speeding through the universe.

He began to see these daydreams as deep-thought experiments, for it was his intention to drift down into as deep a state of reverie as possible, to drift down into a state of consciousness that was almost sleep itself—but he didn't want to actually fall asleep. To guard against this he held a rock in his hand, so that, if he dropped it when he nodded off to sleep, the sound of it hitting the floor would wake him up.

We now know that he was entering the brain-wave state known as Theta—and that Theta is a portal of discovery, a window of access to the highly creative unconscious.

It was while using this deep-thought process that Einstein discovered his theory of Relativity. Or it might be better to say that he daydreamed it. Win Wenger, co-author of *The Einstein Factor*, puts forth a convincing case that Einstein not only revolutionized science and the 20th-century re-conceptualization of the universe, but that he also revolutionized his own mind and creative abilities. By using the deep-thought process, by doing his mental processing in Theta, the young Einstein who flunked his college entrance exams so transformed himself that his very name entered the dictionary as a synonym for "genius."

Blitz-Reading, Supermemory, and Artificial Reincarnation

PhotoReading was developed by Paul Scheele who, like Einstein, didn't excel as a student. But that didn't stop him from inventing PhotoReading, a method that Win Wenger calls an evolutionary leap in human reading skills. Scheele, using a standard speed-reading test, showed that he could PhotoRead a book at the astonishing rate of 68,000 words a minute with 74% comprehension. Skeptical? So were some professors at a Minnesota college where Scheele was going to introduce his new method. Scheele set up a demonstration, monitored by the skeptical professors, wherein a colleague Photoread a volume of U.S. patent law. Scheele's colleague scored 75% on the comprehension test and topped that by drawing approximations of six patent illustrations.

Georgi Lozanov, a Bulgarian psychiatrist, has pioneered a new method of learning that also seems to be a quantum leap. Combining elements of Raja Yoga, slow Baroque music, and a special cadencing for the input of data to be learned, Lozanov's method enabled one group of people to indeed learn about half the working vocabulary of a foreign language in a single day. Lozanov claims that human memory can become supermemory, which is an altered *state of consciousness*, and then "is virtually limitless." The slow beat of Baroque music "also gave an inner sense of time expansion . . . Drs. Robert Masters and Jean Houston later also led people into expanded time, prompting students, for instance, to improve graphic skills that usually take a semester of training, in only a few hours," say Ostrander and Schroeder, authors of *Superlearning 2000*, a book that describes many other techniques for accelerating learning and enhancing creativity.

In the former Soviet Union, a psychiatrist and superb hypnotist named Vladimir Raikov developed a procedure he called "artificial reincarnation." Raikov selected a number of people who up till then had displayed no talent in art. He would then take a person into deep hypnosis, make the person believe he was, say, Picasso or Rembrandt. Artistic talent mysteriously emerged, enabling the person to produce paintings of real expertise. Later, out of hypnosis, the person would deny that he had done the painting, insisting that there was no way he could do a painting of such quality—the very idea was utterly ridiculous! From where did this mysterious talent suddenly emerge? An ancient Zen koan suggests an answer: Who is the Master who makes the grass green? Nietzsche once said, "We are all greater artists than we realize."

Catch The Wave Into Your Neurocosmos

Thoughts are things, a New Age slogan tells us—our personal reality is the manifestation of our thoughts. But is verbal thought per se really *that* creative? Radically creative, I mean. It was not a thought, but an image, an image of the uroborus, the snake swallowing its own tail, presented to him while he was in a light doze, that gave Friedrich Kekulé the key to the hitherto elusive structure of the benzene molecule. Einstein, who said, "I very rarely think in words at all," apparently intuited in the same manner via imagery emerging up from the creative unconscious. Archimedes has his famous "Eureka" experience while soaking in a tub of hot water.

Not verbal thought but an image from a nightmare gave Elias Howe the insight that enabled him to invent the sewing machine. It was not while racking his brain in the lab, but as he was walking down a *spiral* staircase at Oxford that James Watson intuitively glimpsed the *spiral* shape of DNA. It therefore seems to me that radical creativity doesn't happen in the full light of consciousness, but in the darkness of our own inner depths.

Traditionally, brain states are categorized according to frequency: Beta, Alpha, Theta, Delta. As the instrumentation for measurement becomes more sophisticated, new sub-classes of the four major categories are being found. In his book, *Brain States*, Tom Kenyon describes three new sub-classes of Beta: High Beta, K-complex, and Super High Beta. Might not this process be even further refined, so that we find sub-classes of the other three major categories, and maybe even new categories? And since, according to my understanding, the lower portion of Theta seems to be a potently creative state of (un)consciousness—might there not be a sub-class that is a window of access to our creative depths?

The problem would then be how to *get* there and how to *stay* there. In the normal course of a 24-hour day, we do get there on two very evanescent occasions: just before falling asleep and again just before waking up—but we don't stay there. Zen monks can get there and stay there, but only after about twenty years of meditation.

Until the age of around six, children spend most of their time in Theta. Is it mere coincidence that, during this time, they demonstrate their remarkable ability to so easily learn a language? And does not this Theta state, so natural to a child, shed new light on Jesus' saying that we should become as little children?

Consider the internationally acclaimed healer and medicine woman, Rosalyn Bruyere, who has been called "a healer's healer." In the July 1999 issue of *Intuition* magazine, Diane Goldner writes, "Stories of Bruyere's healing prowess are legion. I myself have seen her separate the fused spinal vertebrae of a young minister when doctors urged surgery . . ." Is it not interesting that, when Bruyere is working with a patient, her brain wave state is typically Theta?

Just to mention a few of the technologies now available, there are "mind machines" and psychoacoustic tapes that can, among other things, take you into Theta and keep you there. Flotation tanks can give you what Dr. John Lilly calls "the deepest relaxation available on this planet." Through biofeedback you can learn to access mystical states of consciousness (in one weekend, I'm told). From the founder of NeuroLinguistic Programming, Richard Bandler: "We want you to really use what may have taken years and years of meditation, or disciplined thinking, or perhaps just by chance, but now by a technological advantage—conscious evolution is here at last!" (For extensive information on this rapidly emerging "mind technology," see Michael Hutchison's *Mega Brain Power*.)

Using a computer analogy, the conscious mind has been compared to what is visible at any one time on your monitor screen, while the unconscious is everything else in your computer—I would add: while you're hooked up to the World Wide Web. In other words, what we are conscious of is infinitesimal, compared to what we are (un)conscious of at deeper levels. The great Swiss psychologist, Carl Jung, says we are to make the unconscious conscious. If technology can help us bring these vast resources "onscreen" (to rephrase Jung), should we not take advantage of them?

In her book *The High-Performance Mind*, Anna Wise discusses another intriguing brain-wave manifestation. She describes how Maxwell Cade, using an EEG devise called the Mind Mirror, did EEGs on "a variety of swamis, yogis, healers, and advanced meditators, and found a common thread"—a unique pattern of all four brain waves that reflects the presence of a highly lucid and creative state of consciousness. He called the pattern The Awakened Mind.

When Wise demonstrated the Mind Mirror to a class of chi kung students in Taiwan, they were initially skeptical and even hostile. But their attitude changed to laughter and high interest after seeing that their chi kung master displayed the awakened mind pattern when hooked up to the Mind Mirror.

One technique that Wise discusses to turn off internal chatter and still the mind is simplicity itself. Subvocalization—tenseness and tiny movements of the tongue—seems to accompany most internal chatter. The key to putting a stop to this is learning to relax the tongue completely. Her book describes how to do this and gives simple techniques for accessing The Awakened Mind and other transformational mind states.

Hello, Silicon; Goodbye, Carbon

Raymond Kurzweil makes a fascinating observation in his book *The Age of Spiritual Machines*: "Computers are about one hundred million times more powerful for the same unit cost than they were a half century ago. If the automobile industry had made as much progress in the past fifty years, a car today would cost a hundredth of a cent and go faster than the speed of light."

Kurzweil, who apparently sees Einstein not as an exception but as an example, is the inventor of some of the most innovative technology of our era. A graduate of MIT and recipient of nine honorary doctorates, he is also the author of *The Age of Intelligent Machines*, which was named "Most Outstanding Computer Science Book of 1990" by the Association of American Publishers.

It has been suggested that our next evolutionary leap will come about through our merging with our technology. Indeed, as Kurzweil points out, "technology is the continuation of evolution by other means." But whereas cosmological evolution proceeded at a glacier-like pace, and although biological evolution considerably speeded up the process, technological evolution, especially in the domain of computers, accelerates at an increasingly exponential rate.

According to Kurzweil, at some point in the not-too-distant future, maybe as early as 2099, we will enter the transhuman or posthuman era. If we wish to keep up with our rapidly evolving technology, it will be necessary to scan our brains, say farewell to our carbon-based flesh, and upload our minds into a faster and more powerful computational unit. In other words: a *machine*.

By then, however, Kurzweil says that computers will have evolved to such an extent that they will claim to have consciousness, emotions, and spiritual experiences. Some may even claim to be enlightened, and will be meditating and regularly attending virtual houses of worship. Towards the end of the 21st century, with the widespread use of neural-implant technology by humans, and with machine-based computers modeled more and more on human intelligence, it will become increasingly difficult to tell humans from computers. Those humans who have no neural implants will not be capable of entering into meaningful dialogue with those who do. In speaking of our *descendants* and our *technology*, there is really no distinction to be made. Is this science *fiction*? Maybe, maybe not. The predictions Kurzweil made about computer trendings in his 1990 book, *The Age of Intelligent Machines*, have, for the most part, been right on target.

And when we do upload our minds, so the prediction goes, we will achieve technological immortality—cyberlife everlasting. Just be sure to make frequent backups!

To anyone with a religious orientation, Kurzweil's vision for the future raises many questions and objections. For example:

The discrete contents of the brain and nervous system could, perhaps, at some future date be scanned and uploaded, but not the mind itself, for the mind is more, much more, than just a miscellany or mishmash of data and experiences. As the German philosopher Leibniz cleverly phrased it, "Everything in the mind comes from the senses—except the mind itself!" Mind is not only unity of experience as one viewpoint, one unique consciousness vis-à-vis the world, but also the unified experience of a network of data so incredibly vast and extensive as to defy description. I hold that this unity cannot be scanned or uploaded.

Three of our great mystics (Aquinas, Hildegard of Bingen, Eckhart) tell us that the soul is not in the body, in the sense that the body inclusively and completely contains it. Rather, the soul, which is more than the body, contains and permeates the body with its subtle, invisible, and constitutive essence. Can this essence be scanned? I don't think so.

In "The Myth of the Computer," process thinker Charles Birch argues cogently that Artificial Intelligence can never match, much less supersede, human intelligence or consciousness. Birch says that computers are capable of syntax but not *semantics*, and he discusses how pervasive the *fallacy of misplaced concreteness* is in AI thinking. This is the fallacy of mistaking the abstract for the concrete: to mistake the menu for the meal, the map for the territory, or a computer "virus" for a real living virus.

Some other points that Birch makes: (1) The content of much information is heavily laden with *context* that can't be coded into a computer. (2) No matter how complex or sophisticated, a computer program is always a *simulation* and not the real thing. (3) Computational events cannot produce the mental states produced by the brain since it cannot duplicate the *causal powers* of the brain. (4) A major error in AI is that it evades the "mystery of subjectivity." (5) Computers are aggregates and not individual entities. The micro-constituents of brains are themselves primitive units of feeling that *act and feel as one.* Organisms have evolved from simpler organisms that act and feel as one, however far back our cosmology leads us. Ergo, Mind can never emerge from the no-mind of a computer.

Finally, I can see no way that a machine could be capable of even simple feelings, and certainly not of the complexity, range, and nuance of human feelings. Feelings energize and modulate all aspects of our lives, play an important evaluative role in thought, and are *at the very heart not only of aesthetic experience but of religious experience.* This truth is so basic that it is reflected in our language. We can think *about* God, but no one instinctively says, "I think God's presence." But how natural it is to speak about *feeling* God's presence. And it is just here that the *semantics* of human language transcends the mere *syntax* of computer programs, and that the human heart and mind transcend, once and for all, the computer's central processing unit.

Juggling: Hold Infinity in the Palm of Your Hand

Michael Gelb celebrates the power of play as our most effective way to learn.

Most widely known, perhaps, for his best-selling book, *How To Think Like Leonardo da Vinci*, which has been translated into 24 languages, Gelb is the author of a number of other books and a pioneer in the fields of accelerated learning, creative thinking, and leadership development. As president of High Performance Learning, a management consulting firm, his list of clients include such corporate giants as Microsoft, Nike, DuPont, and Western Union. It may surprise you to learn that, in what he teaches, the art of juggling plays a central role. Learning how to juggle, both literally and metaphorically, enables everyone to become better at what they do—in business, learning, and life.

Gelb first got excited about juggling as he watched a professional juggler and suddenly saw that the three balls, as they wove a pattern in the air, traced the symbol for infinity:

To his friend standing beside him, Gelb exclaimed, "Look: the infinity symbol! He's holding infinity in his hands!" This so inspired him that he decided at that very moment to become a juggler himself so that he could master the infinity pattern. Gelb was familiar with the famous opening lines of a William Blake poem:

To see a World in a Grain of Sand
And Heaven in a Wild Flower,
Hold infinity in the palm of your hand
And Eternity in an hour.

Juggling had suddenly given him a delightful new twist on this and, over time, Gelb took the art of juggling and developed it into a powerful metaphor for the art of learning and the art of living.

The Juggling Metaphor

*The greatest thing by far
is to be a master of metaphor.*
—Aristotle

To explore the art of learning, there are many good metaphors that one might adopt, but juggling is especially powerful and in a class by itself. Here are some of the reasons that Gelb would have us consider:

Although, to you, juggling may at first glance seem next to impossible, it is easy to learn and open to everyone—regardless of gender, or whatever your age, you can become a good juggler. The lesson here is that the same may be true for other "impossibilities" you have avoided.

Learning and other creative activities, whether for business or pleasure, involve keeping a number of things "up in the air" at the same time, and "dropping the balls" is a perfect metaphor for mistakes that will inevitably occur in any learning process. Gelb considers gracefully coping with mistakes to be one of life's most important abilities, and invites us to learn to love our mistakes and see them as "stepping stones on the path to success."

Learning to juggle also requires that you relax and concentrate at the same time, that you cultivate a sense of stillness in the midst of activity, when mind and body are moving in measure, like dancers, to echo a line by T. S. Eliot. Optimal performance in all activities is grounded in this experience of *relaxed concentration*.

Once you have learned to juggle, juggling can be a "moving meditation" that you can use to relax and focus the mind while energizing and balancing the body. As Gelb says, "the ambidextrous movement feels good and helps coordinate the two sides of the brain and body." Ambidexterity, facility of use with both the right and left hands, is a natural outcome of juggling and, as the art is refined through practice, ambidexterity becomes global, to include the whole living system, physical and mental.

When Gelb was researching his book on juggling, he interviewed Raymond Dart, the anthropologist who achieved fame for his discovery of the remains of *Australopithecus africanus*. Asked to sum up his life's work in the study of human nature, as it relates to the development of human potential, Professor Dart exclaimed, "Balance your brain, balance your body! The future lies with the ambidextrous human!" He recommended juggling as a way to cultivate global ambidexterity.

With practice, you will begin to enter the "juggling flow state," where throwing and catching the balls becomes effortless; the juggling seems to happen all by itself as the three balls cascade in the air, weaving and reweaving the pattern of infinity. In the process of flow, what before may have seemed hopelessly complex is now simplicity itself. At such times you will deeply experience the clarity, joy, and poise of optimal performance.

Maybe most important of all: juggling is simply fun! And through this lighthearted activity you enter into the realm of play, one of the most fundamental learning modalities.

Language shows that the Greeks have always known that the secret of learning is to be found in play. As Gelb points out, "Their words for play (*paida*) and education (*paideia*) are slight variations on the same theme." And the word "juggler" derives from the Latin word *joculari*, meaning "to joke or to jest."

Even casual observation reveals that, for young animals and children, play is the primary way they learn. Babies are the true Zen Masters of the art of play and Gelb suggests that there is much to be learned from watching a baby as he or she goes about learning to walk. Except as you become as little children . . .

Juggling for Longevity

Did you ever wonder which profession of people tend to live the longest? Would you be surprised to learn the conductors of music figure as one of those professions. Not only do conductors live longer, they also enjoy a robust and creative old age. Arturo Toscanini, for example, considered by many as the greatest conductor of his era, was still joyously at work (or play) performing, touring, and making wonderful recordings well into his 80s, making his last studio recording in 1954 when he was 86 years old.

One reason given for this longevity is that conducting a symphony requires considerable exertions. A conductor will usually work up a sweat with the energetic and *rhythmic* waving of a baton in time to the music. In this case, hands and arms (rather than legs) are enjoying the workout, and so what comes into play is an *upper-body* aerobic exercise.

If you are with me on this, you already see the juggling parallel coming clearly into view.

Yes, of course!—juggling is also a *rhythmic* activity that can provide excellent aerobics in an upper-body workout. In addition, as Gelb says, "juggling offers a number of other fitness-related benefits: lively muscle tone, quickened reflexes, refined hand-eye coordination, and subtle balance and poise." One way to develop upper-body strength is to juggle increasingly heavier objects, such as 16-pound shot-puts. Just kidding! About the shot-puts, that is. Or, to lighten up, juggling can be combined with running (joggling) and dancing (jiggling) for even higher levels of aerobic benefits.

And so it seems that with the fine art of juggling, we can hold not only *infinity* in the palms of our hands, but also some aspect of *eternity*.

Finally, when you have learned to juggle, you will always know, as Gelb puts it, "a secret for delighting every child and bringing out the child in every adult."

Sometimes a (Not So) Great Notion

Do you sometimes hear a curious notion that, in the context of eternity or, from a God's-eye view, all actions, whether seemingly right or wrong, have a perfect effect? The *logic* of this seems to allow one to nonchalantly dismiss the brutal rape of little girls, genocide, slavery, terminal diseases that cause slow and agonizing deaths, and so on.

Over the years, whenever this idea came up in discussion, I always vigorously opposed it. For the following reasons, it is an idea that I still oppose.

1: This seems an open invitation to set foot on a path that leads to ethical nihilism. If every action, right or wrong, has a perfect effect, then what are the grounds for taking an ethical stance in life? Or for promoting justice? The maverick priest Matthew Fox reminds us of William Hocking's idea that *the mystic is the prophet in action*—and the function of the prophet is to interfere with history, with injustice, and to speak up for those who have no voice. There was a time in American history when Blacks and Native Americans had no voice, a time in German history when Jews had no voice, a time during the Spanish Inquisition when dissenters had no voice. Do not some actions deserve to be condemned and others encouraged?

2: The notion seems to me a coldly "rational" idea that has no heart. An important idea in Alfred North Whitehead's philosophy is what he calls the *feeling of feeling* and this is so basic that it is how the world hangs together. God is the most eminent exemplification of this in that he feels the feelings of all creatures; in Whitehead's words, "God is the fellow-sufferer who understands." Essentially, this *feeling of feeling* is love.

To dismiss the Jewish Holocaust as somehow being "perfect effect" seems a cavalier distancing from *feeling the feelings* of the entire Jewish people, not only the six million men, women, and children who meaninglessly perished under the horrendous evil of Hitler's agenda.

The Holocaust was so apocalyptic to many Jews (bearing radical witness to what they feel was God's "Real Absence" in the death camps) that they have found it necessary to reconceptualize a post-Holocaust theology and even a post-Holocaust God. For some, Whitehead's metaphysics has proven to be fertile ground for such an effort.

3: Another reason to oppose this idea is that it seems a subtle determinism, and thus a denial of freedom and the reality of chance. The notion of perfect effect implies that "The dice of God are always loaded."

The idea of chance, or probabilistic outcomes, is a central feature of both evolutionary and quantum theory. Chance is the *joker* in nature's deck of cards. The idea of perfect effect would seem to fit more neatly into a Newtonian universe wherein exact laws hold sway rather than in a "messy" quantum universe of probabilistic laws that in fact are now viewed more as "habits" than iron-clad laws. If the element of chance enters into every nascent event, it is far from obvious to me how there can always arise a "perfect effect."

This suggests an interesting inference: If, by this hypothesis, God is not in full control of any single event, then, by elementary logic, God is not in full control of the universe. From a process perspective, it's metaphysically impossible that God could be in full and unilateral control of the universe. Real power is multilaterally distributed throughout the entire universe. In this there is no contingency. This is the sound basis for an adequate theodicy.

4: In Voltaire's classic story, *Candide*, the title character, under the instruction of Dr. Pangloss, comes to believe not only that all outcomes are good, but that they are the very best in this "best of all possible worlds." Here's how Pangloss states his case:

"It is demonstrable," said he, "that all is necessarily for the best end. Observe that the nose has been formed to bear spectacles . . . legs were visibly designed for stockings . . . stones were designed to construct castles . . . pigs were made so that we might have pork all the year round. Consequently, they who assert that all is *well* have said a foolish thing; they should have said all is for the *best*."

By the end of the story, after suffering an unbroken string of one calamity after another, Candide is disabused of this idea. Dr. Pangloss, however, still tenaciously holds to his idea for he states:

"There is a concatenation of events in this best of all possible worlds: for if you had not been kicked out of a magnificent castle; if you had not been put into the Inquisition; if you had not walked over America; . . . if you had not lost all your gold; . . . you would not be here eating preserved citrons and pistachio-nuts."

To which Candide answers: "All that is very well, but let us *cultivate* our garden."

5: The notion of "perfect effect" may stem from the idea of pantheism: if "God is all there is" and if God is wholly good, then anything that happens must also be good. Thus, what appears as evil is at best a mere illusion, and can be explained away. *Explained away* is by no means synonymous with *explained*. As mentioned above, rather than the pantheist unilateral idea that "God is all there is," or "God is the only presence and the only power," the process view is that power is multilateral and inherent in *all* creatures. To be is to have power.

6: Rather than being a conclusion that has been carefully thought out and reasoned through, I wonder whether this idea of "perfect effect" is more in the nature of a slogan. Slogans have a notorious tendency to hypnotize thinking.

Process thought does offer another perspective on all this:

Rather than every action somehow ending in a perfect effect, process proposes that every unit of experience begins with "perfect" possibilities, presented by God as *initial aims*, or God's persuasive call, for that experience's best future. Initial aims are windows of opportunity, glimpses of what *might be* in contrast to what *now is*, whispers from the still small voice of God within, intimations of the indwelling Christ, or the Hebrew *dabhar* (Word of God), or what the German poet Rilke calls "the uninterrupted message that comes out of silence."

In the above paragraph, I placed "perfect" in quotation marks because what God offers are the *best possible* aims, given all the details of the present context. Competing with God's persuasive call are a number of other "voices"—our own desires, and the many influences exerted by the pressure of the past and the immediate environment. For example, the best possible aim that God can present to Bill Gates will differ considerably from what can be offered to a strung-out heroin junkie who for decades has followed a life of sometimes brutal crime to support his habit. But, even given the limitations faced by the junkie, growth is always possible: by responding positively to the possibilities offered by God in the present moment we thereby make it possible for God to offer even higher values that can be realized in future moments, and so on, and so on . . .

Jesus of Nazareth, whose very selfhood was so transparent to God's persuasive call that the light of God's presence shone through with breathtaking beauty, shows the power of this process and what can be accomplished by aligning oneself with the initial aims presented by a loving God in every new moment.

Countdown to Silence

Did you ever "go ballistic," or "blow your top" with such steam that someone had to "scrape you off the ceiling"? Have you ever "festered" with resentment, "nursed" a grudge, or "come unglued" in LA gridlock? Do some people so rub you the wrong way that they make you "fly off the handle"? Did you ever lay the blame on someone else for how you feel?

There is a powerful idea, first stated by a Greek philosopher almost 2000 years ago, that can help you avoid such reactions. In one of the key psychological insights of all time, Epictetus made this simple but profound observation: "People are disturbed not by things or events, but by their views of them." This is one of the most liberating insights about human nature ever revealed, for it means that it is always within our power to decide how we shall react to anything. Yes, anything!

The idea that something *must* make you feel a certain way is reflected in a model that you may have learned about in a psychology class or book. It's called the S-R model of behavior—Stimulus-Response—meaning that the stimulus *causes* the response. A notable example of S-R is the classic experiment performed by the Russian scientist Pavlov. After conditioning a dog to associate food with the ringing of a bell, Pavlov had only to ring the bell to cause the dog to salivate.

What the S-R model misses is the crucial step between stimulus and response wherein we exercise our power of choice. We can consciously access this step by using what I call an SOS: a short Sabbath of Silence.

One way to do this is to make a Countdown to Silence . . . When you catch yourself "going negative," simply stop and slowly count down: 3-2-1-0. When you reach "0," the "Oh" (like a circle) is a symbol of silence and also points to the "O" of Options. Placing an O in S-R yields S-O-R and reminds you that in any situation you always have options.

By taking this stand, we own our own power rather than surrendering it to circumstances or other people. I sometimes think of this as mental and emotional Aikido—whereby we can "throw" our problems, rather than being thrown by them.

Psychologist Victor Frankl, a POW during World War II, used this idea to transcend the almost unimaginable brutalities of a Nazi concentration camp. He wrote: "The sort of person the prisoner became was the result of an inner decision, and not the result of camp influences alone." Admiral James Stockdale, a POW for eight years in Vietnam, credits his survival to lessons he learned from his readings of the classics, mainly Epictetus. If this idea is so powerful it works in a concentration camp, think how well it can work with the hassles of everyday life!

I'll close with a summation by Epictetus:

"When, therefore, we are hindered, or disturbed, or grieved, let us never blame anyone but ourselves; that is, our own judgments. It is the action of an uninstructed person to reproach others for his own misfortunes; of one entering upon instruction, to reproach himself; and of one perfectly instructed, to reproach neither others nor himself."

Part Three

Water

The Still Waters
of Morning Silence

During my last term in the three-year course of study and training to become a licensed counselor, I created a spiritual practice that I call Morning Silence. This practice enables anyone to open an "access channel" that leads down to the still waters of creativity within. It's very simple to do:

When I first feel myself beginning to wake up of a morning, when I'm in that in-between state of being not quite awake and not quite asleep, I invite my creative unconscious to provide answers and solutions to whatever project, or whatever topic, I have chosen as the focus for that session of Morning Silence. I place my request on what I call the altar of silence. And then I just lie there in silence, with eyes closed, as close to sleep as possible. Always—well, *almost* always—the images and ideas come. I then write them down as fast as I can, for they can quickly slip away once you open your eyes and drift up from that drowsy state.

Please note that the purpose of Morning Silence is not to *think*, but to *sink* . . . deep down into the brain-state level known as Theta, or even deeper into the upper tiers of Delta. My method of descent into the still waters is to become one with the rhythm of breathing as, like a pendulum, it swings slowly back and forth between inhalation and exhalation.

With practice, Morning Silence becomes like a Muse: a source not only for new ideas but also, on later occasions, for adding depth and breadth to those ideas. If, in your studies or scholarly pursuits, you encounter complex ideas that seem to resist your understanding, you can use this practice to help you digest those ideas. As Milton Erickson reminds us, "Your conscious mind is very intelligent, but your unconscious is a heck of a lot smarter."

This practice can also be used just before falling asleep, to set in motion a healing idea that will resonate in the creative unconscious during the night.

Morning Silence 2.0

In light of new understanding, I've recently "upgraded" this practice to Morning Silence 2.0. To explain how this came about—first, a brief history of our evolving understanding of the human brain, the most complex structure in the known universe.

1. Like the yin-yang symbol ☯, the brain is not a simple unity but a "binity" with a twofold, or two-in-one, structure: a left hemisphere (LH) and a right hemisphere (RH).
2. The two hemispheres of the brain were found to have different modes of operation, different styles, different ways of processing information. Although the distinction is not so simple, nor the polarity quite so "neat," the general idea can be conveyed by these contrasting categories:

LH	RH
math	music
philosophy	poetry
intellect	intuition
logic	liturgy
verbal	visual

3. At any one time, either the LH or the RH is dominant, and at regular intervals, in a natural recurring rhythm, there is a shift back and forth between LH and RH dominance: LH → RH → LH → RH. And this leads to the last piece in the puzzle.

Right Under Your Nose

Did you ever stop and wonder why you have two nostrils instead of one? Science has long been aware of a nasal "dominance" that alternates back and forth between the right and the left nostrils. An increase, for example, of blood circulation to the right nostril causes a tumescence, or swelling, of internal structures in the right nasal cavity, thus narrowing the air passage and restricting the flow of breath.

At the same time, the *opposite* process takes place in the left nostril. In short, one nostril tends to congest or close as the other becomes clear and open. This pattern repeats itself in a rhythm that oscillates back and forth, from right to left, from left to right, throughout the day. And so, an alternating current of *dominance*—in the nose and also, remember, in the brain.

Psychologist Debra Werntz was the first to glimpse a connection, and she went on to make this important discovery: the opening of one side of the nose activates the opposite side of the brain: thus, when the left nostril opens, the right hemisphere becomes dominant. This can be clearly seen in EEG readings of subjects who are hooked up to an electroencephalograph.

Note the elegance of this doubly biphasal process: opening the right nostril shifts dominance to the left side of the brain with its rational, analytical mode, whereas opening of the left nostril engages the more intuitive, holistic mode of the right hemisphere.

In other words, there is a perpetual oscillation between LN and RN that is mirrored, in reverse, by a perpetual oscillation between RH and LH dominance. Here we can marvel at the "wisdom of the body" in providing access to both modes, at regular intervals, so that we can achieve a more integral balance in our mental processing.

Werntz went one step further and showed that this process need not be automatic but could be consciously controlled. And Ernest Rossi, whose writings I draw on heavily in this section, came up with what may be the simplest way to control the cycle. It's as easy as lying down. For it turns out that lying on your right side will cause your right nostril to partially close, and thus activate the right hemisphere of the brain. And vice versa.

And so, to do Morning Silence 2.0, simply add the following variation:

Begin Morning Silence by lying on your right side to activate the intuitive mode. About halfway through, turn over on your left side to switch your "access channel" to the rational mode of the left hemisphere. Finally, turn over on your back, first to "integrate," and then to close the session as you ascend to wakefulness—and you may find yourself enjoying a *really* good stretch and a *really* good yawn—as you open your eyes and brighten the day with a sunny smile of thanksgiving.

The Fourfold Path of Jesus

In Mark 12:30-31, Jesus says: "And thou shalt love the Lord thy God with all thy heart, and with all thy soul, and with all thy mind, and with all thy strength: this is the first commandment. And the second is like, namely this, Thou shalt love thy neighbour as thyself. There is none other commandment greater than these."

More and more it seems to me, that in this statement, the great commandment of Jesus, we have the whole of spirituality, and that anything else is mere commentary. As is often the case with the sayings of Jesus, we have here much wisdom compressed into just a few words. For, if looked at closely, we find that there are four very *distinct* and *subtle* ways we can express our love for God: through Heart, Soul, Mind, and Strength.

HEART has to do with feelings, feelings such as love, devotion, and compassion. The disciple John followed this path, as did Mozart, and, I suspect, most musical geniuses.

With SOUL we are on the mystical path, the path of meditation and intuition whereby we come to the experience of God as a Presence within, and experience our unity with that Presence. This was the path of Meister Eckhart.

MIND is the way of thinking, studying, learning, scholarly pursuits, and intellectual quests. It is the method that Joseph Campbell followed and which he himself called the Path of Books. This path also suggests that we should be open to the ever-changing knowledge and ever-new technological resources provided by science and the Scientific Mind.

When we use our STRENGTH we are in the world of activity, doing the good works, caring for others, actively participating both in the life of our spiritual community and that greater community beyond. Matthew Fox's suggestion that all mystics should also be prophets who speak out against and interfere with injustice is an example of this path.

And is it not tantalizing that these four modes, or paths, correspond to the Four Functions of the psyche as discovered and elaborated by the great Swiss psychologist, Carl Jung. Jung's Four Functions are: Feeling, Intuition, Thinking, and Sensation. Through the integration of these four functions, a person develops into a fully differentiated, balanced, and unified personality, although, as Jung observed, this goal is rarely if ever achieved except by a Jesus or a Buddha. That Jung's four functions correlate wonderfully with the four modalities proposed by Jesus—this suggests that we are onto something that Jesus was onto two thousand years ago.

For many centuries, spirituality has been alive and well in India, so it comes as no big surprise that we find there a variation on this theme of a fourfold path. In the teaching about Yoga, we find that there are four major yogas, or disciplines. As Paul Alan Laughlin has pointed out in his essay "The Yoga of Jesus," where he develops the idea in some detail, these four yogas correspond quite elegantly with the four paths suggested by Jesus.

One is Bhakti Yoga, and this is the "love discipline" that corresponds with the path of Heart. Another is Rajah Yoga: the mystical way of each person who descends into her own depths to find an essential oneness with the One Spirit. This is the path of Soul. And there is Jnana Yoga, the so-called "insight discipline, and this is the way of mind and intellect. Finally, there is Karma Yoga, the "deed discipline," corresponding with the path of Strength. And so it can readily be seen that these four disciplines correspond quite elegantly with the four paths suggested by Jesus.

Yoga in Sanskrit means "union" or, literally, a "yoking together," and it is a means or a discipline whereby, through practice, you become more and more linked to the Supreme Spirit, or Brahman. This is surely what Jesus had in mind with his fourfold method of spirituality— to strengthen and vitalize our connection with God and to bring a measure of balance into our lives and, through this fourfold approach, to cultivate wholeness and health. The words whole, wholesome, health, heal, holy, hale, hallow . . . all these words are intimately related and derive from the same root word.

Are we now done with our fourfold theme? Not quite. Matthew Fox is surely one of the great mystics of our time, and, in his Creation Spirituality, he names the spiritual journey as four ways or paths: the Via Positiva, the Via Negativa, the Via Creativa, and the Via Transformativa.

The Via Positiva is about awe and wonder and the joy and praise that comes from truly beholding Nature and Creation. Rabbi Abraham Heschel says that if you behold God's Creation with anything less than Radical Amazement you're not seeing what's really there.

The next path is the Via Negativa: the way of darkness, suffering, silence, letting go, and even nothingness.

In the Via Creativa we co-create with God; in our imaginative output, we trust our images enough to birth them into existence. This is Path Three.

The fourth path is the Via Transformativa, the transformative way. This is a path of compassion, the relief of suffering, the combating of injustice, of speaking up for those who have no voice.

In his book, _Creation Spirituality_, Matthew Fox writes: "The Four Paths of the creation spirituality represent a distinct paradigm shift from the way in which the spiritual journey was formerly described in the West. Plotinus identified only three paths: purgation, illumination, and union. Creation spirituality rejects as inadequate this way of naming the spiritual journey. It is not biblical, because Plotinus, a Neoplatonist philosopher and mystic, did not know the Bible at all. These paths leave out delight and pleasure, creativity and justice; their goal is not compassion but contemplation and the turning away from earth and all that relates us to it." Matthew Fox says that these four paths also name four dimensions of prayer, and that, through the varied experience of these paths, we have a richer and deeper experience of prayer.

And so we now have, from four widely separated locales, four examples of these four paths:

1) Jesus with his four ways of Heart, Soul, Mind, and Strength

2) Jung's four functions: Feeling, Intuition, Thinking, and Sensation
3) The four disciplines of Yoga: Bhakti, Rajah, Jnana, and Karma
4) Creation Spirituality and its four paths: the positive, negative, creative, and transformative

Although there are close correlations in all four examples, they do not exactly coincide, but present interesting differences and contrasts, and so are creatively supplemental one to the other.

But, some of you may ask, why *four* paths, instead of two, say, or five? The number "four" is so rich in symbolic content that it is deeply archetypal. Four is the number of wholeness, and this is perhaps most clearly seen in the central Christian symbol, the cross, one of the simplest, yet most profound, expressions of a mandala, the universal symbol of wholeness that is found in all cultures and all times. As a symbol, the cross is endlessly suggestive. Rooted in the ground yet aspiring to the sky, the cross, through its *four* parts, unites heaven and earth, above and below, right and left. That a cross of such simplicity has yielded such an abundant harvest of symbolic interpretation, centuries in the making and still going strong, invites endless wonder.

Moreover, as Jungian scholar John Sanford points out in *Mystical Christianity*, the Christian cross is not only a symbol *of*—but also a symbol *for*—transformation: through a sacramental experience of the *mystery* of the cross, we are initiated into a process that brings about a creative change in consciousness. The "mystery" whereof I speak means not "a puzzle to be solved," but derives from the Greek word *mysterion*, and means, Sanford tells us, "a matter to the knowledge of which initiation is necessary." Some things can be known only by experience, and some *mysteries* can be experienced only through initiation. Thus, through the ingenuities of symbol, we can also come to see the cross as a cruciform mirror with four facets, each luminously reflecting one of the fourfold paths of Jesus.

One of the reasons these ideas turn up all over the place is that, everywhere, the inner urge of Life is for creativity and wholeness. And wholeness need not imply completion, in the sense of being finished once and for all. Finished products are manufactured, not created, and I hold that God is no manufacturer. On all levels of actuality the principle of principles, the very essence of reality, is self-surpassing creativity.

And when it comes to metaphysical principles, process philosophy claims that God is not to be treated as an exception, but as their chief exemplification. Therefore, although unsurpassable by all conceivable entities, God—in terms of endless growth through experience and esthetic enrichment—is the self-surpassing surpasser of all. And so, to slightly alter a famous passage of scripture, I say, Be ye therefore self-surpassing, even as your Father which is in heaven is self-surpassing!

What are other values of such a fourfold approach? Such an approach aims at balance, growth, stretching in new spiritual dimensions, trying new things, and the creative advance into novelty as we explore new directions: one way to make sure that our minds stay sharp, and to keep our perceptions, our experiences, our vision—fresh, and green, and open. If one Zen Master is right in saying that Zen Mind is Beginner's Mind, then such a varied approach may help us to keep the freshness and innocence of Beginner's Mind. Although each person may have a natural inclination to primarily practice one of these four ways, by consciously practicing all four we can cultivate wholeness and these other values in our lives.

"Thou shalt love the Lord thy God with all thy heart, and with all thy soul, and with all thy mind, and with all thy strength . . ."

And so, in this "simple" sentence, we find a wonderful guide to the spiritual path, the path illumined as the Way of HEART, SOUL, MIND, and STRENGTH, and that to cultivate all four is to model our lives on the example of wholeness so magnificently exemplified in that truly exceptional young man, Jesus of Nazareth.

Kalogenesis:
Beauty Arising

For some fifteen billion years now, in the upward spiral of evolution, there blooms an ever-widening expansion and inclusiveness, an increase in both depth and height, on the green, growing tip of creative advance. Note these developmental steps: from particles to atoms to molecules to living cells to organisms—and note how one lays the foundation for its successor to build upon, so that, for example, molecules may go beyond but still include the achievements of atoms.

If the "depth" of a molecule is its atomic elements, then even a simple living cell has far more depth because 1) it is made up of, and *integrates*, so much more; and, more importantly, 2) the cell lives by means of *metabolic processes* that mark a new threshold in evolution. With the emergence of the metabolic cell, something decisively new has arisen to prepare the way for a proliferation of life into every habitable niche in nature—first in the watery worlds, and then land and sky.

Science now discerns four levels of evolution:

Cosmogenesis traces the origin and evolution of the physical universe; *phylogenesis*, the evolutionary development of plant and animal species; *ontogenesis*, the life cycle of a single organism or individual. *Microgenesis*, in a radically contracted time frame, traces the split-second developmental steps that lead to a single thought, feeling, or perception within the individual.

Nothing simply pops into the mind instantaneously, or floats in out of the blue from nowhere. Underlying every conscious state—whether a frivolous thought or the most exalted mystical experience—is a sequence of steps that arise and *develop* along both mental and physical pathways.

This developmental moment, microgenesis, *is now where the action is*, for this marks yet another threshold that makes possible *conscious* evolution. According to process thought, each microgenetic moment begins with a phase wherein intuition can hearken to whispers of new possibilities, new horizons, new adventures of spirit. This whisper is a call from God, an invitation in every new moment for us to make more of ourselves than what we currently are, to advance the ongoing process of microgenetic evolution. To use a musical analogy, the *melody* of our personal growth is composed of the *notes* achieved in these microgenetic moments.

God Makes Makers

Evolutionary theology, a new post-Darwinian way of thinking about God, proposes two ideas: first, God does not create all at once, or once and for all. God creates through a process that meanders over vast stretches of time: by *evolution*. And, second, rather than creating directly by divine fiat, God creates through persuasion or *evocation*— by evoking the creativity of all the many centers of power throughout the universe.

What does this mean for us? Simply that God does not make us; rather, God makes it possible that we make ourselves.

As philosopher Donald Wayne Viney has pointed out, this idea began surfacing about 150 years ago, and he cites a number of notable thinkers who apparently came up with the idea independently of one another.[1]

1850: In a letter to a friend, Jules Lequier wrote of "God, who created me creator of myself."

1920: The French priest and paleontologist, Teilhard de Chardin, wrote, "Properly speaking, God does not make. He makes things make themselves."

1932: Henri Bergson, the great French philosopher, wrote of his conclusion that God "creates creators."

Alfred North Whitehead generalizes this idea to go beyond humans and include creatures all the way down, and all the way back, to the very beginning of our cosmic epoch. Stop and think about this: to create, right from the beginning, a universe of countless creatures who are, in a significant way, creators of themselves in every new moment. This is the process view: God makes creatures makers of themselves. We live in a universe that is fairly crackling with creativity.

If you're wondering how creativity is possible on more primitive levels, consider the following excerpt from an essay by biologist James Shapiro:

"The conventional wisdom about bacteria is that they are primitive . . . organisms. Actually, bacteria . . . are essential and sophisticated actors on the stage of life, often outwitting larger organisms for their own (the bacteria's) benefit. . . . Like all cells, bacteria are outstanding genetic engineers, and they have used this capacity to withstand antibiotic chemotherapy. Bacterial antibiotic resistance is one of the best-documented examples of evolution by natural genetic engineering. The discovery that genetic change results from regulated, biological processes instead of random errors and physico-chemical damage to DNA has profound implications for theories of life and evolution."[2]

From Microgenesis to Kalogenesis[3]

If we compare the universe moments after the Big Bang with what it has become today, we see an awesome contrast brought about by the four levels of evolution. Whitehead saw in cosmic process an aesthetic adventure with God calling all creatures to participate in the creation, expansion, and intensification of beauty. Just as this beauty has been expanded by trailblazers such as Socrates, Buddha, and Jesus, so too each individual today has the rare opportunity to be a part of the green, growing tip: to grow in consciousness and transcend to ever higher levels.

In his book *Being and Value*, philosopher Frederick Ferré acquaints us with a beautiful idea that he names with a beautiful word: *kalogenesis*.

"Kalós" (καλός) is the Greek word for "beauty" and "genesis" of course refers to "generating" or "bringing into existence." And so kalogenesis means the creation or coming to be of beauty. According to Ferré, beauty is present, to some degree, in every momentary flash of actuality. The becoming of any actuality is also the becoming of beauty. In short, we live in a kalogenic universe populated by kalogenic entities. To be, on whatever level, is to be a begetter of beauty.

Whitehead is in accord with this, for he says: "The metaphysical doctrine, here expounded, finds the foundations of the world in the aesthetic experience . . . The actual world is the outcome of the aesthetic order, and the aesthetic order is derived from the immanence of God . . . God is the poet of the world, with tender patience leading it by his vision of truth, beauty, and goodness."

In a quantum universe, the fundamental cosmic process is the *coming to be* of each momentary flash of actuality, whether that flash be a moment of human experience or the rhythmic pulsation of a photon. Whitehead calls this *concrescence*, a process that always achieves at least a flicker of originality, arising out of a feeling, however vague, for a range of possibilities that might have made its existential path otherwise. Adventure is inherent in the very structure of reality.

Coming to be always involves the many and the one. In Whitehead's aphoristic phrase, "The many become one, and are increased by one." This describes a process whereby diversity is made one in a prehensive unification of experience. The most fundamental process in the universe, the process whereby actuality is attained in each momentary pulse of experience, is a kalogenic process. To be an actual entity is to be a kalogenic entity.

Mozartian Moments

The musical genius of Mozart is legendary. When creating his music, Mozart never wrote rough drafts that he later polished to perfection. All who observed him at work agree that he could sit down and dash off a musical composition, in its final form, as easily as we might sit down and dash off a grocery list.

He was able to do this because he sometimes conceived an entire movement of a symphony in one single creative thought. Like a beautiful orchid springing into full bloom in the twinkling of an eye, the whole movement came to him as a unity of experience "in one magnificent moment of musical meaning."

We all have experienced magnificent moments, though probably to a lesser degree than this, and Frederick Ferré calls such experiences

"Mozartian moments." These moments have an intrinsic value in themselves; they glow, as Ferré says, with their own worth. When they come to us, in their flashes of momentary splendor, we know truly that our "cups runneth over."

Mozartian moments are integrative—not only do contrasting elements come together, but they are held together in a momentary embrace revealing aesthetic richness and intensity of experience: a unity of diversity, a unity of contrasts. The greater the contrast, the more the intensity. They are adventures of novelty, revealing exciting new vistas, or breakthrough insights, evoking feelings of freshness, zest, and vitality.

Mozartian moments are among our highest experiences of beauty . . . and thus intensely kalogenic. Their beauty sparkles. They come "trailing clouds of glory" and are part of what make us unique as humans. May your Mozartian moments be many!

Endnotes

1. Donald Wayne Viney, "Philosophy After Hartshorne," *Process Studies*, pp. 211-236, Vol. 30, Number 2, Fall- Winter, 2001.

2. James A. Shapiro, "The Smallest Cells Have Important Lessons to Teach," in *Cosmic Beginnings and Human Ends: Where Science and Religion Meet*, Edited by Clifford N. Matthews and Roy Abraham Varghese, p. 205.

3. Certain "modules" of the same thought or idea sometimes find expression in more than one essay. Thus, *kalogenesis* is also discussed in one section of "Adventurous Frontiers in a Process Universe."

The Most Powerful Force
in the Universe

From a process understanding, every unit of experience, including every new moment of human experience, begins with "perfect" possibilities, presented by God as *initial aims*, or God's persuasive call, for that experience's best future. Initial aims are windows of opportunity, glimpses of what *might be* in contrast to what *now is*, whispers from the still small voice of God within, intimations of the indwelling Christ, or what the German poet Rilke calls "the uninterrupted message that comes out of silence."

In the above paragraph, I placed "perfect" in quotation marks because what God offers are the *best possible* aims, given all the details of the present context. Competing with God's persuasive call are a number of other "voices"—our own desires, and the many influences exerted by the pressure of the past and the immediate environment. For example, the best possible aim that God can present to Bill Gates will differ considerably from what can be offered to a strung-out heroin addict who for decades has followed a life of sometimes brutal crime to support his habit. But, even given the limitations faced by the addict, growth is always possible: by responding positively to the possibilities offered by God in the present moment we thereby make it possible for God to offer even higher values that can be realized in future moments, and so on, and so on . . .

Jesus of Nazareth, whose very selfhood was so transparent to God's persuasive call that the light of God's presence shone through with breathtaking beauty, shows the power of this process and what can be accomplished by aligning oneself with the initial aims presented by a loving God in every new moment.

In his loving persuasive call to all creatures, what God is about is the evocation of truth, beauty, goodness, and adventure. Although the newspaper headlines may sometimes make it seem otherwise, in the long run, it is not coercion or brute force, but *persuasive love*, whether enacted by God or by us humans, that is the most powerful force in the universe.

A Science of Spirituality

What is the heart, or core, of science that makes it so powerful? With such dazzling feats as putting men on the moon, science, rather than religion, seems to be the realm where modern miracles routinely take place. One thing that clearly empowers science is its method. The work of science is done by two contrasting but complementary sensibilities: the *theorist* and the *experimentalist*. It is the dynamic interplay between these two that accounts for the amazing vitality of the scientific enterprise.

The experimentalist expands our senses, so that realities, hitherto unglimpsed, may be seen for the first time. The theorist expands our imagination, so that our reach may exceed our grasp (or what's a "meta" for?). As in a dance where one dancer now takes the lead, and then the partner—one is the source of novelty for the other. And through reciprocal testing and analysis, they keep each other honest. A good example of how the experimentalist keeps the theorist honest is Galileo's correction of Aristotle:

Aristotle theorized and came to the conclusion that a falling object falls with a constant speed, and that a heavy object falls faster than a light one. So great was Aristotle's influence that this mistaken view prevailed for two thousand years. And then along came Galileo. By the simple experiment of using an inclined plane that slowed the motion of a "falling" ball as it rolled down the plane, Galileo was able to observe that a rolling ball clearly accelerated, and that a heavy ball rolled down the plane no faster than a light one. Modern *experimental* physics begins with Galileo.

Late in the 19th century experimentalists in their labs were making discoveries that revealed new realities, such as radioactivity (Becquerel, 1896) and the photoelectric effect (Hertz, 1887). Since Newtonian science could not explain these discoveries, it became evident as the 20th century opened that a new theoretical framework was called for. It was thus the work of experimentalists that impelled the formulation of a scientific revolution called Quantum Theory.

The defining moment for a theorist is the *creative* leap of imagination—from the concrete welter of *observations* and experience, he abstracts a general theory that unites them all in a higher synthesis. Rational thought, or *reason*, will then guide him in deducing specific theoretical results or predictions that logically follow from the theory. And it is here that the experimentalist takes over by devising concrete *experiments* that will either confirm or falsify the theory. If an experiment does falsify the theory, then it's back to the drawing-board for the theorist.

If you note the italicized words in the preceding paragraph, you will find the very core (c.o.r.e.) of the method used by science: creativity, observation, reason, and experiment.

Albert Einstein, perhaps the greatest theorist in the history of physics, once drew a diagram to illustrate this method:

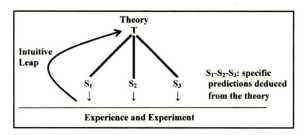

Creativity is crucial for the scientific enterprise; there's simply no other way to make the imaginative leap from experience to theory. Reason alone will never make that leap. As Einstein said, "For the creation of a theory, the mere collection of recorded phenomena never suffices—there must always be added a free invention of the human mind . . ."

At the beginning of his career, Einstein was for a time under the intellectual influence of Ernst Mach, a staunch advocate of positivism in physics. (Positivism rejects any ideas not based on sense-data or verified by mechanistic operations.) Eventually, however, Einstein was persuaded away from this position, partly by arguments from Max Planck and, what was perhaps a stronger reason, by the success of his own new non-positivistic methods of thought. This was fortunate for Einstein and for physics. It was the considered opinion of physicist Heinz Pagels that Einstein would never have discovered the theory of relativity if he had remained a strict positivist!

Another great theorist in the 20th century, Alfred North Whitehead, had the gumption to not only challenge some aspects of Einstein's theory of relativity but also to write a book wherein he expounded an alternate theory (*The Principle of Relativity*, 1922). Here is Whitehead's description of his method of speculative thought:

"The true method of discovery is like the flight of an aeroplane. It starts from the ground of particular observation; it makes a flight in the thin air of imaginative generalization; and it again lands for renewed observation rendered acute by rational interpretation." (*Process and Reality*, 5)

Note the similarities of this to Einstein's diagram and to the general method of science that weds theory and experiment.

Like the left and right hemispheres of the brain, or like yin balancing yang, or like the symbol of medicine, the caduceus, with its two intertwining snakes in an upward spiral—these two, experiment and theory, are a paradigm for the power of complementarity.

The creative rhythm of science is thus a twofold process, a perpetual oscillation between Theory and Experiment, a yin-yang relationship, a flux of the concrete and the abstract.

The Way of Experiment: To Know, Do!

Theory and experiment also play their respective roles in spirituality but not, I think, with the dynamic interplay displayed in science.

It is the task of philosophers and theologians to theorize or speculate about all aspects of the religious life. In the Western tradition the great mystics would seem to qualify as experimentalists, since their vision is grounded in a direct experience of the Holy Reality. But I don't see the fruitful collaboration here that I see functioning between the theorist and experimentalist in science. Nor does experiment play as decisive a role, especially in the West.

Insofar as the word "theory" is not taken in a pejorative sense, the scriptures and sutras of the world's great religions may be thought of as a special case of theory. Granting that such writings are rightly revered, granting even that they may have been inspired, they still tell only half the story, and maybe not even the better half. To use a Buddhist image, they are fingers pointing to the moon, and not the moon itself.

What, then, is the "better half" that the great spiritual luminaries, such as Jesus and Buddha, bequeath to their immediate followers? What is the heart or core of their legacy? The pearl of great price is not dogma or doctrine, not the way of *words*; rather, it is a set of instructions for practice: the way of *experiment*. It is what Ken Wilber calls the Way of Injunction.

A quote from the mathematician G. Spencer Brown will help to make clear what Wilber means by the word *injunction*: "It may be helpful at this stage to realize that the primary form of mathematical communication is not description, but injunction. In this respect it is comparable with practical art forms like cookery, in which the taste of a cake, although literally indescribable, can be conveyed to a reader in the form of a set of injunctions called a recipe. Music is a similar art form; the composer does not even attempt to describe a set of sounds he has in mind, much less the set of feelings occasioned through them, but writes down a set of commands which, if they are obeyed by the reader, can result in a reproduction to the reader of the composer's original experience." (*Laws of Form*, 77)

Whether you're a scientist, a philosopher, or a mystic, Wilber claims that every valid knowledge quest has three strands: 1) Injunction, 2) Illumination, and 3) Confirmation.

The injunctive strand is an experiment with the general form: If you want to know "A," then you must do "B." If you want to know whether the sky is clear or maybe partly cloudy, go outside and take a look. If you want to understand the Pythagorean Theorem, buy a geometry book and study it. If you want to hear "the sound of one hand clapping," find an enlightened Zen Master and let him guide you through several years of work on the one-hand-clapping koan.

The illumination is the actual experience of "A" during the practice. You go outside and see (for yourself) whether the sky is clear or partly cloudy.

Confirmation (or rejection) occurs when you compare your results with a community of like-minded individuals who have also taken up the injunction and stayed with it long enough to experience the second strand: a direct apprehension of knowledge. One must persevere on the path until the "inner eye" becomes adequate to the illumination revealed by the experiment. Like the inquisitors who refused to look through Galileo's telescope, those who do not fully engage the experimental path are not qualified to reject the realities revealed by that path.

Perseverance is required because this is a cumulative process and, in an evolutionary universe, creativity through a developmental process is the very nature of reality. Even mind is not simply a given at birth; it is developmental. The French psychologist Jean Piaget clearly distinguished and described the developmental stages that a child passes through in the process of growing up. Or as Ken Wilber puts it, ". . . mind itself has at least four major stages of growth: *magic* (2-5 years), *mythic* (6-11 years), *rational* (11 onward), and . . . *vision-logic* (adulthood, if then)." Feral children who as infants get separated from the human community and then survive in the wild are a tragic example of what happens when this developmental process is thwarted.

With each new stage, higher levels of understanding become possible. For example, the complexities of math are opaque to a child until she reaches the cognitive level classified as "formal operations," where it first becomes possible to engage in abstract thinking. For a variety of reasons (indeed, variety may *be* the reason), these possibilities are not equally actualized by all: while some delight in math and find it as easy as pi, there are many others who either couldn't care less or are downright terrified at the mere thought of taking an algebra class.

In a universe where creation continues, individual development has no terminal point; indeed, it need never stop! Like expanding ripples on a still pond, consciousness can become ever more expansive, ever more encompassing, ever more *ever more*—and the Way of Experiment is a reliable method for accomplishing this.

Ticket to Athens

The Buddhists can lay claim to what may well be the longest ongoing experiment in the history of humanity. I refer to the practice developed by Siddhartha Gautama, the founder of Buddhism.

After trying, without success, everything the ascetic Yoga of his time had to offer, he streamlined his practice and simply sat in meditation under the Bodhi Tree until he experienced enlightenment upon seeing the morning star. On that momentous morning, under a softly brightening sky, there awakened a Buddha—a threshold had been crossed and, with the crossing, a revolutionary breakthrough in the evolution of consciousness.

What does it mean to say that Siddhartha *awakened*—just what is it that he awakened to? Fundamentally, he awakened to a new way of knowing. And zazen, or sitting meditation, is the injunctive or *experimental* path that enables one to reach this new way of knowing.

Rather than merely reading or hearing about the spiritual breakthrough of the Buddha, this practice enabled his disciples to directly experience that breakthrough themselves—in the laboratory of their own consciousness. Is this not a pearl of great price?

With this practice, that has been handed down, polished, and refined for more than twenty-five centuries, you can sit under the Bodhi Tree not *with* the Buddha but *as* the Buddha, and reproduce, in your own mind, the Master's original insights. Or, to state it another way, you can "let that mind be in you, which was also in Christ Jesus."

Zazen, as an experiment, is a cognitive tool or technology; it is an interior technology on the spiritual quest just as a telescope, for the astronomer, is an external technology. Both reveal realities that the "naked eye" cannot see. With a telescope, the *rings* of Saturn become visible; with a profound interior technology, one can, with poet Henry Vaughn, see "eternity . . . like a great *ring* of pure and endless light." When all three strands of the knowledge quest are rigorously honored, a spiritual experiment is just as valid as one performed by physicists in a laboratory at MIT, and the illumination apprehended in such an experiment is grounded in evidence every bit as solid.

This illumination or direct apprehension transcends the realm of rational thought. Here too, as in Einstein's diagram, there must be a leap of creative intuition. A step-by-step logical process, no matter how subtle or refined, can never blaze a rational trail that arrives where spiritual intuition leaps.

But these "peak experiences" are only a beginning. One must steadfastly continue to practice and, as the practice matures, these momentary states will be transformed into permanent traits. The transformation is from peaks to plateau to permanence.

It is through these deep spiritual practices, or the Way of Experiment, that both the individual (Buddha) and the spiritual community (Sangha) can continue to evolve and ever more completely embody and express the truth (Dharma).

The trajectory of future human development will be on a course empowered by the creation of new inner technologies. Some of these will be integrated with the technology of science, especially the rapidly evolving field of electronics and computers. Already there are "mind machines" that can help you catch the wave into your neurocosmos. In the prophetic words of Ken Wilber, "The coming Buddha will speak digital."

In science, the relation between theory and experiment is a strong, healthy, and fruitful marriage; in spirituality, especially here in the West, the relation is more like a flirtation. I propose a marriage: let there be a wedding, and let the dance begin. If these two ever begin to tango, as they do in science, watch out! The sparks will fly and there will flame a new science of spirituality.

I'll end with a conversation between two people in Aldous Huxley's novel, *After Many a Summer Dies the Swan*:

"I like the words I use to bear some relation to facts. That's why I'm interested in eternity—psychological eternity. Because it's a fact."

"For you perhaps," said Jeremy.

"For anyone who chooses to fulfill the conditions under which it can be experienced."

"And why should anyone wish to fulfill them?"

"Why should anyone choose to go to Athens to see the Parthenon? Because it's worth the bother. And the same is true of eternity. The experience of timeless good is worth all the trouble it involves."

"Timeless good," Jeremy repeated with distaste. "I don't know what the words mean."

"Why should you?" said Mr. Propter. "You've never bought your ticket to Athens."

[Note: this essay owes much to the writings of Ken Wilber, especially *The Marriage of Sense and Soul: Integrating Science and Religion.*]

The Way of Jesus:
Where Ends Are Beginnings

The Way of Metaphor

Jesus was a superb master of metaphor; indeed, the whole thrust of his teaching was primarily through parables and memorable stories. He was also a master of what Jesus scholar Marcus Borg calls "great one-liners," short sayings with an aphoristic bite to them, such as "You strain out a gnat and swallow a camel" or "You cannot get grapes from a bramble bush."

Metaphor is present at the heart of his teachings, for what he taught was not theological doctrine or a set of beliefs, but a Way—a path of transformation. Moreover, as can be seen in Acts 9:2, the movement initiated by Jesus was not at first known as Christianity; it was called "the Way."

Imagery of the way is given a variety of expression in Mark, the earliest gospel. As Borg observes, "The Greek word for 'way' is *hodos*, and Mark uses it frequently throughout his gospel. Its frequency is somewhat obscured in English, for *hodos* is translated with a number of words: 'way,' 'road,' 'path.' Behind them all is *hodos*, the 'way.'"[1]

In the first chapter, verses one through three, we are presented with one of what will be many variations on the theme of the way:

"The good news of Jesus the Anointed begins with something Isaiah wrote: Here is my messenger, whom I send on ahead of you to prepare your way! A voice of someone shouting in the wilderness: 'Make ready the way of the Lord, make his paths straight.'"[2]

On the Way

In the first eight chapters of Mark's narrative, Jesus seems to be "on the road" almost daily as he comes to Galilee and walks around the countryside to bring his message to the people. By the Sea of Galilee, when he calls four men to follow him as disciples, they drop what they are doing at once and follow, going first to Capernaum and then on to the next towns throughout all Galilee. As the excitement begins to grow, and as the crowds become larger and more diverse, we hear of the number of his disciples growing and we hear of their passing through a cornfield on the Sabbath, of their path up into a mountain, and their passage, by boat, over to the other side of the Sea of Galilee. The road then leads Jesus to his own country, near Nazareth, where he makes his way roundabout the villages, teaching. They depart for a time unto a desert place, and then, it's back on the road to the land of Gennesaret, and on to the towns of Bethsaida and Caesarea Philippi.

In the pivotal central section of Mark (8:22-10:52), Jesus, his disciples, and other followers are *on the way* as they make the long journey from Caesarea Philippi to Jerusalem.

A point not to be missed is that this section is framed by two healings by Jesus of men who are blind. The crucial placing of these healings, one at the beginning and the other at the end of the journey, suggests that we are to understand them on more than one level, as metaphors about seeing. As Borg says, "The framing is deliberate, the meaning clear: *to see* means to see that *the way* involves following Jesus to Jerusalem."[3]

On three different occasions while on the journey, Jesus speaks in prophetic words of his destiny, of what awaits him in Jerusalem: that he will be handed over to the authorities, killed, and in three days rise again. And each time, to make clear the crux of his teaching, he concludes by saying that to follow him is to follow him on this path. His invitation is for them to "take up their cross (a symbol of death) and follow me." This is the heart of the matter. This is the *way*.

The remaining chapters of Mark tell the story of the seven last days of Jesus as he comes to the final period of his life's sentence and enacts those events that Christians celebrate as Holy Week. On this *way*, where ends are beginnings, Jesus invites us to follow him as he passes through death to resurrection.

What Is This Way?

It is the final and decisive path that Jesus took on the way to Jerusalem. It is the path of death and resurrection, of dying and rising. Constellated as five aspects:

It is the way of *transformation*: a dying to an old identity and rising to one that is new—and new because radically centered in God and the sacred rather than the "lords" of culture, convention, and the secular.

It is the way of *relations*: (1) our relationship with God founded on what Jesus called the greatest commandment: "And you shall love the Lord your God with all your heart, and with all your soul, and with all your mind, and with all your strength" and (2) our relationship with others, also founded on the second part of this commandment: "and you shall love your neighbor as yourself."[4]

It is the way of *participation*. Rather than the doctrine of substitutionary atonement, according to which Jesus is said to have sacrificed his life in atonement for our sins, Borg's claim is that a close reading of Mark reveals that "it is only by participation in the life, death, and resurrection of Jesus that such 'at-one-ment' is possible. For Mark, it is about *participation with* Jesus and not *substitution by* Jesus."[5] As St. Augustine once said, "God without us will not, as we without God cannot."

It is the way of sacramental *mediation* whereby the sacred becomes present and speaks to us through symbol and mystery. Sacraments are doors or bridges to the sacred and by their use we can mediate both the presence and power of God. Borg says that Christianity, along with all the enduring religions, "is a massive and magnificent sacrament of the sacred."[6]

In contrast to practice in first-century Palestine where access to the holy was mediated and brokered by the high priests and the temple, it is important to add here that Jesus experienced, and enabled others to experience, direct access to God and the power that is always "near at hand" in the realm of the sacred.

It is the way of *imitation*, the *imitatio Dei*, or imitation of God. And, of the attributes of God that we are to imitate, what is the foremost? Jesus would surely answer, compassion.

Love of God and love of neighbor, as the "great commandments," were the heart of the way of Jesus. C. H. Dodd, recognized as one of the great New Testament scholars of the twentieth century, suggests that, rather than stating this as a commandment, Jesus would invite us to think of it in terms of a relationship.

In his book *The Founder of Christianity*, Dodd writes, "Thus, when he is speaking in language of his own choice . . . he says (in effect) 'God is your Father; become what you are, his child.' But there is a further point: the maxim 'Like father, like child' holds good here, and it is in the application of this principle that we can recognize an emphasis which is characteristic of the teaching of Jesus. The child of God will be like his Father, at least to the extent that he will feel himself obliged to try to reproduce in his own behavior towards others the quality of God's action toward his children, and to pursue the direction in which that action points. To love God is to live as his child; to live as a child of God is to treat your neighbor as God treats you."

This suggests a new twist on the Golden Rule: Do unto others as God does unto you. "Be compassionate as God is compassionate," as Jesus says in Luke 6:36. Love as God loves. How does God love? As I learned from Marcus Borg,[7] the Hebrew word for compassion is *rahamin*, the plural of a word that in its singular form means "womb." The intimacy of God's love can thus be likened to the love a mother feels for the children of her womb, a love that is life-giving, nourishing, cherishing, unconditional, and a hundred other words this metaphor so richly suggests.

Two Ways of Believing

Would it surprise you, as it greatly surprised me, to learn that the word "believe" used to have a far different meaning than it has today?

In my Webster's dictionary, the first two definitions of "believe" are: "to take as true or real," and "to have confidence in a statement or promise of (another person)." *To believe*, in the modern sense, means to give assent—intellectual assent—to a set of doctrines, statements, or claims. In this sense, the object of belief is a proposition.

A look at the history of this word, however, reveals a very different story. "I believe" used to share the same meaning as the Latin word *credo*, the first word of the Apostles' Creed. *Credo in Deum Patrem omnipotentem, Creatorem coeli et terrae.* (I believe in God, the Father almighty, creator of heaven and earth.) *Credo*, meaning "I believe," derives from two Indo-European roots: *kerd-*, "heart," and *dhe-*, "to do," or "to place." What does this tell us about the original meaning of the word *believe*?

In short, to say "I believe" used to mean "I give my heart to." "Believe" is also cognate with the German verb *belieben*, which, unlike its English cousin, still means "to cherish, to hold dear, to belove."

In this older and original sense of the word, what, then, does it mean to affirm belief in God? It means to give your heart to God, that is, to give your self, at its deepest level, to God. It means to affirm allegiance and loyalty, to feel that God, as the object of devotion, is worthy of unlimited love and veneration. More than giving intellectual assent to ideas *about* God, it means coming into a heart-felt relationship *with* God. Note how in this, the original sense, the object of belief is not a *proposition* but a *person*.

For what this means in Christian terms, Borg sums it up nicely:

"Believing in Jesus in the sense of giving one's heart to Jesus is the movement from secondhand religion to firsthand religion, from having heard about Jesus with the hearing of the ear to being in relationship with the Spirit of Christ. For ultimately, Jesus is not simply a figure of the past, but a figure of the present. Meeting that Jesus—the living Jesus who comes to us even now—will be like meeting Jesus again for the first time."[8]

For the change in meaning of the word "believe," I am indebted to Wilfred Cantwell Smith, professor emeritus of religion at Harvard, who presents a clear and persuasive case for this in two books: *Faith and Belief* and *Belief and History*.[9]

Jesus—the Only Way?

If Jesus is the way, is he then the *only* way? Many Christians affirm this, citing as evidence John 14:6—"I am the way, and the truth, and the life. No one comes to the Father except through me." However, there are many other Christians who reject this interpretation and perhaps side with Borg who shares the following story that reflects his position:

"The same point is made in a story I heard about a sermon preached by a Hindu professor in a Christian seminary several decades ago. The text for the day included the 'one way' passage, and about it he said, 'This verse is absolutely true—Jesus is the only way.' Then, he continued, 'And that way—of dying to an old way of being and being born into a new way of being—is known in all of the religions of the world.' The 'way' of Jesus is a universal way, known even to millions who have never heard of Jesus."[10]

With the advances in communication and modes of travel that have made the planet Earth into a global village, the reality of religious pluralism, first-hand and up-front, is now a part of our everyday experience. Harvard theologian Harvey Cox relates a personal story that clearly exemplifies this:

". . . a few years ago a student in my course—a typically hardworking premed student—sought me out during my office hours to inquire about courses on the other religions of the world. When I asked him what had prompted him to want to take a course that would pull him away from physiology and quantitative analysis, he said, "Well, my roommate is a Muslim, my girlfriend is a Buddhist, and my lab partner is a Hindu. I'm beginning to think it's time for me to find out where they're coming from."[11]

If, for example, we look to where Zen Buddhism is coming from, we find that the roots of Zen reach down deep into fertile soil that nourishes abundant creative life in Chinese and Japanese culture.

Jesus said, "By their fruits you shall know them." (Matthew 7:20)

To touch on only a few of the fruits of Zen:

In art and esthetics, the spirit of Zen has revealed subtleties of expression and perception that have been either neglected, or missed altogether, in the West.

One can sense both the sense and sensibility of Zen in landscape painting, calligraphy, new poetic forms such as the haiku, the tea ceremony, flower arrangement, the austere beauty of a Zen rock garden, the art of bonsai where the esthetic shaping and dwarfing of living trees and plants creates fresh and original organic forms for contemplation.

The spirit of Zen Buddhism suffuses a creative and vital spirituality that finds expression in the serene atmosphere of Zen temples, religious iconography, the evocative sound of the bamboo flute, the fragrance of aloeswood incense, zazen or seated meditation, koan study, the long lineage of enlightened Zen masters with their robust sense of humor and comic spirit, indeed, saints or masters who equal any in the Christian tradition.

Some of the central metaphors of the two traditions reveal a difference, yes, but one that is complementary or can be *mutually* transforming.

Whereas Christianity uses the metaphor of "born again" to express the essential insight, Zen uses a different one: *awakening*. But the parallel is clear between "death-arising" and "sleep-awaking." Christ *risen* and Buddha *awakened*—both point to a way of radical transformation.

I have also been long impressed, and intrigued, by two sayings, one from the Christian tradition, the other from Buddhist, that sound the same note, or chord, although maybe in a somewhat different key. Philippians 2:5 reads: "Let this mind be in you, which was also in Christ Jesus." There would be an exact parallel if someone in Buddhist scripture had written: "Let this mind be in you, which was also in Gautama Buddha." So far as I know, no such saying exists. However, there is a saying that comes very close, indeed. In the *Diamond Sutra*, a highly revered Chinese text that is dated 868 CE, there is a line that reads:

> You should bring forth (or awaken)
> that mind which abides nowhere.

至應無所住而生其心
zhì yīng wú suǒ zhù ér shēng qí xīn

Buddhist scholar R. H. Blyth awards this saying the very highest praise, for he hails it as "the most profound, the most religious utterance in the world." His enthusiasm becomes understandable when it is realized that "the mind which abides nowhere" is the *awakened* mind—the all-encompassing, nothing-lacking Buddha mind.

There is a famous story about this saying. When he was a young man, Hui-neng, who would later become the Sixth Patriarch in the Zen lineage of great masters, experienced enlightenment upon overhearing this phrase as it was recited by a man who was reading the *Diamond Sutra* aloud.

With all this in mind, we can see that the two sayings are glimpses of the same essential truth. Does this mean that Christ-mind equals Buddha-mind? Not exactly. Buddhism, after all, is not Christianity, and vice versa. But the two sayings do seem to reflect facets of the same precious jewel, the same crystallization of insight, the same *diamond*. Or, as Jesus would say, the same pearl of great price.

The Open Way

Increasingly during the period of Roman domination, as Martin Hengel, a German scholar of religion, observes, "the Hasidic ideal of piety became dominant for the majority of Palestinian Jews."[12] Two movements within Judaism, the Pharisees and the Essenes, intensified this ideal and made it their central concern to live a life of holiness and to center that life in Temple and Torah. The biblical text behind this is found in Leviticus 19:2, where, to paraphrase, the injunction is to "Be holy as God is holy."

The focus of the "quest for holiness" became the avoidance or separation from all that was unclean or impure. Indeed, the word "Pharisee" is derived from the Aramaic word *perishaya*, meaning "separated." This gave rise to a purity system whereby people and things were classified in terms of a basic polarity: clean and unclean, pure and impure. Boundaries, especially *social* boundaries, were clearly drawn, producing a politics of purity and a society structured around the purity system.

Nowhere was this more salient than in the selection, preparation, eating, and sharing of meals—every aspect, every small detail, was meticulously elaborated by the purity code. As Borg observes, "The meal was a microcosm of the social system."[13] Pharisees, and others among the dominant elite, would never even consider welcoming someone who was unclean to sit down at table and dine with them.

Jesus turned this upside down with his boundary-shattering practice of table fellowship, a fellowship so inclusive that all were welcome. The

Pharisees, and those who scrupulously followed the purity code, saw Jesus and his open table as a direct challenge. They sharply criticized him as "a glutton and a drunk, a crony of tax collectors and sinners."

To the politics of purity and the injunction, "Be holy as God is holy," Jesus countered with "Be compassionate as God is compassionate" and a politics of compassion. If we compare these two—a politics of purity and a politics of compassion—note how one divides, the other unites, one is closed and exclusive, the other, open and inclusive. The table of Jesus was always open, open to all, and he welcomed all to his festive table with open arms, an open smile, and an open heart. His way is always the open way.

The Way Out

During the time of Jesus, when the political world of Palestine was ruled by imperial Rome, the Jewish peasantry suffered under a domination system so severely unjust that we can scarcely imagine it. Under this oppressive and exploitative system, peasant existence was harsh, barely subsistent, and the average lifespan was short—only about half the biblical threescore and ten.

A chief characteristic of this system was a stark polarity in social standing. At the top of society were the Roman presence and their collaborators, the Jewish elite, including, as Borg explains, "the ruler, traditional aristocracy, high government and religious officials, and their extended families." Attached to the elites was a service class of "lower-level government officials, the army, some of the priesthood, most scribes, some urban merchants, and the servants of the elites."[14]

At the bottom, and constituting more than ninety percent of the population, was the peasant class. There was no in-between—no middle class that could aspire to upward mobility.

Since this was a pre-industrial, agrarian society, with wealth measured in terms of agriculture and its byproducts, it was the peasants who produced all the wealth. But, through tithes, taxation, and land ownership, the ruling elites, fewer than ten percent of the people, ended up with more than two-thirds of the wealth. The ruling elites were experts in calibrating just how far they could push the peasantry: to the point of starvation—almost, yes—but not so far as to incite open revolt.

Does all this sound familiar? Far from being an aberration, this system has been the general rule throughout history and around the globe. Even today, in the United States, the stubborn remnants of this can be seen in the huge gap that grows ever wider between the very wealthy and the very poor. And this is not simply because, as some seem ready to believe, the poor are unwilling to work harder. The injustice is systemic. This is systemic evil, yet another characteristic of domination systems—evil or injustice built right into the system.[15]

If first-century Jewish Palestine had become the "land of Egypt," a land of bondage, then a new exodus was called for. A *way out*[16] was at the heart of the alternative social vision of Rabbi Yeshua of Nazareth. He called it the Kingdom of God.

The Way into the Kingdom

"Ask any hundred New Testament scholars around the world, Protestant, Catholic, or non-Christian, what the central message of Jesus of Nazareth was, and the vast majority of them—perhaps every single expert—would agree that this message centered in the Kingdom of God."[17] And yet, as Borg observes, "a century of scholarly activity has produced no consensus regarding its interpretation."[18]

What did Jesus *mean* when he spoke about the Kingdom[19] of God? Did he have a single concept in mind that he wished to convey to his listeners? No, for the Kingdom of God is not a *concept*; it is, rather, a *symbol*. Moreover, it is a *tensive* symbol. Unlike *steno*-symbols,[20] which have only one referent, tensive symbols are richly suggestive and have the power to evoke multiple meanings. In this section, with Borg as guide, I will explore the path of one of these meanings.

Some symbols, and the Kingdom of God is such a symbol, have the power to evoke a myth, with *myth* understood as "a story about the relationship between two realms, the sacred and the profane."[21] The myth evoked by the Kingdom of God is *God's activity in the world* as seen in Jewish history and as it unfolded within the Christian community.

As one who was deeply in touch with the realm of the sacred, and whose self-emptying before God was so complete that he was filled and overflowing with Spirit, Jesus was a "holy man" or what Borg prefers to call a "Spirit person." For the Spirit person or shaman, experience—

their direct experience—reveals that reality has at least two levels which have been named variously as sacred and profane, noumenal and phenomenal, or, as in the Lord's Prayer, heaven and earth: "Thy kingdom come, thy will be done, on *earth* as it is in *heaven.*"

A characteristic ability of the Spirit person is to mediate the power of the sacred realm, for the good of those in his community, in such activities as healing and exorcism. Jesus exemplified this to a very high degree, for, as Borg says, "more healing stories are told about him than about any other figure in the Jewish tradition."[22]

And, in Matthew 12:28, Jesus makes a statement that connects his power of exorcism with the Kingdom of God: "But if it is by the Spirit of God that I cast out demons, then the kingdom of God has come upon you."

As Borg summarizes it: "In short, the phrase 'Kingdom of God' in this passage does not refer to a concept or ideal or belief, but to an actual though not physical reality: the beneficent power of the other realm. In the exorcisms, that power 'comes' . . . The phrase 'Kingdom of God' is thus a symbol for the presence and power of God as known in mystical experience. It is Jesus' name for what is experienced in the primordial religious experience and his name for the power from that realm which flowed through him as a Spirit person."[23]

And what is the way into the Kingdom of God? It is, as you no doubt have already guessed, the way of death and resurrection, the way of dying to be born again, the way of self-emptying to be filled by the Spirit, the way of the cross where . . .

"In my end is my beginning." —T. S. Eliot (*Four Quartets*)

Pre- and the Post-Easter Ways

Borg distinguishes between what he calls the pre-Easter and the post-Easter Jesus. The pre-Easter Jesus was a Galilean Jew, a peasant, an itinerant healer and teacher, and a subversive social prophet. As a figure of the past, he was a mortal man, born of woman, in the city of Nazareth, and who died on the cross at Golgotha. After his crucifixion and death, the followers of Jesus continued to experience him as a living reality. As a figure of the present, then and ever after, this abiding *spiritual* presence is the post-Easter Jesus.

Borg[24] compares the two as follows:

Jesus of Nazareth	The Post-Easter Jesus
4 B.C.E. to 30 C.E.	30 C.E. to today
Corporeal (flesh and blood)	Spiritual, nonmaterial
Finite/mortal	Infinite/eternal
Human	Divine
A Jewish peasant	King of kings, Lord of lords
Jesus of Nazareth	Jesus Christ

A metaphor, at the heart of the teaching of Jesus, helps in the understanding of this:

When Jesus spoke to others about being born again, he surely was speaking from the personal experience of having been born again himself, with "born again" a metaphor for personal transformation or the experience of enlightenment. In the Buddhist tradition, the story has come down to us of how Siddhartha Gautama experienced enlightenment upon glimpsing the morning star while sitting in meditation under the Bo tree. Unfortunately, we have no story of the moment when Jesus experienced enlightenment, when he was "born again," but maybe that story lies hidden on an ancient scroll awaiting excavation by an archeologist. Or, following Plato,[25] a "likely story" may be that the moment came on one of the occasions when Jesus went off by himself to spend forty days alone in the desert. But this still leaves one wondering what exactly he was doing, that is, what sort of spiritual practice he was engaged in, when the moment came.

Whatever it was, the experience of God became intensely intimate, intensely personal: God became, in the twinkling of an eye, Abba—Papa.

To extend further the metaphor of being "born again," it can be said that Jesus was once more born again on Easter, in a decisive transformation that brought forth the presence, the living *spiritual* reality, of the post-Easter Jesus. From this perspective, to say that "Christ is risen" is to say that Jesus is born again. Both are metaphors of transformation.

> In the spring of the year
> Came Christ the chrysalis—
> Us to empower.[26]

153

How did Jesus, a figure of the past, become a figure of the present, and the central figure of a worldwide religion? How do we get from the pre-Easter to the post-Easter Jesus, from the human to the divine, from, as Borg puts it,[27] a Galilean Jew to the face of God?

An answer is suggested in process philosophy's understanding of how saltations (or big jumps) can occur in evolution.[28] From a process understanding, every unit of experience, including every new moment of human experience, begins with "perfect" possibilities, presented by God as *initial aims*, or God's persuasive call, for that experience's best future. Initial aims are windows of opportunity, glimpses of what *might be* in contrast to what *now is*, whispers from the still small voice of God within, intimations of the indwelling Christ, or what the German poet Rilke calls "the uninterrupted message that comes out of silence."[29]

God, as poet of the world[30] and through persuasive love, invites all creatures to enjoy ever higher values and novel forms of experience, and these possibilities are first felt mentally and only later does it become possible for them to be realized on the physical level.

On this hypothesis, many incremental steps could be built up within, behind the scenes, so to speak, before the sum of those incremental steps makes a sudden, and observable, manifestation in the body. Behind the apparent saltation lies a series of gradual steps that may have occurred over long stretches of evolutionary time.

Through meditation, prayer, and other spiritual practices, we attune our intuition to these initial aims lovingly offered by God in every new moment and, by our choices and by our practice, reduce the contrast between what our situation *now is* and what it *can be*. Once a possibility is felt, and as it continues to be reiterated and felt across many occasions of experience, it accumulates energy until sufficient massiveness is gained for manifestation to occur. A "process" prayer would not try to get God to do what we want, but instead would create a context wherein the possibility offered by God could be first felt, reiterated many times, and then concretely realized. Our creative work is to complete what God initiates.

Jesus of Nazareth, whose very selfhood was so transparent to God's persuasive call that the light of God's presence shone through with breathtaking beauty, shows the power of this process[31] and what can be accomplished by attuning oneself to the initial aims offered by a loving God in every new moment.

To his disciples, the crucifixion of Jesus seemed at first to be the end but, as the Easter experience would reveal, it became a robust beginning. Easter, as Borg explains, is a vindication, by God, "of how Jesus lived, as well as an overturning of how he died." Easter is not limited to one historical day in first-century Palestine; it is ever present as a sacramental experience, revealing the face of God,[32] as seen in Jesus, a Galilean Jew.

On the Way to Emmaus

Day three after the crucifixion . . .

Two of the followers of Jesus have left Jerusalem, walking along the road on their way to the small village of Emmaus. As they talk about the things that have happened, a stranger approaches and joins them in their journey. (We know the stranger to be Jesus but they do not yet recognize him.) The stranger asks them what they are talking about that seems to make them so sad. One of them, whose name is Cleopas, asks Jesus if he is a stranger here, so that he does not know what has come to pass. Cleopas then tells him about the crucifixion and death of a great prophet, Jesus of Nazareth, how his body was placed in a tomb and how, this very morning, certain of the women, who went early to the sepulcher, found it empty, and then saw a vision of angels who said that Jesus was alive.

As they draw near to the village of Emmaus, the stranger makes as though he will go on alone his own way. But the two men protest, inviting him to "Abide with us, for it is toward evening, the day is far spent."

The stranger accepts their invitation and later, as they sit down to share a meal, he takes bread, blesses it, breaks it, and gives it to them. At that moment, their eyes are opened and they recognize the stranger for who he really is.

And what happened then? He vanished from their sight!

Now, is this a factual account of what took place on that Easter morning? Was it, as Borg asks, something that, say, a CNN photographer could have captured on a video camera? Borg's answer is No, but the story is *true* nonetheless.

John Dominic Crossan, who has been called the premier Jesus scholar in the world today, comes to the same conclusion: the Emmaus story is "the metaphoric condensation of the first years of Christian thought into one parabolic afternoon."[33] Crossan sums it up with six words in a great one-liner: "Emmaus never happened; Emmaus always happens."

As Borg explains, Emmaus happens again . . . and again . . . and again. "To speak as a Christian about this story, the truth of the Emmaus road story is that the risen Christ journeys with us whether we know it or not. Yet there are moments when we do become aware of his presence. Moreover, this foundational experience continues to this day. This, it seems to me, is the truth of Easter. The truth of Easter is grounded not in whether the tomb was empty but in the ongoing experience of Jesus as a living reality, as a figure of the present."[34]

In light of all this, and remembering that Jesus is named the "bread of life" in the gospel of John, the journey can happen again—we can be on our way to Emmaus again—when we pray: Give us this day our daily bread.

The Way from Athens to Jerusalem

The many similarities between Socrates and Jesus have long been noted. One of the earliest to see these similarities was a second-century Christian philosopher, Justin Martyr, who wrote that Socrates was a Christian even before Christ. One similarity is so obvious that it hardly needs pointing out: both of these men taught a subversive wisdom that challenged the status quo and, for this, both were executed. Borg adds, "It is striking that Socrates and Jesus, the two most central figures in the philosophical and religious traditions of the West, were both executed. Clearly, challenging conventional wisdom is often experienced as offensive and threatening."[35]

Although they lived more than two thousand years ago, both became martyrs, and their teachings, and the examples of their lives, continue as a lasting influence. This influence is all the more surprising in that neither wrote or published anything, so that all we know about them we learn from their disciples or followers.

Here, in tabular form, are these and some additional similarities:

Jesus and Socrates—

1. both pursue goodness
2. agree that poverty allows one to see more clearly
3. hear a special voice: Jesus, the Father—Socrates, his *daimon*
4. are teachers who practice an oral tradition
5. use metaphor to help others think for themselves
6. are revolutionaries who challenge established ways of thinking
7. seek to enlighten their cultures and change their worlds
8. leave behind no writings, but each draws in the dirt: Jesus with his finger, Socrates with a stick
9. prepare their followers for their deaths and comfort them
10. are "legally" executed and accept this willingly
11. drink from the cup
    Socrates, the cup of hemlock
    Jesus, symbolism of the cup: "let this cup pass by me"
12. become martyrs and leave behind a group of disciples
13. leave a legacy that lasts to this day

In *Witness to the Truth*, her book about Jesus, Edith Hamilton included a chapter on Socrates because she thought our vision is sharpened to see Jesus if we look first at Socrates. If Justin Martyr is right, as noted above, this accords well with Hamilton's observation.

A Way To Speak from the Depths

Jesus had a way with words. Not only *what* he said, but *how* he said it must have deeply moved many who flocked to hear what he had to say. Was there something in his voice, a bardic quality, perhaps, that sent thrills through the veins of those who heard him, just as modern audiences thrilled to hear the magnificent voice of the Welsh poet Dylan Thomas as he declaimed his poetry?

The freshness and vitality of his way with words also shows in the modes of speech he chose to convey his message: parables, aphorisms, stories: the spontaneous effervescence of his metaphoric mind. C.H. Dodd saw Jesus' way with words as "the natural expression of a mind that sees truth in concrete pictures rather than . . . in abstractions."[36]

Jesus did not lecture to people; he engaged them in direct encounters of give-and-take: face to face, eye to eye, voice to voice, heart to heart.

Jesus also chose to covey his message strictly *viva voce*, "by word of mouth," or with the "living voice" if we literally translate the two Latin words that form this phrase. With a single exception, when he wrote with his finger on the ground as described in John 8:6, Jesus, so far as the gospel tells us, never wrote a word and thus we have nothing by him in writing. "Jesus was a voice not a penman, a herald not a scribe, a watchman with his call in the market-place and the Temple, and not a cry of alarm in the wilderness like John the Baptist."[37] So writes Amos Wilder, and Martin Luther was emphatic about the oral character of the Gospel:

"In the New Testament the proclamation should take place by word of mouth, publicly in an animated tone, and should bring that forward into speech and hearing which before was hidden in the letters and in apparent concealment. Since the New Testament is none other than an opening up and disclosure of the Old Testament . . . therefore it is that Christ himself did not write his own teaching as Moses did his, but gave it forth by word of mouth and commanded that it should be done orally and gave no commandment to write it. . . . Before [the apostles] wrote, they preached and converted men by their living presence and voice. . . . That books had to be written was already a great departure and breach with the Spirit, occasioned by necessity, and not in keeping with the New Testament."[38]

We are told explicitly, in Matthew and in Luke, that people were astonished when he spoke, for he spoke with authority and his word was with power. And in Mark 4, some disciples are at sea with Jesus in a boat threatened by a tempestuous storm. Jesus lies sleeping during this tumult and the disciples, fearful for their lives, awaken him. Jesus speaks to the raging sea, saying, "Peace, be still," and the wind ceases and there comes a great calm. Seeing this, the disciples remark in awe: "What manner of man is this, that even the wind and the waves obey him?" Even if this story be metaphorical, as I believe it is, it still reveals the power and authority of his voice.

The source of this power was surely his intimacy with God. Saint Ignatius of Antioch speaks eloquently of the relation between Jesus and God:

"Jesus Christ, his son, who is his word proceeding from silence."[39]

It is in silence, in the depths of silence, that God speaks, and it is from those depths that Jesus spoke, and spoke decisively, with a voice vibrant with overtones from those depths. Jesus not only *spoke* from the depths, he now *speaks* from the depths, and the fruit of his lips flourishes still in the heart, which is the self at its *deepest* level.

End the Beginning Way

Finnegans Wake, the last work by the great Irish writer James Joyce, is a book wherein ends are indeed beginnings. The novel ends with these words:

A way a lone a last a loved a long the

which lead the reader back to the words that begin the novel:

riverrun, past Eve and Adam's, from swerve of shore to bend of bay . . .

The book thus ends, and begins, in mid-sentence, giving the novel a circular structure so that reading the text is an endless cycle. You can never finish it, so just curl up and enjoy the ride.

As the book comes to a "close," Anna Livia Plurabelle, who personifies the river Liffey, is flowing down toward the estuary of Dublin Bay which then leads out into, and merges with, the Irish sea. In her final monologue, which Joseph Campbell has called "one of the great passages in all literature," she sings the elegy of the river Liffey and gives voice to a simple but lovely line, conflating endings, beginnings, water, worship, and so much more:

I sink I'd die down . . . only to washup.[40]

And, after merging with the vast ocean, where will she washup? Arising from the depths where the world is still fluid, born again of *water* and the spirit, she will flow forth in the *riverrun* that begins the book.

The Way Made Flesh

On his journey to Jerusalem, Jesus literally walked the path, or *the way*, that we are to walk metaphorically, if we wish to follow him.

As Borg observes, "In a quite historical sense, Jesus not only taught the way of death as the path of transformation, but his life and death became an incarnation of the way which he taught. Indeed it is this remarkable congruity between the teaching of Jesus and the way his life ended that accounts in part for the power which his figure has had over the centuries."[41]

The *way* he proposed, the *truth* he proclaimed, the new *life* he promised—for those with eyes to see, these were all present in the person of Jesus. The possibilities he put before others for attainment were not abstractions, but were actualities in his own life. He was a *living* ideal they could look up to. As Edith Hamilton says, "He was what he taught."[42]

Jesus is the way *made flesh*: an incarnation of the way that shows what the way looks like when fully embodied. In Mark 8:34 he spoke his invitation: "If any want to become my followers, let them deny themselves and take up their cross and follow me." And, as Luke reminds us, we are to take up our cross not just one time, once and for all, but *daily*—the way is a lifelong journey of many inns, many roads. To follow Jesus on the way is to go with him all the way, to Jerusalem, the way of the cross, to the very end, yes, but where ends are beginnings.

Endnotes

1. Marcus J. Borg and John Dominic Crossan, *The Last Week: The Day-by-Day Account of Jesus' Final Week in Jerusalem*, p. 24.

2. Daryl D. Schmidt, *The Gospel of Mark: With Introduction, Notes, and Original Text Featuring the New Scholars Version Translation*, p. 43.

3. Marcus J. Borg and John Dominic Crossan, *The Last Week*, p. 30.

4. Mark 12:30-31.

5. Marcus J. Borg and John Dominic Crossan, *The Last Week*, p. 102.

6. Marcus J. Borg, *The Heart of Christianity: Rediscovering a Life of Faith*, p. 215.

7. Marcus J. Borg, *Meeting Jesus Again for the First Time: The Historical Jesus & the Heart of Contemporary Faith*, p. 47.

8. Marcus J. Borg, *Meeting Jesus Again for the First Time*, p. 137.

9. In Smith's analysis, and by way of summary, four major shifts can be traced in the evolution of the word "believe."

   In the first, the object of the verb shifts from a person to a proposition. The subject of the verb, in the second, shifts from first to third person: from "I" to "he," "she," or "they." Whereas "belief" was initially linked with truth, in the third shift there is a descent from true to dubious to false. As the prize example of this trend, Smith cites the 1966 Random House dictionary which defines the word "belief" as "an opinion or conviction" and then offers this illustration: "the belief that the world is flat."

   As Smith observes, "What could be more casually devastating? The first example that comes to mind for the compilers, and then the readers, of this impressive work is a belief that is false. Is it not an eloquent illustration that the word has changed its meaning?"

The fourth shift has to do with what are now called "belief *systems*"— the unconscious or presupposed conceptual framework that underlie an individual's worldview or cultural perspective. If this is *unconscious*, it has no application in first-person statements, that is, I cannot say, "I believe x, y, and z as components of my hitherto unarticulated conceptual framework." Through observation and inference, statements can be made about the belief systems of other people, but not one's own.

10. Marcus J. Borg, *Reading the Bible Again for the First Time: Taking the Bible Seriously but Not Literally*, p. 216.

11. Harvey Cox, "Jesus and Generation X," an essay in *Jesus at 2000*, edited by Marcus J. Borg, p. 95.

12. Martin Hengel, *Judaism and Hellenism*, Vol. 1: p. 179.

13. Marcus J. Borg, *Meeting Jesus Again for the First Time*, p. 55.

14. Marcus J. Borg, *Conflict, Holiness, and Politics in the Teachings of Jesus*, p. 11.

15. For a concrete example of how systemic evil works in American democracy, I quote Borg:

"Moreover, the structuring of our economic policy in the interests of the very wealthy continues. For example, both the tax cut of 2001 and the proposed tax cut of 2003 benefit primarily the wealthiest one percent: approximately one-half of the total dollars involved will go to them. The reason: the very wealthy as a group (there are exceptions) use their political influence to structure tax policy in their own self-interest. But heightened awareness of the justice (or injustice) of economic systems would argue that, if there are going to be tax cuts, the middle and lower economic classes need the extra dollars much more than the very wealthy do." *The Heart of Christianity*, p. 141.

16. The word "exodus" derives from two Greek roots: *ex-*, out + *hodos*, way.

17. John Reumann, *Jesus in the Church's Gospels: Modern Scholarship and the Earliest Sources*, p. 142.

18. Marcus J. Borg, *Conflict, Holiness, and Politics in the Teachings of Jesus*, p. 256.

19. "Kingdom" is the translation of the Greek word *basileia*. John Dominic Crossan points out that this may not be the best translation:

    "I am not particularly happy with the word *kingdom* as a translation of the Greek word *basileia*, but it is so traditional that any alternative might be confusing. It is not only that *king-* is chauvinistic but that *-dom* sounds primarily local, as if we were talking about some specific site or some geographically delineated location on earth. But what we are actually talking about . . . is power and rule, a process much more than a place, a way of life more than a location on earth." John Dominic Crossan, *Jesus: A Revolutionary Biography*, p. 55.

20. An example of a steno-symbol is the mathematical symbol *pi* (π), the ratio of a circle's circumference to its diameter.

21. Mircea Eliade, *Myth and Reality*.

22. Marcus J. Borg, ed., *Jesus at 2000*, p. 11, and also in Marcus J. Borg, *The God We Never Knew*, p. 89.

23. Marcus J. Borg, *Conflict, Holiness, and Politics in the Teachings of Jesus*, p. 262

24. Marcus J. Borg, ed., *Jesus at 2000*, p. 8.

25. In the *Timaeus*, where Plato presents his cosmology, or theory of how the universe came into being, he stipulates that his account is a "likely story" (*eikos mythos*) but adds that he has striven to

make it as likely as any, while granting that it is not definitive or complete.

26. As many will recognize, my little verse carries strong echoes from T.S. Eliot's poem, *Gerontion*:

> In the juvescence of the year
> Came Christ the tiger . . .

27. Borg discusses this from a different perspective, in terms of how, after his death and resurrection, the early Christian community made the leap from Galilean Jew to the face of God. The basic progression is a move from a *foundational experience* to *metaphorical* and then *conceptual development*. First comes the foundational experience: the followers of Jesus continue to experience him as a living reality after his death and, more and more, see him as having the qualities of God. In the second step, they name the Jesus of this experience with such metaphors as Son of God, light of the world, and the bread of life. Finally, as Borg says, "Over time these metaphors became the subject of intellectual reflection and were abstracted and systematized into a conceptual framework. Some of this abstraction ultimately became doctrine."

28. For a process view of saltations, I follow David Ray Griffin, as discussed in his two books, *Religion and Scientific Naturalism* and *Reenchantment without Supernaturalism*.

29. Rainer Maria Rilke, "Duino Elegies," *The Selected Poetry of Rainer Maria Rilke*, edited and translated by Steven Mitchell, p. 153. German text:

> Aber das Wehende höre,
> die ununterbrochene Nachricht, die aus Stille sich bildet.

Mitchell's translation:

> But listen to the voice of the wind
> and the ceaseless message that forms itself out of silence.

30. "[God] is the poet of the world, with tender patience leading it by his vision of truth, beauty, and goodness." Alfred North Whitehead, *Process and Reality*, p. 346.

31. This paragraph is a brief "poetic" statement of a process Christology. For a more substantial treatment, John B. Cobb presents a process Christology in his book *Christ in a Pluralistic Age* and summarizes his position in *The Process Perspective*, pp. 35-51. See also *A Process Christology* by David Ray Griffin.

32. II Corinthians 4:6—For God, who commanded the light to shine out of darkness, hath shined in our hearts, to give the light of the knowledge of the glory of God in the face of Jesus Christ.

33. John Dominic Crossan, *Jesus: A Revolutionary Biography*, p. 197.

34. Marcus J. Borg, *Jesus at 2000*, p. 17.

35. Marcus J. Borg, *Meeting Jesus Again for the First Time*, p. 89.

36. C.H. Dodd, *The Parables of the Kingdom*, p. 5.

37. Amos Wilder, *Early Christian Rhetoric*, p. 13. Wilder emphasizes the fresh and robust character of early Christian rhetoric:

"Throughout our analysis we shall find ourselves recurring to one feature of the *earliest* Christian speech including that of Jesus. It is naive, it is not studied; it is *extempore* and directed to the occasion, it is not calculated to serve some future hour. This utterance is dynamic, actual, immediate, reckless of posterity; not coded for catechists or repeaters. It is only one aspect of this that it is oral and not written. We find ourselves at first and for a rather long time in the presence of oral and live face-to-face communication. The Gospel meant freedom of speech in this deeper sense. One did not hoard its formulas, since when occasion arose the Spirit would teach one what to say and how to witness and what defense to make. The earliest Christians lived on the free bounty of God in this sense also. The speech of the Gospel was thus fresh and its forms novel and fluid; it came and went, as Ernst Fuchs says, with the freedom of sunshine, wind and rain." (pp. 12-13)

And—

"Moreover, when we picture to ourselves the early Christian narrators we should make full allowance for animated and expressive narration. In ancient times even when one read to oneself from a book, one always read aloud. Oral speech also was less inhibited than today. It is suggestive that in teaching the rabbis besides using cantillation also used didactic facial expressions, as well as gestures and bodily movements to impart dramatic shape to the doctrinal material. When we think of the early church meetings and testimonies and narrations we are probably well guided if we think of the way in which Vachel Lindsay read or of the appropriate readings of James Weldon Johnson's *God's Trombones*." (p. 56)

Wilder directly quotes Ernst Fuchs:

"Primitive Christianity is itself a speech-phenomenon. It is for that very reason that it established a monument in the new style-form which we call a *gospel*. The Johannine apocalypse and, indeed, in the first instance the apostolic epistle-literature, these are creations of a new utterance which changes everything that it touches." (Wilder, p. 10, where he lists this citation: Ernst Fuchs, "Die Sprache im Neuen Testament," *Zur Frage nach dem historischen Jesus*, p. 261.) Wilder adds to this by observing that the gospel, as a literary form, is a "wholly new genre created by the Church and the author of Mark receives the credit for it." (p. 28)

And one more observation by Wilder:

"That Jesus confined himself to the spoken and precarious word is of a piece with his renunciation of all cultural bonds such as home and trade and property; and with his instruction to his disciples to 'take nothing for their journey except a staff; no bread, no bag, no money in their belts; but to wear sandals and not to put on two tunics' (Mark 6.8-9)." (p. 14)

38. Quote by Luther cited in Amos Wilder, *Early Christian Rhetoric*, pp. 15-16.

39. St. Ignatius of Antioch, *Letter to the Magnesians*, 8:2.

40. James Joyce, *Finnegans Wake*, p. 628.

41. Marcus J. Borg, *Jesus: A New Vision*, pp. 113-14.

42. Edith Hamilton, *Witness to the Truth: Christ and His Interpreters*, p. 143.

Mansions of Silence: A Meditation

"Silence is golden," the old adage says, but some of our great mystics say that silence is far more precious than gold. Meister Eckhart goes so far as to say that silence is holy, that "Nothing in all creation is so like God as stillness."

Even though it functions without words, silence may be thought of as a kind of language, a language of perfection, a perfect language for communing with Spirit. Not the silence of just closing eyes and mouth, but a deeper silence, an inner silence, the silence of the quiet mind, the silence of "the still point of the turning world."

This true inner silence may be likened to what our Buddhist friends call Sunyata: the void, nothingness, emptiness; but an emptiness that is, paradoxically, fullness itself, fullness to overflowing, inexhaustible creativity, infinite potentiality, expressing everlastingly in truth, goodness, and beauty.

Another elegant insight from the Buddhist tradition shows how pervasive are the secret workings of silence. The sacred syllable OM is said to be made up of four elements: *ooh—uuh—mmm*: representing birth, life, "death," and these three enclosed by the fourth element: the creative silence out of and back into which it unceasingly comes and goes.

Meister Eckhart tells us that in silence, a silence without both words and images, we make room in our soul for God, and that there is no place God more delights to be than in our soul when we have made room for him there.

Should we not then be building mansions of silence in our souls to welcome, and to be worthy of, God's holy presence?

I follow the path of silence that leads to the green meadows of God's loving presence. As I lie down there to drink from the still waters of silence, I am refreshed by God's love, made whole by God's love, energized, vitalized, and lifted high.

Part Four

Fire

An Introduction to Process
Thought in Five Easy Pieces

I

This is the first of "five easy pieces" that will be a short guided tour of one of the most original and creative minds in the history of Western philosophy. Welcome to the "process world" of Alfred North Whitehead. In an age of specialization, Whitehead was a modern Renaissance man, a polymath who distinguished himself not only in philosophy, but also in mathematics, physics, logic, and educational theory. A lifelong teacher, his popularity with students is revealed in the following humorous anecdote:

"At Oxford University, when a professor concludes a course, it is the custom for the students to pound the floor with their feet as a tribute to the teacher for his fine teaching. On one occasion, when Whitehead had finished his last lecture, the pounding of feet was so enthusiastic that in the room below, where a professor of logic was lecturing, the ceiling began to fall. The professor of logic remarked: 'I am afraid that the premises will not support Dr. Whitehead's conclusion!'"

At age 63, while teaching mathematics in London with thoughts of retirement in mind, Whitehead was surprised to receive an invitation to join the faculty at Harvard University as a professor of philosophy. He enthusiastically accepted, telling his wife Evelyn, "I would rather do this than anything in the world!" They left their native England in

1924, crossed the Atlantic, and settled in Cambridge, Massachusetts, near Harvard where he then taught for more than a decade. The vitality of Whitehead's thought in his final years is amazing—during his time at Harvard, a period of exuberant creative expression, he wrote nine ground-breaking books wherein he worked out and refined his revolutionary new cosmology.

Adventures of the Mind

In the winter of 1947, Whitehead died at his Cambridge home at the age of 86. By his instructions his body was cremated and there was no funeral. Nor is there a grave. What he left as a lasting monument is a new metaphysical system—an adventure of the mind—unsurpassed in its beauty, suggestiveness, and sublimity.

Whitehead's conceptual breakthrough about a new frontier in philosophy began with his understanding of the radical revolution in science initiated by Albert Einstein and Max Planck. Quantum and relativity theory are not just steps in a different direction, but a cosmic leap into a new universe. Whitehead was among the first to realize that the new science involved a complete breakdown of the old Newtonian worldview, and thus a radical challenge for other fields of thought. Whitehead answered this challenge with a revolution of his own: process philosophy.

To see how Whitehead's view contrasts with the Newtonian, let's first take a look at how the universe, with the rise of modernism, is conceived in mechanistic terms.

The Mechanization of Nature

The controlling image of the Newtonian worldview is the machine. The very universe itself, and all living creatures in nature, are ultimately reducible to the mechanical workings of their inorganic parts. They are, in a word, *machines*. Some are marvelously elaborate, as is the "human machine," but machines they are, nonetheless. What science seeks to discover are the internal mechanisms that drive these machines, or "what makes them tick," to use a fitting clock metaphor. Although its luster has begun to tarnish in some quarters, for the most part "mechanistic" is still a positive word in the modern scientific community. The origin of this image becomes apparent with a realization that the only makers of machines are humans, and very recent humans at that. As biologist

Rupert Sheldrake has noted, "The mechanistic worldview involves projecting modern man's fascination with machines onto the whole of nature."

Newton's atoms, conceived like billiard balls, are the basic units of nature, the so-called "building blocks" of the universe. In Newton's own words, "It seems to me that God, in the beginning, formed matter in solid, massy, impenetrable particles." These particles have no interior and their behavior is governed from without, and governed strictly, by mechanical laws. Whitehead dismissed such particles as "vacuous actualities."

As to some of the other flaws in the mechanistic worldview, such a view is _Materialistic, Atheistic,_ and _Deterministic._ In a fully determined universe there is no creativity, no freedom, no spontaneity. God is no longer a holy reality, but is reduced to a neurological episode in the so-called _God spot,_ "a tiny locus of nerve cells in the frontal lobe of the brain that appears to be activated during religious experiences." In other words, so-called "spiritual" experiences have an entirely physical basis—the "fire from heaven" turns out to be only the mundane "firing" of neural machinery.

We humans are somewhat better off than all other animals in that we have "minds," but this "mind" is a mere "ghost in the machine" and is ultimately explainable in terms of some sort of electro-chemical activity. A complete materialism requires mere matter as the ultimate reality, and rejects "mind" as a category of existence.

Inspired by the mechanistic model, scientists dissected the living body of the cosmos, eviscerated all vital ideas such as spirit or soul, and assembled it back together as a clockwork machine. If the universe is God's body, then the mechanistic revolution turned it into a cadaver or a corpse.

If you feel little sympathy with such a view, neither did Whitehead. In fact, the whole thrust of his philosophy was to overturn such a distortion of reality.

Hello, Silicon; Goodbye, Carbon

The mechanistic model has mesmerized most of the scientific community _for more than three centuries_—and is still going strong, as the following clearly reveals: In his book _The Age of Spiritual Machines,_

Raymond Kurzweil suggests that our next evolutionary leap will come about through our merging with our technology.

According to Kurzweil, at some point in the not-too-distant future, maybe as early as 2099, we will enter the "transhuman " or "posthuman" era. If we wish to keep up with our rapidly evolving technology, it will be necessary to scan our brains, say farewell to our carbon-based flesh, and upload our minds into a faster and more powerful computational unit. In other words: a *machine*.

By then, however, Kurzweil says that computers will have evolved to such an extent that they will claim to have consciousness, emotions, and spiritual experiences. Some may even claim to be enlightened, and will be meditating and regularly attending virtual houses of worship.

Towards the end of the 21st century, with the widespread use of neural-implant technology by humans, and with machine-based computers modeled more and more on human intelligence, it will become increasingly difficult to tell humans from computers. Those humans who have no neural implants will not be capable of entering into meaningful dialogue with those who do. And when we do upload our minds, so the prediction goes, we will achieve technological immortality—cyberlife everlasting. Just be sure to make frequent backups!

Those who hold this "posthuman" vision of the future make it sound like a silicon Shangri-La; from a process perspective it sounds more like the "dying gasp" of the whole mechanistic agenda.

II

In sharp contrast to the mechanistic model, Whitehead called his new metaphysical system "organic philosophy" or the "philosophy of organism." The term "organism" suggests only biological entities, but Whitehead extends the meaning to include the physical entities studied by physics, such as electrons, atoms, and molecules. This radical shift from mechanism he saw as the new basic idea for science. As he put it, "Biology is the study of the larger organisms; whereas physics is the study of the smaller organisms." With his philosophy of organism, Whitehead breathes new life into the universe, from top to bottom.

To say merely *that* an organism is "alive" is a great improvement over the mechanistic view, but *how* it is alive is what makes a subtle and decisive difference in Whitehead's metaphysics.

The many parts (or cells) of an organism, and the relations and interdependence among these parts, constitute a complex unity, and a complex "environment," wherein a higher level of actuality can emerge. This new actuality is the "presiding subject" of the organism. We can even call it "mind," if "mind" is understood as a variable and not as a constant. This means that no matter how lowly the life form, or how primitive the particle, "mind," or at least the "germ" of mind, is active in all the dynamic unities present in the natural world.

Note carefully that this new actuality is more than the sum of the parts of an organism; it is numerically distinct from them, exerts real power and purpose, and enjoys the most intimate relations with the constituent cells of the organism, feeling their influence, and exerting influence on them.

Indeed, In Whitehead's system this new actuality is *the primary reality* to be found in all of nature. He calls it an "actual entity."

Actual Entities: "Atoms" of Process

An *actual entity* is simply Whitehead's term for what he conceives as the most fundamental unit of nature.

For Sir Isaac Newton, atoms were the basic units of nature, the so-called "building blocks" of the universe. These atoms have been likened to billiard balls, and Newton himself described them as "solid, massy, impenetrable particles." They are inert, have no inner reality, and, since they are governed strictly from without by mechanical laws, are capable of no spontaneity whatsoever. Such atoms were seen as enduring substances with uninterrupted existence.

Unlike Newton's billiard-ball atom, an actual entity is internally dynamic: it is an atom" of process, a pulsation, a throb of actuality that endures only for a split-second. At the very base of things, at the very heart of reality, we find not matter or substance, but *process*—units of dynamic process wherein possibilities can become actualities.

An actual entity does not endure in a state of static completion. So process-oriented is Whitehead's conception that he says of an actual entity that "it never really is." This is what the quantum revolution is all about. This revolutionary view reveals a vibratory atomic world—fairly sizzling with energy—wherein atoms emerge and vanish in incredibly brief quantum pulsations that come and go, one after the other. Inert as it may seem at first glance, a solid block of granite, at the quantum level, is so internally dynamic that its micro-constituents enjoy a veritable fiesta of rhythmic adventures.

As the name "quantum" implies, the movement of process is not a steady flow but, rather, in successive drops, or discrete units, of experience. Nature *pulsates*. This means that even the famous saying of Heraclitus, that all things flow, must be revised to read: all things flow, yes, but *quantumly*—i.e., in a series of vibratory reiterations.

In a quantum universe, existence is not a given, but must be achieved, over and over again, by all actual entities: with the closure of each pulsation, one fleeting moment of actuality ends, and the next pulsation begins a new adventure of self-actualization.

It should probably be emphasized that you are already intimately acquainted with actual entitles. You directly experience them, though perhaps mostly on an unconscious level, *more than a million times* each day. Since they flicker by so fast—10 to 12 times each second—they're easy to miss and seem a steady stream. A good analogy would be the movies where separate frames of the film are projected onto the screen at just the right speed, so many frames per second, to give the illusion of a continuous flow.

An actual entity is simply a single moment of experience, a pulse of actuality, whether the experience be that of a human person, a cat, a single living cell, or even an electron.

As an electron flashes along its quantum way, each tiny pulsation throbs its own actuality into existence, just as quickly fades away, and is immediately followed by another. This vibratory signature underlies the nature of all reality—from the most primitive particles to the human mind, or soul, and, yes, even to the nature of God. The very essence of all reality, including the divine reality, is self-surpassing process.

As one of the first to see that Newton's universe was topsy-turvy, Whitehead set about reversing many basic ideas. And so: the old Newtonian notion of *static stuff* is replaced by the new idea of *fluent energy*—*substance* thinking, by *event* thinking. In Whitehead's new language and "grammar" of reality, the subject, whether of a sentence or a moment of experience, is no longer a noun—but a Verb!

III

Whitehead's fundamental insight—his novel intuition about the nature of reality—he expressed in a simple but aphoristic phrase: "The many become one, and are increased by one." These nine simple words describe what Whitehead was perhaps the first to glimpse: that actual entities are where the real action is. Actual entities are the *creative heartbeats* of the universe, and underlying all reality is the twofold rhythmic work done by these robust "units of process."

"The many become one" describes how an actual entity integrates the many influences flowing in from the past to self-actualize as a new quantum individual. How it passes on to future actualities what it has thus achieved is described by "and are increased by one." These two kinds of universal process Whitehead calls *concrescence* and *transition*, and it is chiefly in reference to them that Whitehead's system is called *process* philosophy.

Every throb of actuality is not only a present achievement to be enjoyed in and for itself, but also a thrust beyond: into the future. The whole point of the process is to achieve actuality over and over and over again—and, each time, to introduce the possibility for novelty, for adventure.

Creation Continues

On the creative path of evolution, from the initial chaos to the first micro-individuals such as electrons and protons, from electrons and protons to atoms, and then on to molecules, living cells, multicellular animals, animals with a central nervous system, and finally to the human body and soul—note how each creative advance is not only a good in itself, but lays the foundation for, and makes possible, a greater good in the future. Atoms, for example, make it possible for molecules to later emerge, and so on. And thus we have the emergence of ever higher levels of actuality, and these evolving actualities are capable of ever higher intensities of experience.

As creation continues, as it has now for over 15 billion years . . . as creation continues, from one end of the universe to the other, and in every new moment . . . as creation continues within the countless myriads of actual entities in effervescent pulsations of spontaneity—

shining through all the variety, the diversity, all the *multiplicity* of the vast universe is the *unity* of this incessant twofold process.

"The many become one, and are increased by one"—this single sentence, though simplicity itself, is a "skeleton key" that unlocks the universe and the metaphysical treasure chest of Whitehead's idea of *universal process*.

This is beautifully illustrated in that paragon of creation, the human body.

What's It All About, Alfie?

From a process understanding, the central nervous system of all vertebrate animals, including the human animal, has two main functions, one practical and the other aesthetic.

For practical purposes, the central nervous system enables a complex organism (with a multitude of cells) to achieve the same dynamic unity of experience enjoyed by more primitive individuals such as, in descending order, single living cells, molecules, atoms, and sub-atomic particles. The complex organism can act and react *as one*, but on a much higher level.

As for the aesthetic purpose: Did you ever stop and wonder about the many causes that flow into the creation of one unitary moment of human experience? It is an astonishing multiplicity! Consider the past impinging on the present with the vast saga of personal memory; consider the vivid presentations of all five senses. Merging also into the new moment are millions, billions, even trillions upon trillions of micro-experiences contributed along the neural nets by bodily cells and, finally, by the streaming neurons of the brain—the human brain itself the most complex structure in the known universe.

Through a process of emergent synthesis this vast multiplicity becomes one of the most beautiful, fragile, and fleeting of flowers: an efflorescence of novelty known as a single moment of experience.

The human body, with what Whitehead calls its "miracle of order," makes possible astounding adventures, beauties, and complexities of experience. And, indeed, on the process view this is the whole thrust of evolution, and explains why we humans can be *happier* than clams.

But the good news, the really good news, is that the evolutionary emergence of the human body makes possible the experience of a whole new dimension of reality. For it is the higher synthesis, or higher unity, made possible by the body, that enabled some primal human pioneer, maybe a million years ago, to soar through the most adventurous threshold of all and consciously feel, for the first time ever, a numinous Presence in the world of nature.

We have here our first Buddha, or Awakened One, our first mystic, and the prototype of Cosmic Consciousness whereby we humans can experience, through the creative matrix of the human body, the Holy Reality we call God. Was it something such as this that the apostle Paul glimpsed when he said that the body is the temple of the Holy Spirit?

IV

Whitehead's philosophy is called process-*relational* because it presents a robust "social conception" of reality. It is "social" because we socialize on many levels that, hopefully, will be more obvious after you have read this essay.

Our relations with the natural world, on all levels, are with other *individuals*, other centers of experience, and not with mere inert matter, as the materialists would have us believe. These other individuals are the "natural unities," or the primary units of reality, that I have mentioned more than once: atoms, molecules, living cells, vertebrate animals, human souls. We live in a world that, at every level, is teeming with sentience.

In this social structure of reality, there is a continuous sharing of experience, both receiving and giving, an interweaving ebb and flow of mutual influence. Unlike classical metaphysics which exalted such abstractions as the *absolute* and disparaged the merely *relative*—in a metaphysics of process, "relativity" is a positive word and simply means that we are abundantly "rich in relations."

The Body as Social

Your relationship with your body is a social relationship: a relationship of the one self, or soul, to the many micro-individuals that make up your living body—the hundreds of thousands of different kinds of cells whose total number ranges in the trillions. Each cell in turn is a vast society of molecules wherein each molecule in turn is a teeming society of atoms, and each atom a society of elementary particles. All of these micro-individuals are, to some degree, taking account of one another, or "socializing."

Any moment of human experience is a highly complex social event. Consider stopping for a moment to behold a beautiful rose. This is a "social" event made possible by the contribution of many individuals: photons of light, living cells in the eyes, optic nerve, and brain. All sense perception is entirely dependent on the prior functioning of our bodies; what we experience is derived from extensive and interconnected chains of antecedent experiences that occur within the body.

No Thinker Thinks Twice

What is this invisible entity we call the human self, or soul? How does it endure over time? Is it always there, day and night, underlying all our activities? The process answer is No.

As one of the *emergent* natural unities in the universe, the human self is no exception, but is quantum in nature. It is made up of actual entities: discrete drops or buds of experience. There is no self that is first somehow *already there* and *then* has these experiences. The experiences themselves are all there is. Whitehead puts it in a way to make you stop and think—he says, "No thinker thinks twice."

The concrete life of the psyche is in discrete moments of experience, one after the other, each sharing elements of a common character, but with no two exactly alike. The human self, in process terms, is a temporally ordered "society" of momentary occasions of experience.

A *temporal* society is unique in that, rather than having many coexisting members, only one member exists at a time. As a temporal *society*, each member enjoys close relations with the preceding member, reenacting the common form that characterizes members of the society, and passing on this pattern to the succeeding member. Continuity is thereby established but a *discontinuous* continuity, thus satisfying the quantum requirement while also supporting social solidarity between discrete events.

If there are about 12 such experiences per second, then each 24-hour day adds more than a million new actualities to this society. Walt Whitman's poetic intuitions were right on the mark when, in *Song of Myself,* he said, "I am large, I contain multitudes."

The Kingdom Within

A moment of experience begins with a *social* or public phase, with influence flowing in from other sources, and is completed by an *individual* or private phase wherein the self, alone, decides how to integrate this influence. Indeed the basic rhythm of the universe is a *perpetual oscillation* between the social and the solitary, the public and the private, the receiving of influence, and the private "processing" of that influence. Both are required—one is necessary for the underlying solidarity of the universe; the other, for its creative advance.

By interweaving a contrast between actuality and possibility, between what *already is* and what *might be*, this biphasal unit of action breaks the impasse of sheer continuity. Rather than being determined by the past, the self, in the private phase, decides what to make of the past, and, in its split second of sovereignty, self-actualizes as a new quantum individual.

In that moment resides freedom, creativity, and all evolutionary advance. It is the most minute of moments, small like a mustard seed, and yet, as the matrix of creativity and adventure, it provides a fresh perspective on "the kingdom of heaven within."

This "kingdom of heaven within" is God's most precious gift to all creatures, for what it makes possible, in addition to the above, is *selfhood* itself.

Atoms as Social Beings

In this social conception of reality, even atoms are social beings. Consider the simplest case: the hydrogen atom with its one proton and electron. Did you ever stop and wonder what holds such an atom together—that is, what holds the electron and proton *together*, and at the same time *apart*, in dynamic and elegant unity? The new physics has revealed that what holds atoms together are virtual photons that are said to "carry" a fundamental force called the ElectroMagnetic Interaction.

The photons are called "virtual" because they arise on the electron and, after an incredibly brief life-journey, almost instantaneously vanish on the proton, thereby creating "a tie that binds." How many photons are busy at work "holding together" a hydrogen atom? Physicist John Jungerman places the number at a mind-boggling trillion billion each second: that's "1" followed by 20 zeros!

And so the hydrogen atom, far from simple, is a buzzing hive of social activity. It takes astonishing creativity, from almost countless micro-entities, for a "simple" hydrogen atom *just to be* a hydrogen atom. If this is the case for a mere atom, pause for a moment and consider the underlying "social activity" required for you . . . *just to be you.*

V

If our knowledge about the universe is growing, it would be strange if our knowledge about God were not also expanding. In fact, since there was so major a revolution in physics that it represents "a cosmic leap into a new universe," it would be strange if no comparable revolution had occurred in metaphysics or theology. Were there no thinkers, of comparable stature with Einstein and Planck, who accomplished revolutionary work in metaphysics and in our human musings about God? Indeed, there were, and the seminal figure was Alfred North Whitehead.

The Einstein of Religious Thought

But of equal importance is one of the most gifted minds of the twentieth century: the American philosopher Charles Hartshorne, a thinker of such brilliance that he has been hailed as "the Einstein of religious thought, someone whose discoveries and insights will be influential for centuries."

Not only is Charles Hartshorne my personal hero, he truly made the hero's journey. He was the Indiana Jones of philosophers; but, rather than daring escapades, books and ideas were the great adventures of his life. The sheer fertility of his thought is astonishing. In addition to a vast correspondence, he published twenty books and over 500 essays and reviews in professional journals. Hartshorne lived to the age of 103, and was especially prolific in his eighth and ninth decades. So far as I know, he is the only philosopher to have published a major new book in his hundredth year.

He credited to his longevity, which he called his secret weapon, some of his most important insights. As Hartshorne put it: "With Plato I strongly believe that philosophy, of all subjects, requires maturity. One of my advantages over most of my contemporary rivals is that, decade after decade, in eighty or so years I have gone on gaining additional clarity on a number of topics which interested me from the start." Among 20th-century philosophers, Hartshorne stands out as a premier metaphysician and *the* most influential proponent of a process conception of God.

Here in Part Five I will focus on one of the most distinctive features of this new process understanding: the dipolar nature of God.

Traditional ideas about the nature of God derive largely from medieval theologians who replaced a relational understanding found in the Hebrew Bible with what has been called the "icy absolutes" of Greek thought. According to this view, which is called "classical theism," God is said to be a *perfect being* (complete in every way) who is *immutable* (devoid of change or process), *impassive* (impervious to influence), *eternal* (nontemporal), and *simple* (excluding diversity or distinction). This is a prime example of the human tendency for oversimplification. And so the basic process critique of these ideas is that they tell only *half* the story.

Is God Relative? Absolutely!

In the table below are two columns of polar terms, or what Hartshorne calls ultimate contrasts:

R-terms	A-terms
relative	absolute
change	permanence
contingency	necessity
complexity	simplicity
temporal	nontemporal
concrete	abstract
becoming	being
finite	infinite
passible	impassible
dependent	independent
social	nonsocial
R-perfection	A-perfection

The classical ideal is to characterize God exclusively by the A-terms, with the clear implication that R-terms were unworthy of God. Hartshorne called this the *monopolar prejudice*, a prejudice that has reigned as the dominant paradigm in Western theology for some twenty centuries. When the wheels of thought run in deep ruts, it's hard to get them going in a new direction. To designate God by strictly abstract terms also tears asunder the unity-in-diversity of polar contrasts exemplified in the yin-yang symbol ☯, an ancient symbol reflecting the wisdom of dipolar wholeness. Modern science reveals the same open secret with a new and more complex mandala: the yin-yang beauty of the double helix. Also note that classical theism requires that we value the abstract over the concrete, and this entails that we value the map over the territory, or the menu over the meal.

Classical theists were doubly wrong in assuming the absolute to be wholly good, and the relative, altogether bad. Hartshorne shows how the idea of absoluteness, like that of relativity, has both good and bad aspects. Whereas classical theism oversimplifies the issue thus:

$$\text{bad - Relative} \qquad\qquad \text{Absolute - good}$$

process theism invites us to see it as:

$$\begin{array}{cc} \text{good} & \text{good} \\ > \text{Relative} \quad \text{Absolute} < & \\ \text{bad} & \text{bad} \end{array}$$

This is yet another variation on the dipolar theme.

By affirming *both* R- and A-terms together, instead of one to the exclusion of the other, Hartshorne attains polar balance and discovers a new way of thinking about God. True, he follows Whitehead on this, but, as George Allan wrote, "Hartshorne's axiom of dipolar divinity is surely his most distinctive . . . contribution to philosophy. He follows Whitehead's lead, but has elaborated the notion and its implications in ways that carry him far beyond his sometime mentor. *The Divine Relativity*, his first book-length presentation of the matter, has rightly become a classic in the philosophy of religion."

Moreover, it is not enough to simply say that God is relative, and leave it at that. It is necessary to stipulate that God, as *relative*, enjoys a unique metaphysical status that makes crystal clear the radical difference between human and divine relativity.

Remember—to be relative simply means to be rich in relations. As the individual most rich in relations, God is so robustly relative that he enjoys mutual immanence with all actualities throughout the universe. This is surely a positive excellence not only to rival, but to infinitely surpass, the negative attribute of bare absoluteness. As the only omni-relational individual, God is, as Hartshorne says "unsurpassably influencing as well as unsurpassably influenced." To describe this special case of God as the most relative of all individuals, and the goodness of this relativity, Hartshorne coins a new term: *surrelative*. God is *supremely* relative.

As supremely relative, God is, contrary to what Aristotle thought, the individual most subject to change. With his idea of God as the "Unmoved Mover," Aristotle has had a "mesmerizing influence" on theistic thought for well over two thousand years. The doctrine of divine immutability reveals both a Greek and a male bias, and a long habit of thinking in *substance* rather than in event or *process* terms.

The Thomas Edison of Philosophy

Charles Hartshorne's writings scintillate with so many new ideas, so many new "metaphysical inventions," that he indeed rivals Edison on this score. To overturn one long-standing error, Hartshorne invented a new logic that he called The Logic of Ultimate Contrasts. This new logic corrects, and reverses, centuries of upside-down thinking about how the absolute is related to the relative—in fact, about how all A-terms are related to their corresponding R-terms. The relative is the inclusive category, which means that A-terms are related to R-terms as part to whole. This is clearly seen in the relation holding between the abstract and the concrete where, by definition, the abstract is abstracted *from* the concrete.

Using this as a standard, Hartshorne invites us to reverse centuries of ossified thought that exalted the absolute over the relative. To get things right, we are to think *just the opposite* of what the classical theists would have us think. This means that the *relative* is primary, and inclusive of, the *absolute*, rather than vice versa. Thus the divine relativity, God's concrete actuality, is inclusive of what is absolute: God's abstract essence. And the same pattern holds with such contraries as effect and cause, becoming and being, finite and infinite. In other words, the classical theists, in their intoxication with abstractions, got it *exactly backwards*. Their topsy-turvy "logic" implies that we should value objects over subjects and that the movement from cause through effect is a descent from better to worse, from more to less. As Hartshorne says, if this indeed is the case, then "pessimism is a metaphysical axiom."

Another innovation by Hartshorne has to do with the following question, How can we think adequately about the idea of God and the relation between God and the world until we know all the options? It was not until after his 90th birthday, after many years of reflection, that he finally solved to his satisfaction the arrangement of a 16-fold matrix that presents an exhaustive list of the formal options for thinking about God and the world—in terms of permutations of contrasting pairs such as *necessity* and *contingency*.

Hartshorne's Matrix

	I	II	III	IV
1.	N.n	C.n	NC.n	O.n
2.	N.c	C.c	NC.c	O.c
3.	N.cn	C.cn	**NC.cn**	O.cn
4.	N.o	C.o	NC.o	O.o

Key to Interpretation
I.   God is wholly necessary
II. God is wholly contingent
III. God is diversely necessary and contingent.
IV. God is impossible or has no modal status.

1.   World is wholly necessary.
2.   World is wholly contingent.
3.   World is diversely necessary and contingent.
4.   World is impossible or has no modal status.

Since, of all his metaphysical discoveries, Hartshorne felt that this was the most original and the most important, it will surely repay our efforts to understand what it means.

In Hartshorne's matrix, capital letters designate *divine* and lower case letters the *worldly* attributes. Take, for example, N.c—this means that God is wholly necessary; the world, wholly contingent. The use of capital and lower case letters (as well as the reversal of order: NC ~ cn) symbolize the categoreal difference between God and the world.

Careful analysis of the matrix reveals both elegance and subtlety: Just as column III includes what is positive in the first two columns, so does row 3 include what is positive in rows 1 and 2. The diagonal (running from top left to bottom right) includes only those cases where the variables display a symmetrical pattern. This suggests, especially to the mathematical eye, that something significant occurs at the point where these three intersect.

To be clear on this, imagine three lines superimposed on the matrix: one straight down through column III, one straight across through row 3, and one through the diagonal running from N.n to O.o. Note the position where these three lines intersect: NC.cn—the most *complex*, and the most *positive*, of all sixteen views. This is Hartshorne's position, the dipolar or social view of reality that he calls "neoclassical theism." NC.cn also neatly represents his doctrine of dual transcendence.

It is Hartshorne's claim that, of the sixteen possible views or positions, only one can be true. If this is accurate, then the other fifteen will all be false, with varying degrees of implausibility. The candidate for least plausibility is O.o which, as most simple and most negative, denies reality to both God and the world. If O.o is the *least* true of the formal options, then should not its opposite be the *most* true? Hartshorne argues, convincingly I think, that this is indeed the case, thereby showing that his position, NC.cn, as the *exact opposite* of O.o, is the one true option on the matrix.

The following table illustrates how Hartshorne compares with some other theistic (and atheistic) positions:

classical theism ....N.c

Spinoza and the Stoics.......................N.n

acosmic Advaita Vedanta ....N.o

William James ....C.c

John Stuart Mill ....C.n

mechanistic worldview*....................O.n

atheism (à la Sartre).........................O.cn

Aristotle ....N.cn

Jules Lequyer.....................................NC.c

Charles Hartshorne ....NC.cn

(*the MAD version: *m*aterialistic, *a*theistic, *d*eterministic)

A point to notice is that the matrix reveals far more formal options than 16. As Donald Wayne Viney, a notable Hartshorne scholar, observes, "comparable tables can be constructed for any pair of metaphysical contrasts, such as infinite-finite or eternal-temporal. For any pair of metaphysical contrasts there is a 4 x 4 table (= 16), and hence, for any two pair in conjunction, the number of formal alternatives is 16 x 16 (= 256). To generalize, if *n* equals the number of pairs of contrasts to be included, the number of *formal options* is 16^n."

As seems fitting for a cosmic leap into a new universe, Hartshorne's matrix is light-years ahead of what was offered by classical theism. These are just a few of his many innovations and discoveries. Indeed, in an Addendum to this essay, I list 42 Examples of metaphysical and philosophical truths discovered by Hartshorne, ancient truths that he revealed in a new light, and intellectual errors he helped to overturn.

Variations on a Twofold Theme

The dipolar idea finds expression in the new physics where, to tell the full story of the nature of light, the polar concepts of particle and wave are both required. Although both are "true," either taken separately tells only half the story. As primary as yin and yang, this dipolar or twofold theme is pervasive throughout the universe, and is so basic to a process understanding of reality that I have mentioned it several times in the course of this essay, especially in terms of "the many and the one."

Indeed, if dipolarity is a fundamental principle, and if Whitehead is correct in holding that God can be no exception to such principles, then the divine nature *must* be dipolar. Moreover, not only is God conceived as dipolar, but as *doubly* dipolar.

One dimension of the dipolar idea involves what Hartshorne calls God's *abstract essence* and his *concrete actuality*. To get an idea of what this distinction means, consider the following: What factors or elements enter into any concrete state of human experience to make it just what it is? One major factor is a person's "character," that collection of enduring traits a person embodies that for the most part, but not wholly, determine the specific acts of behavior. These concrete acts themselves are not the person's character; but, from the general patterns these various acts display, the character, or essence, of the person can be inferred or abstracted. So character is an *abstract* essence that is expressed in various ways through the *concrete* actuality of specific actions. Taking this as a clue, process theism draws an analogy: just as we have characters that play a decisive role in our everyday activities, so too does God have a "character" that is exemplified in all divine actions. The difference is that, whereas our characters can and in fact do change, God's character, his abstract essence, does not change. In terms of unsurpassable power, goodness, wisdom, and love, God is always perfectly steadfast and reliable. But, in response to an ever-changing universe, God's concrete actuality does change.

In contrast to Aristotle's Unmoved Mover, God is also dipolar in how God relates to the world: both exerting influence *upon*, and receiving influence *from*.

Here's how process theism understands this as working: Because of the quantum nature of things, all individuals, including God, endure as "societies" that exemplify the two types of process (concrescence and transition) discussed in Part Three. This means that all actualities perpetually oscillate between two phases: as subjects experiencing other objects, and as objects experienced by other subjects. All experience, including God's experience, is social in nature and has this irreducible duality of structure. One big difference is that God enjoys the unique double distinction of being the only subject who experiences all objects, and the only object who is experienced by all subjects. In each momentary divine *concrescence*, through an unimaginably complex "intuition whose datum is the universe," God receives or *prehends*, and perfectly knows, all that the world cumulatively has become— both individually and collectively. This then becomes the basis, in the *transitional* phase, for God to pour back into the world, and to each quantum occasion throughout the universe, relevant ideals or possibilities for that occasion's best future. In this way God is said to provide "particular providence for particular occasions."

Some critics charge that the God of process theism is not transcendent enough. To this charge Hartshorne has made a witty reply: he said that the God of process is *twice* as transcendent as the God of classical theism. He was able to make this reply through his doctrine of *dual transcendence*. By this, Hartshorne means that only God has uniquely excellent ways of being both absolute and relative, necessary and contingent, immutable and capable of change. As the one and only universal individual, God enjoys not one, but two kinds of perfection: absolute and relative. God is perfect being, yes, but also perfect becoming; moreover, becoming is primary, that is, inclusive of being.

Hartshorne is only one of many who have pointed out serious defects in classical theism; where he does stand alone, however, is in revealing how nearly all of these are related to a neglect of divine relativity, or a truly *social* conception of God. How important is all this? Hartshorne's view is that "The future of theology depends . . . above all upon the answer to this question: can technically precise terms be found which express the supremacy of God, among social beings, without contradicting his social character?"

You Take It from Here!

A perennial intuition in religious experience is the idea of *Deus est caritas*, or God is Love. But, as many over the centuries have wondered, how can this be if God is wholly immutable and impassive? In an effort to answer this, the writings of some classical theists offer laboriously contrived convolutions of thought. But, far from making sense, these pretzels of logic merely make your head swim. No God conceived strictly in terms of the icy absolutes of classical theism can enjoy the reciprocity of love, but only a God conceived concretely and socially, that is, as a living person with the balance of a dipolar nature, a nature capable of both giving and receiving influence.

Process theism teaches that every momentary occasion of experience throughout the universe *begins* with the touch of God. In human terms, and to use an analogy from the NASA space shuttle, God provides "lift-off" and an initial aim in the right direction. But it is then up to us to make the in-flight decisions that take us to our destination. God is always reliably there *in the beginning* to help us get started, but at a crucial point in the creative process, God says, "You take it from here!" We complete what God initiates.

What we and all creatures achieve in this process of self-actualization then becomes a part of God's concrete actuality. Our achievements are "cells" in the body of God. God and the world are thus sources of novelty one for the other, and, to some degree, constitutive of one another. Without this mutual immanence, made possible by the divine relativity, both God and the world would be completely static. All that can be surveyed in the vast saga of evolution, all the glory, all the grandeur, is the result of this mutual immanence of God and the creatures, of God and the world.

As a concluding statement, and to summarize some of the ideas presented in this essay, there is a "process" poem on the following page that I wrote for just this occasion:

Process and Presence

In the beginning, once upon a void,
A pulse, *first* quantum throb, felt and enjoyed:

From the many random emerges one,
In dipolar rhythm where before was none;
One after another now, pulsing free—
A social process of self-creativity.

If, in nature, consciousness be the crown,
Experience, at least, goes all the way down.
In people, yes, but in photons too we find,
As in all natural unities, the light of mind.

And now a Presence—silent, soft as air,
Flowing within, without, and everywhere.
Through renewal from this divine connection
Life endures by constant resurrection.

Every new moment, in a twinkling of eyes,
Numberless minds perish, and as quickly arise.
Fresh in the flow of this interweaving stream,
Mutual immanence is the universal theme.

Rhythmic adventures, process ever new,
A quantum world where time is quantum, too.
Each quantum a threshold, another chance
For beauty, goodness, creative advance.

In the beginning, God and creatures meet;
What God begins, the creatures then complete.
This, alone, the way of God's creation—
Not through fiat, but by evocation.

Power is relational, not only from above:
Not almighty force, but all-persuasive love.

Addendum

42 EXAMPLES of metaphysical and philosophical truths discovered by Charles Hartshorne, ancient truths that he revealed in a new light, and intellectual errors he helped to overturn:

1. Doctrinal Matrices: exhaustive sets of theoretical options.

2. The distinction between "existence" and "actuality."

3. The reality of chance or contingency—as opposed to the idea that "there are no accidents," and that "chance" is merely a word for our ignorance.

4. The Prosaic Fallacy.

5. The Anselmian Principle.

6. Contributionism: through our creativity, we "enrich the divine life itself."

7. The Logic of Perfection.

8. We know very little about God (existence/essence, but not much about actuality), but what we do know is important and can't be written off as mystery or theological paradox, nor should it be dismissed because of some putative revelation.

9. The idea that God's existence is a metaphysical not an empirical question.

10. The idea that "Is there a God?" is a loaded question since it presupposes an answer to the question "What is God like, supposing there were a God?"

11. The idea of dual transcendence, that God can be characterized by both sides of metaphysical contrasts (provided one makes the existence/actuality distinction).

12. Divine love is not mere outflowing benevolence but includes an eminent form of passivity. God is not the unmoved mover but the most and best moved mover.

13. Divine power and creativity are not all-determining, but power or creativity over other beings with power. This transforms the traditional problem of evil.

14. Divine knowledge is primarily a knowledge by acquaintance and propositional knowledge is based on this.

15. The divine actuality is constantly changing in creative response to the world. God is, nevertheless, unsurpassable. God is the self-surpassing surpasser of all.

16. Closely related to the previous: The future is best described with a triad of options: "X must occur, or X must not occur, or X may or may not occur." Taking "X will occur or X will not occur" as exhaustive is problematic since it makes of genuinely contingent alternatives matters of our ignorance.

17. The Humean or empiricist dictum that the distinguishable is the separable is false. It is inconsistent with a world in process, a world where things undergo development, a world where evolution is true.

18. Relations of asymmetry, even in logic, are more fundamental than relations of symmetry. This relates to the points about chance and indeterminism.

19. Multiple freedom is inherently unstable and risky. Chance is real (3). Determinism is ignorance parading as knowledge.

20. The distinction between God and the creatures is not the distinction between the infinite and the finite but the distinction between the whole and fragmentary. Religion is acceptance of our fragmentariness.

21. Genetic identity is not strict identity. In the jargon of the philosophers, the personal pronoun "I" is an indexical, acquiring

a partly new reference even when the "same" individual uses it at successive times.

22. The Phenomenological Principle, that is, Prehension, or nonsensory perception. "Prehension" is Whitehead's term and idea, but, as David Ray Griffin observed, "it is Hartshorne who has called attention to this achievement. One could well read through Whitehead's writings several times without realizing that such a powerful generalization had been accomplished. It is also Hartshorne who has called attention to the similarity between this accomplishment and the type of unity that scientific thinking in general seeks. For these reasons, the achievement is one in which Hartshorne shares. Fully recognizing and naming an insight of genius can be as important as the insight itself."

23. The Cosmic Variables.

24. The Compound Individual.

25. *Deus est caritas*, or, God is love.

26. The compatibility of Objective Independence and Universal Objectivity.

27. Reality as the content of divine knowledge.

28. The correction of defects in traditional versions of Idealism.

29. Contingency in God.

30. Memory and perception belong to the same genus, and both are retrospective. Perception is *impersonal* memory.

31. The Zero Fallacy.

32. The reality of time or, in the words of Charles Peirce, time as "objective modality."

33. A social theory of reality, or, reality as social process.

34. The Affective Continuum.

35. There is progress in philosophy.

36. Causality is crystallized freedom, freedom is causality in the making.

37. Errors in traditional, or classical, theism.

38. The Principle of Moderation.

39. Hartshorne's "global argument" for the existence of God.

40. Experience cannot generate its own data.

41. Psychology as inclusive of physics.

42. To add one more, and thus bring the total to 42, the year of my birth, I will mention another insight. In "A Reply to My Critics,"* Hartshorne discusses Twenty Metaphysical Principles. The last principle, P20, will repay reflection: "The foregoing nineteen principles must, if true, be mutually compatible; any one fully understood is, except in emphasis, equivalent to any other. They all define that abstract Something that could not fail to have instantiation or concrete realization."

*Charles Hartshorne, "A Reply to My Critics," in *The Philosophy of Charles Hartshorne*, edited by Lewis Hahn, p. 583.

[Note: numbers 8 through 21, were contributed by Donald Wayne Viney.]

The Prosaic Fallacy

Everyone has heard about the pathetic fallacy, but there is another fallacy, the exact *opposite* of the pathetic, that is of far more importance. This fallacy, which was first named and analyzed by Charles Hartshorne, is called the prosaic fallacy.

Science tends to cast a cold eye on life and the world of nature, and all of us have, in differing degrees, learned to see with the eye of science. This is good, as far as it goes. But when it goes too far, as it does in a strictly materialistic science, it can constrict our ways of seeing and perceiving.

Our vision can be so impaired that we miss the wildness and the beauty of the world around us. The world of sensory experience offers an aesthetic width and depth of feeling that we miss when looking from a perspective that abstracts from the concrete totality of living nature.

"The child and the artist, being less obsessed with practical and intellectual concerns, find the world more vivid and absorbing. But most of us select out aspects of experience for attention and use. We are thus left," as Eugene H. Peters says, "with a pragmatic skeleton of concrete experience."[1]

And when we are left with only a skeleton, what is missing is life itself.

One of the core doctrines of process philosophy is the idea of panexperientialism: that the enjoyment of experience goes all the way down in nature. The world of nature, on every level, is an ever-moving, never-ending "ocean of feeling."[2] We can even call it "mind," if "mind" is understood as a variable and not as a constant. This is a basic intuition of all poets and it finds vibrant expression in the works of William Wordsworth.[3]

If feeling, or experience, is enjoyed by all the dynamic or natural unities in the universe, then to deny such experience, or "mind," to the lower members of this ascending scale, and to assert that they are lifeless stuff—this is to commit the *prosaic fallacy.*

To see nature in this way is to see only what Whitehead calls *vacuous actualities* (empty shells, mere surface, mere behavior)[4] and not to behold robustly living entities who enjoy creative experience, individual unity, initiative, and purpose—with each of the foregoing four terms understood as variables that can be generalized to include an extensive range of values.

Under influence of the prosaic fallacy, the world of living nature is still there in all its freshness and fullness and wildness, but our perception delivers a domesticated version. Rather than perceiving, and *feeling*, the full spectrum, we take in only a narrow band. As Hartshorne observes, we suppose "the world to be as tame as our sluggish convention-ridden imaginations imply."[5]

After commenting on the pathetic fallacy, Hartshorne writes, "But there is another fallacy, more insidious among trained minds, which one may call the prosaic fallacy: the error of supposing that what is not, for our casual inspection, obviously endowed with a life of its own is thereby shown to be mere lifeless stuff or bare structure without inner quality. Surely the world is not obvious. Think of the history of science, of the microstructure or megalostructure of things, both different even in principle from what direct perception for ages led people to think."[6]

To supplement the eye of science, we need to learn to see with the eye of a poet, for, as Hartshorne adds, "The world is not so tame as prosy people are apt to suppose."[7]

Continuing with Hartshorne:

"What I call the prosaic fallacy is almost as naturally human as the poetic or pathetic fallacy. The world is neither the fairyland of primitive cultures nor the great machine of early modern science. Nor is it merely a vast but mindless organism. It is rather a vast many-leveled 'society of societies.' Enormous imagination and courage, combined with careful weighing of rather complicated chains of evidence, are required if we are to arrive at much idea of this cosmic society. There is no easy path, whether sentimental or cynical. But we are not even fairly started on the right path if we overlook or deny the *pervasive indistinctness of human experience or the evidence in direct awareness of two levels of feeling,* the second derivative, logically and temporally, from the first."[8]

Endnotes

1. Eugene H. Peters, *Hartshorne and Neoclassical Metaphysics*, 97.

2. Alfred North Whitehead, *Process and Reality*, Corrected Edition edited by David Ray Griffin and Donald W. Sherburne, 166.

3. For example, from a poem by Wordsworth called The Simplon Pass:

   Black drizzling crags that spake by the wayside
   As if a voice were in them, the sick sight
   And giddy prospect of the raving stream,
   The unfettered clouds and region of the heavens,
   Tumult and peace, the darkness and the light—
   Were all like workings of one mind, the features
   Of the same face, blossoms upon one tree,
   Characters of the great Apocalypse,
   The types and symbols of Eternity,
   Of first, and last, and midst, and without end.

4. If the idea of "mind" is sufficiently generalized, then mind, as Hartshorne says, "is not confined to a corner of nature but is everywhere in it, just as behavior is. But *mind is the substance*, and mere behavior, in the sense of spatio-temporal change, is the shadow, the skeletal outline only, the causal geometry, of nature." Hartshorne, "Physics and Psychics: The Place of Mind in Nature," in *Mind in Nature: Essays on the Interface of Science and Philosophy*, edited by John B. Cobb, Jr. and David Ray Griffin, 90.

5. Hartshorne, "Physics and Psychics: The Place of Mind in Nature," 95.

6. Charles Hartshorne, *Creativity in American Philosophy*, 173.

7. Charles Hartshorne, unpublished manuscript.

8. Charles Hartshorne, *The Zero Fallacy*, 159.

Here are two more statements by Hartshorne about the fallacy:

"But, as I am fond of remarking, the 'pathetic fallacy' is a danger of which the prosaic or apathetic fallacy is the opposite counterpart. Reality is not as dull as many sober souls imagine. One scientist recently remarked, 'Nature is stranger than we think. Perhaps it is stranger than we can think.' 'Feelings of atoms' or cells are strange enough; but they may fit the evidence better than feelings of planet earth, or of the oak tree beside my house, which may have been alive when the Pilgrims first crossed the Atlantic." —Charles Hartshorne, *Insights and Oversights of Great Thinkers*, 250.

"Wholly mindless matter can never be demonstrated, it can only be asserted. And Popper claims no certainty for his negation here. His only argument for mindless matter is that mind requires memory, and atoms can have none. My reply is that memory is shown by the influence of the past of the individual on its present, and I wonder how physics can reduce such influence to zero while still maintaining even partial individual identity. All causality is influence of the past on the present. I feel my ignorance here and I admire Popper in that he does offer a definite argument against psychicalism. Otherwise all I ever find are vague appeals to common sense or to the 'pathetic fallacy,' against which I balance the 'prosaic fallacy.' Unimaginative people—and to talk about the feelings of atoms does make demands on imagination—are not going to understand nature." —Charles Hartshorne, "Some Under- and Some Over-rated Great Philosophers," *Process Studies* 21, no. 3 (Fall): 171-72.

And another by Eugene Peters:

"Each unit event is an aesthetic creation. In each the world issues into novel concretion and achieves intrinsic value. And the whole is summed up, in majesty and beauty, in the life of the 'self-surpassing surpasser of all others.' Not realizing all this, distracted by pedestrian cares, one may commit the prosaic fallacy (Hartshorne's term) of thinking the world less exciting, more humdrum, than in fact it is. Some even deny that it is meaningful at all. Hartshorne argues that this denial is nonsensical. But beneath the argument, there is his insight that life is essentially affirmation and hope, the reaping of intrinsic values and the expectation of future harvest." —Eugene H. Peters, "Philosophic Insights of Charles Hartshorne," *Southwestern Journal of Philosophy,* VIII/1:17, 1976, p. 170.

Light and Levity in
Mysticism and the New Physics

What is it about the nature of light that causes a great mystic to say, "There is no more worthy, more glorious, or more potent work, than to work with light." Why is it that Nobel Prize winner Richard Feynman felt an enchantment that would last for a lifetime when he heard his high-school physics teacher say: "Light always follows the path of the beautiful"? What is it about the nature of light that prompted Albert Einstein, early in his career, to say, "For the rest of my life I will reflect on what light is!"?

Why is it, throughout human history, that the divine presence has so often been imaged as light? What is it about light that makes it the most enduring metaphor for the divine presence, and so natural a metaphor that we image God in countless ways as light, and these images of light find constant and pervasive expression in all sacred literature?

Why is it that God seems so at home in the light? Why do we sometimes hear the great mystics say, "God *is* light"?

Mysticism and Light

From the very beginning, the theme of light intertwines with the history of mysticism, and a vision of light often forms the central luminous core of the mystical experience.

Unity with the Light of the divine presence has been called the very signature of mysticism, and descriptions of this event by mystics tell of their feeling of unity, oneness, and a feeling of the inter-connectivity of the many and the one, a feeling of what Gregory Bateson has called "the pattern that connects."

What is this pattern that connects? At a fundamental level it is light—as *messenger* photons—that mediates relations and change on all levels.

Analogy and Metaphor

When the mystic tells us that God is light, are we to take him literally, or is there a better interpretation? In his excellent book *Electromagnetism and the Sacred*, physicist Lawrence W. Fagg provides a helpful distinction. God is not light, he suggests, nor is electromagnetism God, but light is an analogue for the immanence of the divine presence. He writes:

"This hypothesis is based . . . on *how* [light] on the physical level can be seen to be analogous to God's immanence at the spiritual level. First, they both share in the property of [omnipresence]: both are all-pervasive in our world. Second, they have analogous ranges of intensity from the most subtle and sensitive of experiences . . . to the most powerful and awesome. Third, they are analogous because light is so often used as a sign, symbol, or metaphor for God's presence. Light, however, is electromagnetic radiation. Just as God's light extends far beyond what we can sense, so analogously the spectrum of [light] extends far beyond what is visible. Fourth . . . just as the speed of [light] is constant, so is the abiding, eternal constancy of God's Light . . ."

Analogy shows similarities where before only differences were seen, and can awaken us to the presence of unity in variety.

Advance in science, and advances in thought generally, frequently come about through analogy or metaphor. When Newton saw a similarity between a falling apple and the moon in orbit round the earth, his thinking by way of analogy led to his discovery of universal gravitation. In what he called the happiest thought of his life, Einstein saw a deep analogy between gravity and steady acceleration, and this allowed him to further generalize his Special Theory of Relativity to include gravitation. James Watson glimpsed the *spiral* shape of DNA as he was walking down a *spiral* staircase at Oxford. I could cite many such examples.

The Electromagnetic Interaction

Like the mystic and his quest for unity, so too is the scientist in search of the "one," a unitary principle behind all the multiplicity of nature. The quest of science is also for an ever higher synthesis as illustrated in the evolution of thought concerning electricity, magnetism, and light which, not so long ago, were thought to be entirely separate categories. And then along came Michael Faraday and James Clerk Maxwell who showed that these three—electricity, magnetism, and light—like the three persons of the trinity, were really one, or better, manifestations of one underlying force: electromagnetism, which includes light.

In what may be called a revolution in light, Einstein, with his theory of relativity and the discovery of the photon, integrated light ubiquitously into every nook and cranny of the cosmic architecture. Further revolution came quickly as human consciousness was ushered into the strange and paradoxical world of very small things such as atoms and the elementary particles described by quantum theory.

Next, about halfway through the last century, we have the culmination of the work of Richard Feynman, Julian Swinger, and Sin-itiro Tomonaga who put the final touches on the field theory of quantum electrodynamics, for which these three men were awarded the Nobel prize in physics in 1965. And with this, an even higher synthesis, all the forces of nature were reduced to what are called the fundamental four: the strong force, the weak force, gravitation, and the electromagnetic interaction.

The electromagnetic interaction is abbreviated as the EMI, and when I use this I'm not speaking about something other than light, for the EMI is light. Think of the EMI as light in action. It is this force, the EMI, that is so pervasive in the workings of nature, secret and otherwise, as to be virtually omnipresent.

Atoms, molecules, and clusters of molecules are elegantly held together (and apart) through the workings of the electromagnetic force and specifically though the photon which is said to "carry" the electromagnetic force; and any change, for better or worse, seems to be mediated by photons in their role as "messenger" particles.

It is through the EMI that all living systems hang together from moment to moment, cohere as a unity, as one thing: a dynamic singular, and, at death, this coherence falls apart, and the process of bodily decomposition begins. The beauty of sunrise and sunset, the fragrance of a rose, the sound of a babbling brook, the taste of a ripe peach, the feeling of a lover's kiss and caress: all five senses operate through the EMI, or light in action.

Photons

As tiny, as diminutive, as micro-minute as it is, a photon has inexhaustible energy in that it can propagate everlastingly—witness the photons that make up the cosmic background radiation that has been around ever since the Big Bang, and is it not amazing that these particles of light wave to us all the way from the very birth of the universe itself: fifteen billion years ago!

One of the paradoxes about light is that a photon, as a particle of light, has no mass and therefore no weight, and thus it may be said that a photon is "light" in more ways than one.

Levity

By "levity" I mean both "lightness in mood, behavior, or word" and "lightness in weight" as the action of a counter-force that is the "opposite of gravity."

Gravity is a "down" force—a force that causes, when the time is ripe, the fall of such things as apples, and also keeps our feet planted firmly on the ground. Gravity is what makes a bushel of apples hard to lift. Gravity makes things *heavy*. Blow on a dandelion puffball and watch the gossamer seed-puffs sail away in the breeze. Inflate a yellow balloon with helium, release it, and behold as it floats up, up, and away. This is levity. Levity makes things *light*. Frown, which rhymes with "down," is a word of obvious gravity, just as its opposite, a sunny smile, fairly shines with levity.

Levity was once a scientific term, and the *Oxford English Dictionary* defines it thus:

". . . a positive property inherent in bodies in different degrees . . . in virtue of which they tend to rise, as bodies possessing gravity tend to sink . . ." The force of levity is not directed solely up, but also outward. Levity is the force that expresses as growth, extension, and expansion. Mix flour with water and leaven with yeast and, as the dough begins to rise, this is levity in action as is, later, the aroma of the freshly baked bread.

In fire we find, perhaps, one of the purest expressions of levity. What is lighter than a dancing flame of fire? Like a photon, that paragon of levity, fire is "light" in both senses of the word. Since to be a photon is to be never at rest but always on the move, at the speed of light, the universe has to keep expanding to make room for light, and in this expansion we see yet another expression of levity.

Such Stuff As Snowflakes Are Made On

Consider for a moment the beautifully patterned integrity of a single snowflake: one of the sparkling icy stars that fall like diamonds in profusion from the skies during any snowstorm . . . consider this tiny constellation of ice . . . this crystal masterpiece in miniature, this natural mandala, this hexagonal prism of light . . . consider the purity of form of this paragon of symmetry, elegance, and beauty . . . that seems suddenly and simply to appear out of thin air.

Suddenly? Not quite, for the snowflake comes trailing clouds of glory, and that glory turns out to be our old friend, the EMI, as light in action, that mediates the step-by-step process of crystallization, and then holds the elegant pattern in place.

Simply? On the contrary, for, in a complex process, many, many water molecules must be orchestrated, oriented, and articulated by the EMI to form a single snowflake. The number turns out to be "one" followed by 18 zeros. That so many do indeed become one coherent whole seems no small miracle.

To add to the complexity, it is no isolated process, but must take account of, and adapt to, the sometimes rapidly changing conditions within a blustery storm cloud: change of temperature, wind velocity, humidity, barometric pressure, and the changing velocity of its own swirling fall. In fact, the more complex the historical path a snowflake takes, the more complex, elegant, and beautiful is its final form. Can the same not be said of ourselves?

All snowflakes are similar, variations on a sixfold theme, yet they all differ, like our fingerprints, in that no two are alike. Not only is this an example of "unity-in-diversity," one of the definitions of beauty, but it suggests that even in the inorganic world there is an urge, an appetition, for novelty, beauty, and adventure.

Diamonds & Rainbows: The Path of Beauty

The presence of light is behind much of the beauty we behold. The essence of a diamond is its interaction with light, and a diamond sparkles with light because the many facets are cut in such a way that the rays of light enter and leave by many different shimmering paths. Light, remember, always follows the path of the beautiful.

Sunlight is the source of all the wonderful colors that "light up" Nature. Just as the universe is overflowing with the immanent but invisible presence of God, so too does sunlight contain all hues and all colors, invisible to the eye, until the light is shone through a prism, revealing thereby the primary colors so wonderfully hidden within.

Let us not forget a natural prism that comes with every spring shower: that magical mirage moment we call a rainbow. Is not a rainbow, woven in mist by rays of sunshine, a mystical epiphany of light?

What did God choose as a symbol of his covenant with humankind? In Genesis 9:13 we read that it was a rainbow: an arc of light linking in its sensuous curve both heaven and earth. And recollecting that in Greek mythology the goddess Iris was the personification of the rainbow, I feel amazement that there is a rainbow in the eye that mirrors the rainbow in the sky—a ring of bright color we call the iris. Indeed, what we are looking *for*, is what we are looking *with*.

Many-in-One

How the many become one is elegantly shown in our own somatic beginnings. The human embryo begins its life adventure as one cell: a fertilized female ovum that divides into two cells . . . two become four, and then: 8, 16, 32, 64, 128. . . . At some point in the process of simple cellular division "a miracle of creativity occurs" with the emergence of a rudimentary brain and nervous system that unifies all the micro-constituents into one unit of experience, one subject.

This process culminates with the birth of a bouncing baby boy or girl in which billions of cells, and a multiplicity of organs, glands, tissues, enzymes, hormones, amino acids, and living fluids are constellated beautifully as one unique individual.

As the organ that unifies, the brain and its network of nerves, on the quantum level, not only confers unity, but is itself a unity, through an intricate web of undulations of light. This is the language of light that whispers between cells.

A photon is perhaps the most diminutive of experiencing subjects, and, as the unification of particle and wave, the simplest exemplification of the many-in-one.

Rose Windows

Just like the green leaves of plants, Rose Windows, and other windows of stained glass in cathedrals, are designed to interact with light, to play with light and color, suffusing the interior of a sanctuary with a mystical light.

Leonardo da Vinci, who knew a thing or two about light and color, said that the power of meditation can be enhanced tenfold if practiced in the presence of violet rays coming through the stained glass windows of a quiet church.

One of the overall functions of beauty in a sanctuary is the elevation of the human spirit. And in the word "elevation" note letters 2, 3, and 4: L-E-V: the root of "levity." And so: light and levity: the entwined theme of this essay.

Dante's Mystic Rose

The Divine Comedy, written by the Italian poet Dante, is one of the world's literary treasures, and it ends, in its four last cantos, with a great metaphoric symphony of light: after his blindness is healed by immersing his face in a flowing river of light, there blooms, in Dante's vision, a flower of pure light, a Mystical Rose, white in color and of galactic size; at the center: a golden corona whose splendor far outshines any sun or star, and the white petals that radiate outward are freshened by a glorious rainfall, not of water, but a golden shower of joyful light.

Photosynthesis

Long ago, almost four billion years in the past, an event occurred that has been called "one of the greatest works of creativity" in the entire history of the living earth. There were no humans around then since our ancestors, *homo sapiens*, made their first appearance only two-hundred thousand years ago. But there were a host of many individuals, and among these many, one heroic individual stood out prominently.

Cosmologist Brian Swimme and geologian Thomas Berry, in their book *The Universe Story*, have christened this individual Prometheo, naming him after the Titan in Greek mythology who stole fire from heaven.

Prometheo was one of the prokaryotes, single-celled organisms with no nuclei, the very first life forms on earth. It was the high distinction of Prometheo to invent a new ability, the ability to weave "a molecular net with the power to capture photons in flight," thereby establishing a new intimacy with sunlight. Suddenly, photons became food, and new life itself was woven wondrously out of thin air by Prometheo's alchemy with light. In an act so elegant that it passes all understanding, Prometheo, measuring a mere one millionth of a meter across, had discovered photosynthesis. It is also part of Prometheo's everlasting legacy that he may be thought of, metaphorically, as being the first mystic who became one with the Light.

The complex chlorophyll molecule, the key to photosynthesis, is itself shaped like a flower: a daisy—and it is this "molecular flower" that works directly with photons, absorbing their energy so that it can be used to split hydrogen from oxygen in water molecules. In yet another dance of the many and the one, this is the first step in a chemical process whereby many atomic elements are orchestrated into the unity of new carbohydrate molecules. And it is these carbohydrates, these basic sugars and starches, that underlie and support all life on this planet.

Since oxygen is also a by-product of photosynthesis, it is this process, this interaction of light and leaf, that is the ultimate source not only of all the food we eat, but also of all the air we breathe.

The leitmotif of flower and sun can be further extended. The word daisy derives from "day's eye," meaning the sun, and when we look at a daisy with its golden orb in the center and white petals radiating out like rays, do we not see the very image of the sun itself? All of this reveals how Mother Earth, using the language of light, speaks eloquently to us in a poetry of luminous analogies and natural metaphors.

Light as Unity

Let us take a moment to look at the word "photosynthesis" itself. If we analyze this word we find that *photo* is the Greek word for "light," and that *synthesis* means the process of making a whole by putting together its separate component parts. Well, this is exactly what light does on all levels.

Light is how the many constellate as one. Light integrates and makes whole, light unifies—light and unity are inextricably intertwined. No light, no unity.

And so, in the word photosynthesis, we find revealed a process of unification that is integral to the very structure of the universe itself.

Is this why light is at the center of the mystical experience: that experience of wholeness, of being *one* with the *Light?* The writings of the great mystics tell us about two kinds of light: the light of everyday experience and a mystical light of the Divine Presence. If the EMI, as light in action, makes for unity and wholeness on the physical level, could it be that, on a spiritual level, the mystical light does the same thing?

Language of Flowers, Language of Light

And so, we have seen how the chlorophyll molecule resembles a daisy, and the daisy, or day's eye, reveals a radiant image of the sun. In the tiny crystal flowers of snowflakes we see a similar pattern, and the poet Ezra Pound spoke of "the rose of steel dust" seen in iron filings sprinkled round a magnet. A rainbow is a flowering of light and color that we behold through the iris of our eyes, and there's the Star of David, and a white flower that grows wild in the Holy Land called the Star of Bethlehem, and a beautiful crystal flower called fulgurite: a blossoming of electricity and silica, sometimes created when a bolt of lightning strikes a dune of sand. Then there are Rose Windows in Gothic cathedrals, Dante's Mystical Rose . . .

In sacred geometry there's an archetypal symbol known as the Flower of Life, a symbol so pervasive and so ancient that it is found in all places and all times. The Flower of Life, properly understood, is said to reveal the pattern of creation and the language of light by which life unfolds.

In the spirit of levity, in the spirit of the incredible lightness of being, flowers reach up and stretch outwards in an expansive desire for sunlight: the source of life. Some flowers, known as heliotropes, even open their blossoms at first light in the morning and turn to face the sun and then follow the arc of its path from east to west, from horizon to horizon, some closing their delicate petals at dusk in a fare thee well to the setting sun.

Conclusion

Just as Einstein ran joyously with light in his youth and saw the first glimmerings of Relativity, just as the great Bulgarian mystic Aïvanhov saw in rays of sunshine a light so mystical that he called them love letters from God, just as so many for so long have been transformed through an experience of light, so too have I been blessed and changed by immersing myself in the study of light for these past weeks.

Cardinal Newman begins one of his poems, Lead, kindly Light— lead thou me on!

Soon after I began researching and writing this essay, I decided to follow the path of light, trusting that the light would lead me on an illuminating journey. For me personally, there was much exhilaration throughout the journey and, by the time I reached what is thus far the end a few days ago, I was, and am still, experiencing many luminous rewards.

In the exhilaration I felt a wonderful levity or lightness of spirit, and in the subtleties of light I began to glimpse a marvelous interconnectivity that links all manifestations of the many and the one, and that "unity-in-diversity" constellates a pervasive principle as to how the universe, and everything in it, hangs beautifully together through the sometimes secret workings of the EMI, or light in action.

References:

The Ancient Secret of the Flower of Life, Drunvalo Melchizedek

Awaken Healing Light of the Tao, Mantak & Maneewan Chia

The Body of Light, John Mann and Lar Short

Catching the Light: The Entwined History of Light and Mind, Arthur
    Zajonc

The Cosmic Code, Heinz Pagels

Cosmic Consciousness, Richard Maurice Bucke

Electromagnetism and the Sacred, Lawrence W. Fagg

The Elegant Universe, Brian Greene

$E = mc^2$: *A Biography of the World's Most Famous Equation*, David
    Bodanis

$E = mc^2$: *An Equation That Changed the World*, Harald Fritzsch

Empire of Light, Sidney Perkowitz

Facing the Word With Soul: The Reimagination of Modern Life,
    Robert Sardello

*From Science to God: The Mystery of Consciousness and the Meaning
    of Light*, Peter Russell

The God Particle, Leon Lederman

Gathering the Light: A Psychology of Meditation, V. Walter Odajnyk

Gravity and Levity, Alan McGlashan

The Hidden Heart of the Cosmos: Humanity and the New Story, Brian
    Swimme

The Idea of the Holy, Rudolf Otto

The Importance of Light, Omraam Mikhaël Aïvanhov

Light Is a Living Spirit, Omraam Mikhaël Aïvanhov

The Marriage of the Sun and Moon: A Quest For Unity In Consciousness,
    Andrew Weil

Matter and Light: The New Physics, Louis de Broglie

The Mystery of Light, Georg Feuerstein

Natural Grace, Matthew Fox & Rupert Sheldrake

One River, Many Wells, Matthew Fox

The Paradiso, Dante (Translated by John Ciardi)

Photonics: The New Science of Light, Valerie Burkig

The Physics of Angels, Matthew Fox & Rupert Sheldrake

The Pound Era, Hugh Kenner

QED: The Strange Theory of Light and Matter, Richard P. Feynman

Quantum Questions: Mystical Writings of the World's Great Physicists, Ken Wilbur (Ed.)

Quantum Reality: Beyond the New Physics, Nick Herbert

Rainbows, Halos, and Glories, Robert Greenler

Sacred Geometry, Robert Lawlor

Science, Order, and Creativity, David Bohm & F. David Peat

The Self-Organizing Universe, Erich Jantsch

The Seven Mysteries of Life: An Exploration of Science and Philosophy, Guy Murchie

Sins of the Spirit, Blessings of the Flesh, Matthew Fox

"The Smallest Cells Have Important Lessons To Teach," James A. Shapiro

The Splendour of Tiphareth: The Yoga of the Sun, Omraam Mikhaël Aïvanhov

Synchronicity: The Bridge Between Matter and Mind, F. David Peat

Toward a Solar Civilization, Omraam Mikhaël Aïvanhov

Trialogues At the Edge of the West, Ralph Abraham, Terence McKenna, Rupert Sheldrake

The Universe of Light, Sir William Bragg

The Universe Story, Brian Swimme & Thomas Berry

Wheels of Light, Rosalyn L. Bruyere

When Science Meets Religion, Ian G. Barbour

Permanence and Change

A deeply entrenched prejudice against the idea of "change" in Western religious and metaphysical thought goes all the way back to Plato, with his Eternal Realm of Perfect Forms. There's a certain irony in this since Plato himself moved away from this position in his later writings. The basic misconception ties in with the idea of perfection. To move either toward or away from perfection is construed as negative, the former implying an initially incomplete state; the latter, a degradation. But why cannot change be seen as positive, even as applied to deity, in the sense of self-surpassing, with God as the unrivalled but self-surpassing surpasser of all? Surely the vast saga of evolution, with its billions of years of adventure and novelty, has been something on the order of aesthetic satisfaction for God.

Using the metaphor of God as supreme dramatist, Charles Hartshorne writes, "But the drama would be nothing if the players had no decision-making power of their own; in subtle ways the actors always ad lib, make up their own speeches. If God's world were merely the exact echo of divine thoughts coming back to God it would be pointless."

Indeed, it is far from obvious that the so-called idea or ideal of immutability is always a positive value. The movie *Groundhog Day*, starring Bill Murray, seems to suggest that the realm of the unchanging, or ceaseless repetition, may be more hellish than heavenly. Sartre's *No Exit* is another variation on this time-honored theme. Rather than paying a metaphysical compliment, perhaps there can be no greater insult than attributing to God complete immutability.

Among process thinkers, the primacy of "becoming" over "being" is so non-controversial as to be axiomatic and accords with the revelations of contemporary physics. This, along with the primacy of subjectivity over objectivity, is what partly constitutes *the revolution in metaphysics* that I discuss in an essay by that title.

It boils down to a question of the concrete or the abstract, the dynamic or static, event or substance, change or permanence. Western thought still suffers a bad hangover from the old Greek intoxication with abstractions and with a Newtonian addiction to "substance" abuse.

The process solution is to see these "ideal opposites" as requiring each other, with the concrete as the inclusive category. I invite you to turn to a single moment of your own experience as a clue to the nature of all reality.

All natural unities in the universe—particulate, atomic, molecular, cellular, vertebrate, human, divine—are self-creative, from moment to moment, through a definite process of becoming. Mind is quantum, or episodic. What endures is abstract essence, character, or what Whitehead calls "defining characteristic." We are personally ordered "societies" of momentary occasions of experience.

Surely it is not God's abstract essence that thrills in our veins, nor are the "icy absolutes" of medieval theology the object of our veneration; rather, it is God's living actuality that is worthy of worship. To exalt the abstract over the concrete implies that we should value objects over subjects, the possible more than the actual, and that the movement from cause through effect is a descent from better to worse, from more to less. It seems to me that we sometimes have a tendency to forget, or to selectively ignore, some of the obvious insights and implications of evolutionary theory.

In a splendid little book by John B. Cobb, called *The Structure of Christian Existence*, Cobb identifies and offers an analysis of the various "structures of existence," of different dimensions and of ever greater complexity, that have arisen during the human journey of evolution.

After an Introduction, and a chapter about the psyche (or soul), he goes on to discuss "primitive existence" wherein a threshold was first crossed dividing humans from our simian ancestors. What he finds distinctive about the first humans is the autonomous development of psychic life as its own end, a decisive increase in unconscious activity through the growth of symbolization that eventuates in what he calls the "mythical mind," and an advance from mere receptive awareness to reflective consciousness.

He then discusses, in this order:

Civilized Existence
Axial Existence
Buddhist Existence
Homeric Existence
Socratic Existence
Prophetic Existence
Christian Existence

Axial existence, which arose during the middle of the millennium before Christ, was a pivotal threshold crossing, and the five categories that follow this can be thought of as "modes" of this structure of existence. These structures of existence are cumulative, they build upon one another, and each successive stage enables the realization of possibilities that were not available for the previous stage. Indeed, it seems self-evident that even the brightest among the first "apes" who crossed the threshold into primate existence could not even begin to think like Einstein or make music like Mozart. This is simply more evidence that makes it clear to me that "mind" is not a constant, but a variable. It evolves just like everything else, including so-called "immutable" Laws.

Mention of the word "apes" brings to mind a phrase from Whitehead who speaks of "the dim recesses of our ape-like consciousness." Indeed, although the human mind does have simian roots, it can also soar, on the wings of Daedalus, free from the labyrinth of determination by the past—up, up, and away!

As the Moody Blues remind us in song:

And you can fly
High as a kite if you want to
Faster than light if you want to
Speeding through the universe
Thinking is the best way to travel . . .

Adventurous Frontiers
in a Process Universe

The general, or popular, notion of "process" goes back at least as far as the Greek philosopher Heraclitus who declared that all things flow, and who came up with an analogy so memorable that it has become part of our common vocabulary: you can't step into the same river twice.

Process philosophy, however, as conceived by Alfred North Whitehead, one of the most profound and original thinkers of all time, is a unique creation of our era. Whitehead's thought is of such quality that it has been characterized as ". . . some of the most careful and elegant thinking in the history of Western philosophy." (RE 412) Whitehead made significant contributions not only in philosophy but also in mathematics, physics, and formal logic. When quantum physics dematerialized Newton's billiard-ball atom into a vibrational "structure of activity," it took a genius of Whitehead's breadth to glimpse that such a structure could be further dematerialized into a non-substantial "unit of experience," and to conceive the entire universe in terms of dynamic units of living process. From this new process perspective Whitehead was able to upgrade the saying of Heraclitus by making a rather startling statement. He said that "no thinker thinks twice." *No thinker thinks twice.* Hold that thought—it will become clearer as this discussion unfolds.

Process philosophers today, as in the 20th century, differ among themselves in how they accommodate, or oppose, the complex metaphysical system conceived and developed by Whitehead. Some, like Nicholas Rescher, try to distance themselves as much as possible from Whitehead. Others are more intent on refining and advancing the intellectual task that Whitehead initiated.

Such a philosopher is Charles Hartshorne who independently came up with some of the same ideas he later found in Whitehead. Hartshorne originated electrifying new insights himself, clarified many process ideas, and corrected some of Whitehead's oversights. It can hardly be overstated how much Hartshorne has done to strengthen the case for process philosophy. Among 20th-century philosophers, Hartshorne stands out as one of the premier metaphysicians and the most influential proponent of the process conception of God. In contrast to Hartshorne, Frederick Ferré is among those in process thought who prefer to get along without introducing the notion of God into their systems.

Given all this, is there any agreement or consensus as to what constitutes the basic ideas of process philosophy? Hartshorne identifies fifteen common theses accepted by most process philosophers and David Griffin has set down what he calls the Ten Core Doctrines of Process Philosophy. (see Appendixes B and C) Donald Wayne Viney finds Griffin's list laudable but problematic, and defines process philosophy in terms of four propositions:

(1) The fundamental constituents of reality are processive—involving change, motion, time, and/or contingency;

(2) Whatever is *not* processive is part of or grounded in what is processive. As Hartshorne argues, becoming includes being, not vice versa;

(3) Reality is social—Hartshorne has the most coherent doctrine of social relations, saying that the present moment is internally related to the past but partly externally related to the future;

(4) Value is inherent in process.

My essay is divided into six main sections, each dealing with what I see as basic and important ideas in Whitehead's system, and a final section wherein I make variations on a theme introduced by the philosopher Frederick Ferré. These are:

(1) the centrality of the body in human experience

(2) the idea of panexperientialism: there is experience in everything

(3) dipolarity: an essential two-foldedness that runs through all nature

(4) the two basic types of "process" in process philosophy

(5) A Holographic Universe

(6) God and the World

(7) A Kalogenic Universe (*kalogenic* means the "creation of beauty")

All of these are tied together by the unifying theme of the idea of experience.

Coming to Terms

Before I go any further it may be helpful to briefly discuss some of Whitehead's key technical terms that I will be using in this essay, terms some of you may not be familiar with. First—

Actual Entities

What are the basic units of nature, what are the most fundamentally real things in the world? Strictly speaking, this is not a scientific, but a metaphysical question. To answer this question, Whitehead began with a single moment of human experience. For surely the one thing we cannot doubt is the reality of our own experience. If we can't start here, then there's simply no starting at all.

The first thing to be noticed is that a moment of experience is a discrete unit: experience comes in drops or buds. Experience is quantum in nature. Whitehead's analysis of a single moment of experience also revealed a tripartite structure:

First, a moment of experience is heavy with the presence or pressure of the immediate past. This accounts for our distinct sense of continuity. From this there arises a feeling or valuation of what is thus received with the felt possibility of novelty, or deviation from the past. Finally, there is a "decision" for either originality or conformity with the past, and a handing on of this as influence on the future. Whitehead then generalized that this basic structure must hold throughout all reality: a moment of experience in anything—from people to protons, from elephants to electrons—will exemplify this structure, or better: this process.

For Whitehead, this is the most basic process in the universe, and he calls this universal process an *actual entity*.

An actual entity is Whitehead's term for the basic units, or building blocks, of nature. It is a dynamic unit of process, a pulsation, a throb of self-achieved actuality that endures only for a split-second. In contrast to Newton's billiard-ball atom, note how Whitehead's actual entity is a *unit of creative experience*. The universe of Alfred North Whitehead is an adventurous universe—right down to the very core.

The next term is—

Prehension

Undergirding sensory perception is a more basic and primitive form of nonsensory perception that Whitehead calls "prehension." Before sensory perception arose in evolutionary history, this was how creatures were able to take account of their immediate environment. Thus, a single-celled life form, such as an amoeba, will retreat from what it prehends as danger and advance toward, and engulf, what it prehends as possible food.

Or, I can remember my favorite dog when growing up, a beagle. When I played with him, and spoke to him in a warm and friendly way, he would become very animated and frisky, and begin to bark and wag his tail and jump all over me. He was feeling, or prehending, my affection and approval, and responding in kind. A scolding, however, with sharp words and tone, would cause him to hunker down with his tail between his legs.

Another example may help to make clear how this works. When Laker basketball star Kobe Bryant ate a tainted hamburger in Sacramento during the NBA playoffs, he fell ill with food poisoning and began to feel very sick at his stomach. What Kobe experienced were not sense perceptions. He was directly feeling the causal influence of his body. He was prehending the cells of his stomach, feeling their feelings of acute distress. In fact, Whitehead's most concise definition of "prehension" is the "feeling *of* feeling."

An example from the botanical world would be heliotropic flowers. In a prehensive "taking account of" sunbeams, or photons, such flowers turn their blossoms to follow the sun, from morning till evening, from horizon to horizon. Underground the same sort of thing happens with the roots as they meander here and there in a prehensive search for water and essential nutrients. This surely illustrates a primitive form of "awareness."

Even in the inorganic world something of this can be seen. The mutual "attraction" of oppositely charged particles is made manifest in magnets, for if you hold two magnets close together, you can feel them straining for union. Does this illustrate a primordial form of "yearning?"

The third term is—

The Ontological Principle

Whitehead's philosophy is strongly empirical, meaning that it is grounded in experience. Reflecting this empirical commitment, his ontological principle states that only actual individuals can act. All explanation, in metaphysical discussion, is to be in terms of, or referable to, an actual thing or fact. Paraphrasing his words, "nothing simply floats into the world from out of the blue." An example of a violation of the ontological principle would be to say that laws, such as the laws of nature, cause or make things happen. Laws merely describe the relatively stable but evolving "habits of interaction" of the many entities that populate the universe.

A Psychosomatic Universe

"I sing the body electric." — *Walt Whitman*

Whitehead derived his metaphysics, in part, from a keen observation and analysis of his own everyday experiences as a human subject. Much of the time we tend to ignore the body, or to take it for granted. But for Whitehead the human body is "the starting point for our knowledge of the circumambient world." (PR 81)

All sense perception is entirely dependent on the prior functioning of our bodies; what we experience is derived from extensive and interconnected chains of antecedent experiences that occur within the body. We experience other experiences.

For example, what happens when we see a patch of red before us? As Whitehead says, a datum of information is passed from the excited "cells of the retina, through the train of actual entities forming the relevant nerves, up to the brain. Any direct relation of eye to brain is entirely overshadowed by this intensity of indirect transmission . . . the predominant basis of perception is perception of the various bodily organs, as passing on their experiences by channels of transmission and enhancement." (PR 118, 119) And even this account abstracts from the complexity of the biological details underlying our experience of "red."

What you are seeing is a presentation made possible by many antecedent processes occurring in your body. From this David Griffin observes: "So even though the *data* of sensory perception give us a purely spatial world, the *process* of sensory perception itself suggests that the cells in our bodies are not purely spatial but are *prehensive unifications of data from prior events*, being in this respect analogous to moments of our own experience." (RS 106-07)

The body is a vast ocean of feelings—a labyrinth of elegant routes of communication whereby information of various kinds is passed on, amplified, enhanced, integrated, and reintegrated. Whitehead again:

It is a set of occasions miraculously coordinated so as to pour its inheritance into various regions within the brain. There is thus every reason to believe that our sense of unity with the body has the same original as our sense of unity with our immediate past of personal experience. (AI 189)

Your relationship with your body is a social relationship: a relationship of the one self, or soul, to the many micro-individuals that make up your living body—the hundreds of thousands of different kinds of cells whose total number ranges in the trillions. Each cell in turn is a vast society of molecules wherein each molecule in turn is a teeming society of elementary particles. All of these micro-individuals are, to some degree, taking account of one another, or "socializing." Electrons are very "attracted" to those flirtatious entities we call protons. We are complexly social through and through.

෮

So closely do we identify with our bodies, that we tend to lose sight of an obvious fact: that the body is *in the world*. Far from being apart from the external world, the body is only the most intimate part of the environment we experience.

As Whitehead puts it, "We think of ourselves as so intimately entwined in bodily life that a man is a complex unity—body and mind. But the body is part of the external world, continuous with it. In fact, it is just as much part of nature as anything else there—a river, or a mountain, or a cloud. Also, if we are fussily exact, we cannot define where a body begins and where external nature ends." (MT 21)

Given that our bodies are the most intimate part of nature that we can observe most directly, Whitehead took this as a clue as to what was happening in the rest of nature, and he surmised that "other sections of the universe are to be interpreted in accordance with what we know of the human body." (PR 119) "The human body," Whitehead says, "provides our closest experience of the interplay of the actualities of nature." (MT 115)

Whitehead calls the body "a miracle of order" and indeed it is the extraordinary structure of the human body that makes possible what may be called high levels of experience. The body, and I mean the body itself, is structured for conceptual adventure. The body is that locus, or matrix, wherein the possible and the actual intersect. On this fundamental contrast is based all novelty.

On this matter of the body, Teilhard de Chardin is in agreement with Whitehead, for he has written:

> Hitherto, the prevailing view has been that the body (that is to say, the matter . . . attached to each soul) is a *fragment* of the universe—a piece *completely detached* from the rest and handed over to a spirit that informs it. In future, we shall say that the Body is the very Universality of things, in as much as they are centered on an animating Spirit, in as much as they influence that Spirit—and are themselves influenced and sustained by it. . . . My own body is not these cells or those cells that *belong exclusively* to me: it is *what*, in these cells *and* in the rest of the world, feels my influence and reacts against me. *My* matter is not a *part* of the universe that I possess *totally*: it is the *totality* of the Universe possessed by me *partially*. (SC 12-13.)

226

A Panexperiential Universe

During the 300-year reign of science over which the analytical spirit of Sir Isaac Newton presided, the universe was viewed as a gigantic clockwork machine, ticking away in timeless perfection, a perfection created once and for all by God, who then stepped back, according to that view, to dispassionately contemplate his handiwork for all eternity.

The world the scientist looked out upon was, in essence, a fixed world, a changeless world, governed by immutable laws. It was a predictable world of force and matter, ruled by a rigid determinism, a mechanical world of billiard-ball cause and effect. Now, one undeniable attribute of a machine is that it has no life in it. So too, said science, was the material universe devoid of life: sheer matter acted upon by mechanical force. And back of it all, a changeless God—Aristotle's Unmoved Mover. In a deterministic universe such as this, there's not much room for adventure.

Modern science has, in a sense, eviscerated the basic units of nature. As a consequence, they are seen as inert, completely insentient, nonpurposive, devoid of experience, incapable of self-movement. Whitehead calls such matter "vacuous actualities," meaning that it has no interiority.

Enter panexperientialism: this is a long eight-syllable word with a simple meaning but some rather complex and surprising implications. It simply means that experience is the basic reality. In sharp contrast to Newton's vacuous actualities, the fundamental units of nature, what Whitehead calls "actual entities," are experiencing subjects. The basic units of nature are units of process and that process itself is a momentary flash of experience. Whitehead is clear and emphatic about this when he says that "apart from the experiences of subjects there is nothing, nothing, nothing, bare nothingness." (PR 167)

Whitehead makes an important distinction between actual entities and what he calls enduring objects, entities that endure, or persist in time. These enduring entities are the real individuals that you can see and touch in the everyday world: all life forms that act and feel as one, such as dogs and fish and birds. Or the simple life forms that can be seen through a microscope: the cells of the human body, bacteria, protozoa, and plankton. And those inorganic enduring entities that can be, if not seen, at least detected by scientific instrumentation: molecules, atoms, subatomic particles, photons of light.

An actual entity is a single moment of experience in any one of these enduring entities. A moment that begins and ends very quickly—in a fraction of a second. When an actual entity achieves its moment of actuality, it "perishes," to use Whitehead's word, and is immediately followed by a new pulse of actuality.

Simply put, actual entities arise and "perish" whereas enduring entities persist through time. Whereas an enduring entity has a history, and sometimes a very long history, an actual entity happens "all at once."

Whitehead states the importance of making this distinction:

> The real actual things that endure are all [enduring entities]. They are not actual occasions. It is the mistake that has thwarted European metaphysics from the time of the Greeks, namely, to confuse [enduring entities] with the completely real things which are the actual occasions. . . . Thus [an enduring entity] enjoys a history expressing its changing reactions to changing circumstances. But an actual occasion has no such history. It never changes. It only becomes and perishes. (AI 204)

In making this distinction Whitehead is insisting on the essential quantum nature of all reality, as opposed to the view of an enduring substance that somehow persists over time while exhibiting changing qualities. This includes the human mind or psyche, and so it is proper to speak in terms of the *quantum soul*. As David Griffin has stated, "The enduring self, understood as an enduring substance, is deconstructed." (FC 202) Such a quantum view of the soul has been commonplace in Buddhist thought for centuries.

∞

For panexperientialism to be a tenable doctrine, two other distinctions are required, and to overlook either is to invite confusion.

Some critics of process like to make fun of the idea of panexperientialism. They misconstrue the doctrine to mean that everything has experiences—everything without exception. They can then talk about how silly it is to claim that a chair has feelings, or that a stone or a rock can think.

The "pan" in panexperientialism means not that *all* things experience, but that there is experience *in* all things. A rock, for example, enjoys no unified experience, but a rock is teeming with a multitude of micro-individuals who do experience—molecules, atoms, elementary particles, and so forth. Internally, on the quantum level, a rock is roaring with activity. Even though a rock itself cannot be said to experience, there is experience, and plenty of it, *within* the rock.

Which brings me to the second distinction:

Experience varies vastly as to complexity, beauty, and intensity. This is the whole thrust of evolution, which began with very primitive units of experience, and only much later, after billions of years, evolved consciousness and self-awareness. Although experience does go all the way down, consciousness does not. As Whitehead puts it, "consciousness is the crown of experience . . . not . . . its base." (PR 267)

Thus, those who ridicule the idea of panexperientialism by pointing out the obvious—that rocks can't think—have completely overlooked these two essential distinctions.

For clarity, it should be pointed out that not all actual entities are exactly alike. In fact, Whitehead distinguishes four different grades:

In the actual world we discern four grades of actual [entities]. First, and lowest, there are the actual [entities] in so-called 'empty space'; secondly, there are the actual [entities] which are moments in the life-histories of enduring non-living objects, such as electrons or other primitive organisms; thirdly, there are the actual [entities] which are moments in the life-histories of enduring living [entities]; fourthly, there are the actual [entities] which are moments in the life-histories of enduring [entities] with conscious knowledge. (PR 177)

They differ among themselves . . . But, though there are gradations of importance, and diversities of function, yet in the principles which actuality exemplifies, all are on the same level. The final facts are, all alike, actual entities; and these actual entities are drops of experience, complex and interdependent. (PR 18)

In short, although there are great differences among actual entities, they all exemplify the same fundamental process of coming to be.

We are rarely, if ever, consciously aware of actual entities. In John B. Cobb's words:

> These individual occasions are only detectable either by intense introspection or by scientific instruments. None of the entities of which we are conscious in common experience are individual occasions and only rarely do these appear even in the sciences. For the most part, our conscious experience is concerned with entities that are groupings of occasions rather than individual occasions. (CN 40)

∾

There are three very distinctive features of human experience. First, the inwardness of experience. We are more than our bodies and our mere behavior as glimpsed by others. Experience is something that transpires within and in a very real sense is hidden from the rest of world.

The second feature is that experience is not continuous but comes in discrete units, or "quanta." William James called them drops or buds of experience. As we've seen, Whitehead uses the technical term "actual entities" or sometimes he refers to them as "occasions of experience."

To use a cinematic analogy, we flash along our quantum way at about ten to twelve frames per second. This would seem like slow motion to an electron for whom a minute must seem like a millennium.

As mentioned previously, for Buddhists the quantum nature of reality is nothing new. In a book entitled *The Secret Oral Teachings in Tibetan Buddhist Sects*, we find this:

> The tangible world is movement, say the Masters, not a collection of moving objects, but movement itself. There are no objects "in movements," it is the movement which constitutes the objects which appear to us: they are nothing but movement.

This movement is a continued and infinitely rapid succession of flashes of energy (in Tibetan "tsal" or "shoug"). All objects perceptible to our senses, all phenomena of whatever kind and whatever aspect they may assume, are constituted by a rapid succession of instantaneous events . . . the movement is intermittent and advances by separate flashes of energy which follow each other at such small intervals that these intervals are almost non-existent.

The third feature is creativity. Every moment of experience provides windows of opportunity for creative advance—for adventure. Whitehead's thought is adventurous because he found reality itself to be adventurous.

Whitehead was an empiricist and, as such, he founded his epistemology, his theory of knowledge, and his ontology, his theory of reality, on that concrete reality we know best, most directly, and most intimately: our own experience as human subjects. Indeed, it would be no exaggeration to characterize Whitehead's entire conceptual system as "the metaphysics of experience."

Whitehead made the bold conceptual move of generalizing this to include all of reality: experience, inner experience, goes all the way down, from people to protons. Human experience is thus a high-level exemplification of reality in general. Or, as Frederick Ferré puts it:

Coherence would strongly suggest that the one precious sample of reality to which we have intimate access should be taken instead as our best clue to whatever else is real and effective in itself. It is our *only example* of the interiority of an existing being; and it provides the *inescapable context* for every bit of data we receive. (BV 351)

Since our experiences are the "only complete data" given to us directly, and since we *are* those experiences, it is difficult to see how knowledge could be any more intimate than this. With this in mind it is far from obvious that the other units of reality are completely different in principle than what we most intimately feel and directly know.

To attribute feelings "all the way down" is one aspect of Whitehead's attempt to reflect, in his metaphysical system, the unity of nature. Whitehead was the first philosopher to formulate the doctrine of panexperientialism with conceptual clarity. As so formulated, this doctrine has been hailed as "one of the greatest philosophical discoveries of all time."

℘

Panexperientialism is a powerful conceptual tool that provides many theoretical benefits. I'll briefly mention only two.

First, the mind-body problem.

For over three centuries, the mind-body problem has proven highly resistant to solution by philosophers. This problem has been so difficult to untangle that Arthur Schopenhauer called it the "world-knot." With regard to our era, philosopher John Searle has said that, "contrary to surface appearances, there really has been only one major topic of discussion in the philosophy of mind for the past fifty years or so, and that is the mind-body problem."

In 1998 David Ray Griffin published a book (UW) devoted to the problem and some of us believe that he has at last unsnarled this perplexing knot, arguing from the vantage point of panexperientialism. If mind and matter are completely different in kind, the problem to overcome is how they could possibly interact. From the point of view of materialism and dualism, the problem, according to leading theoreticians, appears to be insoluble. But what they miss seeing is that these are not the only options.

Panexperientialism, with its view that mind and so-called matter differ in degree but not in kind, provides a clear understanding of how interaction between the two is possible.

Another long-standing problem concerns evolution.

Some scientists have concluded that the problem of how first life, and then consciousness or mind, evolved out of mere inert matter is theoretically insoluble. From the perspective of panexperientialism, this is only a pseudo-problem in that whatever entities emerged following the so-called "Big Bang" enjoyed some form of experience, however slight and primitive. As William James has said, "If evolution is to work smoothly, consciousness in some shape must have been present at the very origin of things."

A Dipolar Universe

Another feature that Whitehead found in his analysis of experience was its essential dipolarity.

Imagine pausing for a moment to look at yourself in a mirror, and become aware of the double perspective—you see your body as others see you, but you are also aware of your own inner experience. Your body, from without, is what you are as you appear to the sensory perception of others. Your mind, or inner experience, are what you are for yourself. Griffin reminds us that this provides the basis for a distinction between mind and matter: "What we call matter is then the outer appearance of something that is, from within, analogous to our own experience." (FC, 203)

The French paleontologist Teilhard de Chardin said that "coextensive with their Without, there is a Within of things." And physicist David Bohm is thinking along the same lines in his distinction of two orders in nature: the *implicate* and the *explicate*.

Whitehead called these two aspects of experience the *mental pole* and the *physical pole*; hence, the word "dipolar."

He then generalized this dipolarity to be ingredient in all actualities all the way down to the most fundamental units of nature.

Though many have tried to describe what subatomic particles look like as matter, that is, as seen from without, Whitehead was perhaps the first to try to imagine what an electron feels like from inside. To Newton's inert mass particles, he thus resuscitated not only some interiority, but a lively inner experience with each pulsation of actuality. And thus philosopher Charles Hartshorne came to speak of how an electron can "enjoy its almost incredibly lively career of rhythmic and not too rigidly rhythmic adventures." (BH 202)

Whitehead's anatomy of a single pulsation reveals a beginning, a momentary phase of creative development toward a completion that ends with a thrust beyond itself into the next new pulsation. As an electron flashes along its quantum way, each tiny pulsation throbs its own actuality into existence, just as quickly fades away, and is immediately followed by another.

At the deepest level, in electromagnetic wave propagation, this same polarity is vividly exemplified in that such waves are propagated by a sheer reversal of field as a pulsation of negative charge begets positive and positive begets negative in a segue of polar reversals. In this perpetual rhythm of vivid contrasts, nature can be seen as dipolar through and through.

The strange, charmed, beautiful, and truly upside-down microworld of quantum physics reveals the presence of this same dipolarity, for there are two types of elementary particles, quarks and leptons, and the individual particles themselves are linked in pairs—the six quarks: up-down, charmed-strange, truth-beauty (or top-bottom in more prosaic terms), and the six leptons: electron neutrino-electron, muon neutrino-muon, tau neutrino-tau. To extend this biphasal omnipresence even further, each particle also has an antiparticle, such as the neutrino-antineutrino pair.

Charles Hartshorne proposed that "in basic contrasts or polarities, both poles must be asserted if either is." If this is true, and if there is life after death, as some of us believe, then we can look forward not to lives of pure spirit but to post-terrestrial careers of *dipolar immortality*.

Change, or the oscillation between two phases, operates at every level of reality—from subatomic particles and atoms to planets and galaxies. If dipolarity is so fundamental to the very nature of reality, what does this suggest about the nature of God?

The Divine Dipolarity

Process proposes what at first glance may appear to be an apparent paradox: that God both changes and does not change. Can any sense be made of this paradoxical proposal? The process answer is that a coherent explanation can be made by conceiving God as dipolar.

Indeed, if dipolarity is a fundamental principle, and if Whitehead is correct in holding that God can be no exception to such principles, then the divine nature *must* be dipolar. Moreover, not only is God conceived as dipolar, but as doubly dipolar.

One dipolarity is in terms of a distinction between two aspects of God: God's concrete actuality and God's abstract essence. God's abstract essence does not change, is timeless, necessary . . . in fact, all the mostly negative characteristics attributed to God by classical theism. But as a concrete actuality, God does change, through increase of experience and value, and is temporal, contingent, and relative. Hartshorne emphasizes just how relative God is by proposing that God is the most relative of all actualities and coins the term "surrelative" to describe this. God is super-relative.

In sharp distinction to Aristotle's Unmoved Mover, God is also dipolar in how God relates to the world: both exerting influence *upon*, and receiving influence *from*.

Some critics charge that the God of process theism is not transcendent enough. To this charge Hartshorne has made a sagaciously witty reply: he said that the God of process is *twice* as transcendent as the God of classical theism. He was able to make this reply through his doctrine of *dual transcendence*. By dual transcendence, Hartshorne means that only God has uniquely excellent ways of being both absolute and relative, necessary and contingent, immutable and capable of change, and so on.

Ideal Opposites

Dipolarity is only one of many variations on a twofold metaphysical theme that weaves its way through Whitehead's work: the unification of contrasting pairs such as the many and the one, order and novelty, permanence and change. The last pair, permanence and change, is maybe the most general expression of the underlying rhythms of process in nature. Whitehead calls these contrasting pairs *ideal opposites*. The point to be noticed is, that in all of these contrasting pairs, one *requires* the other. They cannot, in Whitehead's words, "be torn apart." There is an ultimate complementarity in the very nature of things, including the nature—the dipolar nature—of God.

In Whitehead's words, "Opposed elements stand to each other in mutual requirement. In their unity, they inhibit or contrast. God and the World stand to each other in this opposed requirement." (PR 348)

Not only do God and the world stand in mutual requirement, either one is the source of novelty, and adventure, for the other. This is the basis for Whitehead's statement that "It is as true to say that God creates the world, as that the world creates God." (PR 348)

In Whitehead's scheme what appears as an opposition, or self-contradiction, is converted to a vivifying contrast. Since "all the 'opposites' are elements in the nature of things, and are incorrigibly there," (PR 350) there can be no final reconciliation of permanence and change in a process universe. The world will never reach a state of static completion, and neither will God. Creation continues, forevermore and everlastingly, and so: adventure!

Getting It Exactly Backwards

Charles Hartshorne has taken Whitehead's idea of "ideal opposites" and developed it considerably into what he calls a logic of ultimate contrasts. Consider for a moment pairs of contrasting terms such as absolute and relative, cause and effect, object and subject, being and becoming—Hartshorne calls these ultimate contrasts, or contraries. For many centuries it has been customary in theology to exalt one side of these contraries at the expense of the other—to such an extent that one side has been used exclusively as names or designations of deity. Thus we have God as Absolute, Universal, Cause, Infinite . . .

In thus exalting the absolute over the relative, being over becoming, Hartshorne argues that the medieval theologians did not get it right once and for all, but, on the contrary, they got it exactly backwards.

One of the many surprising adventures of reading Whitehead is to discover what to some may seem an outrageous claim: that much of our received wisdom is not only wrong but that some of our most venerated thinkers got it exactly backwards. Whitehead reminds us that "the doctrines which best repay critical examination are those which for the longest period have remained unquestioned."(AI 177) In his book *Process and Reality*, time and time again he will cite an established idea only to say, "but the converse is true." And then proceed to show why this is so. Is this not reminiscent of Jesus' saying, "It has been said . . . but I say unto you."

Two Types of Process: Concrescence and Transition

In Whitehead's system of thought there are two types of process: *concrescence* and *transition*. What he means by these two terms can be shown by drawing a distinction between two types of causation:

efficient and final. Efficient causation is how one thing, or occasion, influences another. It is the causal influence *between* two occasions, and is objective, or physical. Final causation is self-determination. This is how an entity influences its own self-formation, or self-completion. As such, it is the causal influence exerted *within* one occasion on itself, and is subjective, or mental. Final causation, with its glimpse of possibilities beyond what is given by the past, is how determinism is transcended and novelty enters the world.

An analysis of our own experience reveals that we are not completely determined by the past, but are constantly deciding how to react to circumstances. For example, if I feel hunger while working at my computer, I'm not thereby compelled to make a mad dash for the refrigerator, but can decide to wait until later to have a slice of apple pie.

From this analysis, Whitehead generalizes that the same sort of process, different in degree but not in kind, occurs in other individuals, all the way down. Although they differ in richness and complexity, the momentary experiences of a molecule and a Mozart all share the same basic structure.

Here's how Whitehead analyzes a moment in the life of an actual entity:

Remember, all experience comes in quantum pulsations. Each pulse of experience begins physically by receiving the efficient causation of the past, followed by a mental, or subjective, phase wherein it feels not only this influence but also a range of possibilities for deciding how to respond. Once this decision and response is made, the subjectivity comes to an end, and the objective datum of what has thus been achieved is then passed on to the succeeding pulse of experience. The ending of subjective experience is the beginning of objective existence as efficient causal influence.

New possibilities for an actual entity are felt as contrasts between what *now is* and what *might be*. What "might be" are a range of possibilities, provided by God in terms of an initial aim. The initial aim both initiates the occasion and aims at its best outcome, given all the myriad factors that make up the present concrete situation. Through an initial aim that is relevant to the context, God provides "particular providence for particular situations."(PR 351) This is how

God is present, and participates in, every concrescence and transition in the entire universe.

Simply put, *concrescence* is how an entity achieves actuality and *transition* is how it passes on what it has thus achieved to future subjects that follow. Underlying every reality is the cosmic rhythm wherein transition follows concrescence to beget yet another concrescence. Note the beautiful symmetry of this interweaving of transition and concrescence, efficient and final causality, objectivity and subjectivity, permanence and change.

And so all the enduring entities of nature, including all humans, are biphasal in nature with two modes of existence: subjective and objective. As David Griffin observes, to be an enduring entity is to be in "*perpetual oscillation* between the two kinds of process, concrescence and transition. The creative advance of the world, therefore, involves a perpetual oscillation between efficient and final causation." (RS 115)

Perpetual oscillation: is this not reminiscent of the reversal of field, from negative to positive, seen in wave propagation as described by quantum theory? Whitehead's two kinds of process, concrescence and transition, reveals another instance of the twofold theme. The whole point of this twofold process is to achieve actuality, over and over and over again, and to each time introduce the possibility for change, for novelty, for adventure.

A Holographic Universe

For Whitehead the universe is not a competitive arena for rugged individualists but a close-knit web of intimate social relationships, so close-knit, in fact, that every item in the universe is involved in the concrescence of each actual entity. In the initial phase of concrescence, an actual entity takes account of, or prehends, all other actual entities in its immediate past. As Whitehead says,

In fact if we allow for degrees of relevance, and for negligible relevance, we must say that every actual entity is present in every other actual entity. The philosophy of organism is mainly devoted to the task of making clear the notion of 'being present in another entity.' (PR 50)

Actual entities are internally related, which means that the relations are essential and constitutive of what each actual entity becomes. To the question, what are actual entities made of—the reply is that they are made of other actual entities, *plus* what they achieve by self-completion. And so, another aspect of what is meant by the word "process" is to say that reality is a *social* process.

Whitehead repeatedly insists that the *entire universe* conspires to create each new actual entity:

The whole world conspires to produce a new creation. It presents to the creative process its opportunities and its limitations. (RM 113)

In the first place, no event can be wholly and solely the cause of another event. The whole antecedent world conspires to produce a new occasion. (MT 164)

Each task of creation is a social effort, employing the whole universe. (PR 223)

If Whitehead is right about this, and also about saying that every actual entity prehends all other actual entities in its immediate past, and this entails that they be present, in their objectified state, in that actual entity, this has a startling implication.

Indeed, philosopher Jorge Luis Nobo takes us for a quantum leap by pointing out that Whitehead's adventurous thinking along these lines anticipates the holographic paradigm. In this light, every actual entity is revealed to contain a "metaphysical hologram" of the entire universe; and thus Nobo says:

. . . the metaphysical chronology and topology of the universe are forever captured and enshrined in . . . its actual occasions.

Noting that the universe is never at a standstill, Nobo qualifies what he means:

[The universe so captured], it must be noted, is a fleeting momentary state of the universe, which, nevertheless, is permanently captured in the crystallized modal structure of [an actual entity's] own extensive standpoint.

Thus, the holographic conception of reality—the conception which physicist David Bohm, psychologist Karl Pribram, and other contemporary scientists are beginning to find so illuminating in their respective disciplines—has been an essential, but generally unacknowledged, ingredient of Whitehead's metaphysical thought since 1924, if not earlier. (WM 327)

Nobo pushes the envelope even further:

. . . the causal objectification of each occasion in [an actual entity's] immediate past presents for [that actual entity] the entire history of the universe up to the birth of the occasion in question, thereby leaving out only some of the information concerning the complete determinateness of its own contemporaries. (WM 328)

And so each momentary throb of actuality constellates within itself a replication, in marvelous miniature, of the entire universe, showing how all things are interdependent, interwoven together in a wonderful pattern of connectedness, a pattern linking all things together in dynamic relatedness.

Not only does an actual entity contain the whole of the past universe, it pervades the whole of the future by passing on what it achieves, an achievement that will be taken account of, or prehended, by all subsequent entities. As a holographic entity, each fleeting pulse of experience is Alpha and Omega, with prehensive roots stretching all the way back to the primordial flaring forth of the universe fifteen billion years ago, and branches of influence reaching forward into the future . . . for as long as forever is.

Of course, some of our poets, especially those of a mystical turn of mind, have previously sounded at least *intimations* of these depths. For example, William Blake begins one of his poems with these lines:

To see a World in a Grain of Sand
And Heaven in a Wild Flower,
Hold infinity in the palm of your hand
And Eternity in an hour.

But even though some mystical poets have glimpsed this, it was left to Whitehead to formulate this penetrating insight into a rigorous metaphysical system that stands up to the rational criteria of consistency, coherence, applicability, and adequacy.

Our Buddhist friends have a wonderful image of the holographic universe. They call it The Jewel Net of Indra. It pictures the cosmos as an infinite network of glittering jewels, all different. In each one we can see the images of all the others reflected. Each image contains an image of all the other jewels; and also the image of the images of the images, and so ad infinitum. The myriad reflections within each jewel are the essence of the jewel itself, without which it cannot exist. Thus, every part of the cosmos reflects, and brings into existence, every other part.

And thus an actual entity is a *holographic* entity whose datum is the boundless universe itself, stretching to the farthest reaches of intergalactic space and back to the beginning of time. If this is true of an actual entity, then it must also be true of our own momentary occasions of experience. This means that the entire universe, as a metaphysical hologram, flashes forth in our unconscious experience a dozen or so times every second.

God and the World

To discuss how God and the world interact, in Whitehead's view, it may be helpful to first say a few words about creativity.

Creativity is so fundamental an idea in process thought that David Griffin argues that there are two ultimates: God *and* creativity. Process denies the idea that only God is creative, or that the creativity of the creatures comes from God. In no way does this deny God's all-surpassing eminence in the creative process, for without God no process would even be possible, creative or otherwise.

Just as there are no actual entities without some degree of creativity, there is no creativity without, or apart from, some actual entity. Apart from God and actual entities, creativity has no actuality of its own, and yet it transcends them both. Whitehead reveals just how interconnected are his three fundamental ideas:

> But, of course, there is no meaning to 'creativity' apart from its 'creatures,' and no meaning to 'God' apart from the 'creativity' and the 'temporal creatures,' and no meaning to the 'temporal creatures' apart from 'creativity' and 'God.' (PR 225)

Again, this is Whitehead's "ontological principle," according to which "there is nothing which floats into the world from nowhere." For Whitehead the ultimate metaphysical category is creativity, the form of forms, and universal of universals. In *Process and Reality*, he writes,

> Neither God, nor the World, reaches static completion. Both are in the grip of the ultimate metaphysical ground, the creative advance into novelty. Either of them, God and the World, is the instrument of novelty for the other. (PR 349)

Creativity is pervasive, spanning the entire spectrum of reality, from God all the way down to atoms, electrons, and quarks, though in these elementary particles the degree of creativity is so minimal as to be almost (but not quite) negligible. This is an aspect of the idea of panexperientialism—that all actual entities or dynamic singulars (units of process that act and feel as one) enjoy experience to some degree.

To be a creature, any creature, is to be creative, is to be a creator, though not of course *the* Creator. And rather than claiming that God is the only Power, process proposes that all creation is co-creation, and that the creative process is just that: a process involving both God and creatures. God does not unilaterally provide any finished products. Jesus made essentially the same point when he said, "My Father worketh hitherto, and I work."

First, God provides the ultimate ground and order necessary for any experience whatsoever to occur. God also begets the subjective immediacy of each beginning actual entity, endows it with possibilities, the freedom to choose among those possibilities, and an aim towards its own self-completion.

From a process perspective, God is always present in the very midst of our becoming, offering perfect possibilities in every new moment for each individual's highest good. Such possibilities Whitehead calls *initial aims*, and these aims are directive and persuasive, but never coercive. And so every becoming occasion begins with God as creative love: everlastingly leading, luring, urging all actualities to new heights of fulfillment and enjoyment.

Whitehead puts it eloquently:

> Every event on its finer side introduces God into the world. The power by which God sustains the world is the power of himself as the ideal. He adds himself to the actual ground from which every creative act takes its rise. The world lives by its incarnation of God in itself. (RM 155-56)

The point to be noticed here is that all creation is co-creation—the co-creation of God *and* the world.

ဆ

In the closing pages of *Process and Reality*, Whitehead presents a litany to this ultimate complementarity of God and the world:

> It is as true to say that God is permanent and the World fluent, as that the World is permanent and God is fluent.
>
> It is as true to say that God is one and the World many, as that the World is one and God many.
>
> It is as true to say that, in comparison with the World, God is actual eminently, as that, in comparison with God, the World is actual eminently.
>
> It is as true to say that the World is immanent in God, as that God is immanent in the World.
>
> It is as true to say that God transcends the World, as that the World transcends God.
>
> It is as true to say that God creates the World, as that the World creates God.

When I first read this it sounded like a paragon of paradox. I thought to myself, this cannot be! But then Whitehead gives an intriguing clue: "The concept of 'God' is the way in which we understand this incredible fact—that what cannot be, yet is." (PR 350) Remember, in Whitehead's view God is dipolar with both an abstract essence and concrete actuality. With this in mind, let's take another look at the second sentence:

> It is as true to say that God is one [as abstract essence] and the World many [the many becoming actualities], as that the World is one [unified in God's concrete actuality] and God many [the many actual entities as they are initially prehended into God's concrete actuality].

The conclusion to be drawn from this I'll phrase in Whiteheadian terms:

It is as true to say that the world requires God, as that God requires the world. It is as true to say that the World cannot exist without God, as that God cannot exist without the world. It is as true to say that God contributes to the World, as that the World contributes to God.

What God contributes to the world are possibilities for actualization; what the world contributes to God is the actualization of those possibilities, possibilities that hitherto God, as abstract essence, had only known abstractly and conceptually.

In the everlasting cosmic rhythm of the many and the one, the many creatures are the source of actualized adventures for the one God just as the one God is the source of possibilities for adventures and novelty for the many creatures. In Whitehead's words:

> The theme of Cosmology, which is the basis of all religions, is the story of the dynamic effort of the World passing into everlasting unity, and of the static majesty of God's vision, accomplishing its purpose of completion by absorption of the World's multiplicity of effort. (PR 349)

A Kalogenic Universe

In his book *Being and Value*, philosopher Frederick Ferré acquaints us with a beautiful idea that he names with a beautiful word: *kalogenesis*. "Kalós" (καλός) is the Greek word for "beauty" and "genesis" of course refers to "generating" or "bringing into existence." And so kalogenesis means the creation or coming to be of beauty. The adjectival form of this word is "kalogenic."

According to Ferré, beauty is omnipresent, everlasting, and present in every momentary flash of actuality. The becoming of any actuality is also the becoming of beauty. In short we live in a kalogenic universe populated by kalogenic entities. To be, on whatever level, from protons to people, is to be a begetter of beauty. It seems Whitehead is in accord with this, for he says:

> The metaphysical doctrine, here expounded, finds the foundations of the world in the aesthetic experience . . . All order is therefore aesthetic order, and the moral order is merely certain aspects of aesthetic order. The actual world is the outcome of the aesthetic order, and the aesthetic order is derived from the immanence of God. (RM 104-05)

> God is the poet of the world, with tender patience leading it by his vision of truth, beauty, and goodness. (PR 346)

In co-creation with God, the fundamental cosmic process, the coming to be of each momentary flash of actuality, represents a real achievement, a flicker of originality, arising out of a feeling, however vague, for a range of possibilities that might have made its existential path otherwise. Adventure is inherent in the very structure of reality.

If, on this hypothesis, the coming to be of every actual entity involves at least some measure of self-completion and, therefore, real freedom, it follows that every occasion is of intrinsic value. Value is inherent in the very texture of reality.

Coming to be always involves the many and the one. In Whitehead's pithy phrase, "The many become one, and are increased by one." This describes a process whereby diversity is made one in a prehensive unification of experience. Probably the most general definition of beauty is "unity in diversity." The culmination of coming to be is a feeling of "satisfaction" upon achieving this accomplishment. It follows that every momentary flash of actuality not only produces beauty, but also "enjoys" the experience of beauty. Beauty is inherent in the most basic dynamics of reality.

The most fundamental process in the universe, the process whereby actuality is attained in each momentary pulse of experience, is a kalogenic process. To be an actual entity is to be a kalogenic entity. The "process" of process philosophy is a *kalogenic* process.

Beauty also has to do with contrasts held together in harmony. The wider the contrast, the more intense the expression and the experience of beauty. In the becoming of every individual there is always, however slight, some feeling of contrast between what is actual and what is possible.

Ferré observes that:

> . . . in its process of becoming actual every fundamental entity must result in a unified harmony of definite elements held together in experience. In this way, every pulse of actualizing energy represents in itself an act of kalogenesis. The universe comprised of kalogenic entities and their combinations is therefore, strictly speaking, the by-product of beauty. (BV 358)

With the advent of sexual reproduction new experiences and expressions of beauty became possible. In Ferré's words:

> Sexual reproduction makes the search for beauty even more intense and gives advantage to decorations, iridescent fins and fine feathers, prowess at dance, attractive odors, and the like, throughout the sexually animated kingdoms, botanical as well as zoological. The universal quest for satisfactory experience, for subjectively enjoyed beauty, draws organisms whether or not their experience (compared to ours) is dim and unselfconscious. At the biological level, we find ourselves within an intensely kalogenic universe. (BV 361-62)

Primordial Trailblazers

From a process perspective, even pre-biotic evolution tells a tale of high adventure. In the beginning of our universe, what science rather unpoetically calls the Big Bang, electrons and protons emerged in a fraction of a second.

Over the course of about 300,000 years these two types of entities enjoyed their own careers, their own individualities, if you will, as they flashed along their solitary quantum ways. But then something exciting happened. For these primordial individuals somehow managed to suddenly weave themselves together into new more complex entities called atoms. The simplest, and probably first to emerge, is the hydrogen atom with a nucleus of one proton and its single electron.

The path leading from electrons and protons to atoms is a creative path, and the ontological principle requires that creativity be explained in terms of actual entities, in this case: electrons and protons. In short, this means that these two were not mere inert particles but throbs of adventurous actuality. It was somehow through their creative interaction, their "decision" for novelty, that a new creature, a new atomic entity, came into being. This is the first social interplay, a romance if you will, between two opposites who continue to attract each other by one of the strongest forces in the universe.

This is an astonishing achievement. The leap from electrons and protons to atoms is a quantum leap of breathtaking beauty, and these two worthy pioneers may be seen as the first trailblazers.

In _The Universe Story_, a book that can be described as deeply kalogenic, cosmologist Brian Swimme and geologian Thomas Berry describe the adventure story of hydrogen in much the same way:

> The universe bloomed into existence, settled on its fundamental laws, and stabilized itself as baryons and simple nuclei. For several hundred thousand years it expanded and cooled and then, in an instant, at the very end of the fireball, the universe transformed itself into the primordial atoms of hydrogen and helium. Our wandering proton snapped into a new relationship with one of the erstwhile freely interacting electrons. These bonded relationships were impossible during the violent former eras, but now they became the predominant mode of reality.

> The creation of the atoms is as stunning as the creation of the universe. Nothing in the previous several hundred thousand years presaged their emergence. These dynamic twists of being leapt out of the originating mystery and immediately organized

the universe in a fresh way. Is it the electron trapping a proton? Or vice versa?

It is rather an event initiated by the universe, and completed by the mysterious emergent being we call hydrogen, a new identity that has the power to seal a proton and an electron into a seamless community. (US 29)

In a creative explosion, other new atomic entities quickly followed, bringing forth all the basic atoms, the elements that make up the periodic table. And from these arose molecules and macromolecules, one of stunning beauty and complexity we now call DNA.

A hydrogen atom, with its union of one electron and one proton, is perhaps the simplest exemplification of unity and diversity, and shows forth a simple beauty. And thus it can be readily seen that kalogenic entities were present, and prolific, at the very birth of the universe. The scientists of today no longer see atoms as inert bits of matter. For example, here's how Swimme and Berry describe the simple helium atom.

In actuality each helium atom roars with activity. In the time it takes a human to sneeze, a single helium atom has had to organize a billion different evanescent events to establish its helium presence in the world. Just one of its accomplishments is to keep its electrons free from interacting with most of the photons rushing at it. To exist as an invisible gas is a major achievement, one requiring instant-by-instant action, an accomplishment that transformed the universe. (US 33)

Mozartian Moments

And, speaking of accomplishments that transform the universe— The musical genius of Mozart is legendary . . . astonishing . . . breathtaking.

When creating his music, Mozart never wrote rough drafts that he later polished to perfection. All who observed him at work agree that he could sit down and dash off a musical composition, in its final form, as easily as we might sit down and dash off a grocery list.

He was able to do this because he sometimes conceived an entire movement of a symphony in one single creative thought. Like a beautiful orchid springing into full bloom all at once, in the twinkling of an eye, the whole movement came to him as a unity of experience "in one magnificent moment of musical meaning."

We all have experienced magnificent moments, though probably to a lesser degree than this, and Frederick Ferré calls such experiences "Mozartian moments." These moments have an intrinsic value in themselves; they glow, as Ferré says, with their own worth. When they come to us, in their flashes of momentary splendor, we know truly that our "cups runneth over."

Although they can aspire to intense elevation, Mozartian moments are grounded in the body, for they come charged with deep feeling, and are made possible by the human brain which, as Ferré reminds us, is "the most complex system in the known universe."

Mozartian moments are integrative—not only do contrasting elements come together, but they are held together in a momentary embrace revealing aesthetic richness and intensity of experience: a unity of diversity, a unity of contrasts. The greater the contrast, the more the intensity. They are adventures of novelty, revealing exciting new vistas, or breakthrough insights, evoking feelings of freshness, zest, and vitality.

Mozartian moments are among our highest experiences of beauty . . . and thus intensely kalogenic. Their beauty sparkles. They come "trailing clouds of glory" and are part of what make us unique as humans.

And so in conclusion, I make this wish: may your Mozartian moments be many, and may there be one that stands out above all. And may that one be an adventure of the spirit, of such breathtaking beauty that it transforms the universe!

Key to Abbreviations

SC Chardin, Teilhard de. *Science and Christ.*

CN Cobb, John B. *A Christian Natural Theology: Based on the Thought of Alfred North Whitehead.*

RE Cooper, Robert M. "God as Poet and Person at Prayer," *Religious Experience and Process Theology*, Ed. Harry James Cargas and Bernard Lee.

BV Ferré, Frederick. *Being and Value: Toward a Constructive Postmodern Metaphysics.*

FC Griffin, David Ray, John B. Cobb, Marcus P. Ford, Pete A. Gunter, and Peter Ochs. *Founders of Constructive Postmodern Philosophy: Peirce, James, Bergson, Whitehead, and Hartshorne.*

RS Griffin, David Ray. *Religion Without Supernaturalism: A Process Philosophy of Religion.*

UW Griffin, David Ray. *Unsnarling the World-Knot: Consciouness, Freedom, and the Mind-Body Problem.*

BH Hartshorne, Charles. *Beyond Humanism.*

WM Nobo, Jorge Luis. *Whitehead's Metaphysics of Extension and Solidarity.*

US Swimme, Brian & Thomas Berry. *The Universe Story: From the Primordial Flaring Forth to the Ecozoic Era.*

AI Whitehead, Alfred North. *Adventures of Ideas.*

MT Whitehead, Alfred North. *Modes of Thought.*

PR Whitehead, Alfred North. *Process and Reality.* Corrected Edition. Ed. David Ray Griffin and Donald W. Sherburne.

RM Whitehead, Alfred North. *Religion in the Making.*

Appendix A

Whitehead's Six Main Principles

In his Harvard lectures of 1926-27, Whitehead announced "the six main principles of my metaphysics":

1. The principle of solidarity. Every actual entity requires all other entities, actual or ideal, in order to exist.
2. The principle of creative individuality. Every actual entity is a process which is its own result, depending on its own limitations.
3. The principle of efficient causation. Every actual entity by the fact of its own individuality contributes to the character of processes which are actual entities superseding itself.
4. The ontological principle. The character of creativity is derived from its own creatures and expressed by its own creatures.
5. The principle of esthetic individuality. Every actual entity is an end in itself for itself, involving its measure of self-satisfaction individual to itself and constituting the result of itself-as-process.
6. The principle of ideal comparison. Every creature involves in its own constitution an ideal reference to ideal creatures: (1) in ideal relationship to each other, and (2) in comparison with its own self-satisfaction.

Process Studies 4, no. 3. (Fall 1974): 204.

Appendix B

Ideas and Theses of Process Philosophers

A. Process Philosophers of the Past
  A — Samuel Alexander (1859-1938)
  B — Henri Bergson (1859-1941)
  Bou — Emile Boutroux (1845-1921)
  Bu — Buddhists (ca. 100-)
  D — John Dewey (1859-1952)
  F — G. T. Fechner (1801-1884)
  H — David Hume (171 1-1777)
  J — William James (1842-1910)
  L — Jules Lequier (1814-1862)
  M — Karl Marx (1818-1883)
  N — Friedrich Nietzsche (1844-1900)
  NB — Nicolas Berdyaev (1874-1948)
  P — C. S. Peirce (1839-1912)
  S — Fausto Socinus (1539-1604)
  Sch — F. W. J. von Schelling (1775-1854)
  W —A. N. Whitehead (1861-1947)
  WPM — Wm. Pepperell Montague (1873-1953)

There is a case for including Hegel in the above list. Indeed, since Kant, and with the exceptions of Bradley, Royce, Russell, Nicolai Hartmann, Santayana, Weiss, and Findlay, metaphysics or speculative philosophy has been almost exclusively process philosophy, taking the term in a broad sense. Yet the critics of metaphysics tend to ignore process philosophers, among whom Croce, Collingwood, and Heidegger should probably be included. Several thinkers in modern India, e.g., Sri Jiva, Mukerji, and Iqbal, could be added. Also Renouvier and Teilhard de Chardin in France; DeWitt H. Parker and E. S. Brightman in the United States; and, with more reservations, Bernardino Varisco in Italy.

B. Common Theses (accepted, or at least not denied, by all or most process thinkers).

1. Becoming includes being; there is a partly new universe each time it is referred to.

2. The future is really open or partly indeterminate (even for God: F, L, NB, S, P, W, WPM).

3. Causal determinism is not absolute; creative freedom (not fully determined, though influenced, by causal conditions) is real: B, Bou, D, F, J, L, N, NB, P, S, W, WPM.

4. "Substance" is defined through "event" or "process", and not vice versa: A, Bu, D, H, J, M, N, W.

5. The laws of nature evolve: B, Bou, P, W.

6. Experience (human or nonhuman) is coextensive with reality (psychical or nonmaterialistic monism, panpsychism or psychicalism). Exceptions: D, M; not decided or clear: J, L, NB.

7. Memory, as givenness of the past, is basic in reality. Especially B, P, W.

8. There are both internal and external relations, both dependence and independence (moderate pluralism). Especially J, P, W.

9. Social relations are pervasive in experience and reality: P ("agapism"), W ("feeling of feeling").

10. Self-interest is *not* the principle of all motivation or the justification of altruism: Bu, H, M, P, W.

11. Some version of the pragmatic theory of meaning is correct: D, J, M, N, P, W.

12. The "ontological principle" (W) that universals, abstractions, are real only in concrete actualities (Aristotle) seems to be affirmed, at least implicitly, in all process philosophies.

13. God is in some aspect in process and is influenced by the creatures: A, F, J, L, NB, P, S, Sch, W, WPM. Nontheists: D, M, N; undecided: H.

14. Aesthetic categories are primary: B, P, W.

15. There are incompossible but genuine values: NB, W.

Charles Hartshorne, "Ideas and Theses of Process Philosophers," *Two Process Philosophers: Hartshorne's Encounter with Whitehead*, Lewis Ford, Ed., 100-01.

Appendix C

Core Doctrines of Process Philosophy

1. The integration of moral, aesthetic, and religious intuitions with the most general doctrines of the sciences into a self-consistent worldview as one of the central tasks of philosophy in our time.
2. Hard-core commonsense notions as the ultimate test of the adequacy of a philosophical position.
3. Whitehead's nonsensationist doctrine of perception, according to which sensory perception is a secondary mode of perception, being derivative from a more fundamental, nonsensory "prehension."
4. Panexperientialism with organizational duality, according to which all true individuals—as distinct from aggregational societies—have at least some iota of experience and spontaneity (self-determination).
5. The doctrine that all enduring individuals are serially ordered societies of momentary "occasions of experience."
6. The doctrine that all actual entities have internal as well as external relations.
7. The Whiteheadian version of naturalistic theism, according to which a Divine Actuality acts variably but never supernaturally in the world.
8. Doubly Dipolar Theism.
9. The provision of cosmological support for the ideals needed by contemporary civilization as one of the chief purposes of philosophy in our time.
10. A distinction between verbal statements (sentences) and propositions and between both of these and propositional feelings.

David Ray Griffin, *Reenchantment Without Supernaturalism*, 5-7

Appendix D

Books by Whitehead and Hartshorne

ALFRED NORTH WHITEHEAD (1861-1947)

The Aims of Education. 1929. New York: Free Press, 1967.

Adventures of Ideas. 1933. New York: Free Press, 1967.

The Concept of Nature. Cambridge: Cambridge UP, 1920.

Essays in Science and Philosophy. New York: Philosophical Library, 1947.

The Function of Reason. 1929. Boston: Beacon, 1958.

Interpretation of Science. Ed. A. H. Johnson. Indianapolis: Bobbs-Merrill, 1961.

Modes of Thought. 1938. New York: Free Press, 1968.

The Organisation of Thought. London: Williams and Norgate, 1917.

Principia Mathematica with Bertrand Russell. 2 ed. Cambridge: Cambridge UP, 1929.

An Enquiry Concerning the Principles of Natural Knowledge. Cambridge: Cambridge UP, 1919.

Process and Reality. 1929. Corrected Edition. Ed. David Ray Griffin and Donald W. Sherburne. New York: Free Press, 1978.

The Principle of Relativity. Cambridge: Cambridge UP, 1922.

Religion in the Making. 1926. New York: Fordham UP, 1996.

Symbolism: Its Meaning and Effect. New York: Macmillan, 1927.

Science and the Modern World. 1925. New York: Free Press, 1967.

CHARLES HARTSHORNE (1897-2000)

Anselm's Discovery. La Salle: Open Court, 1965.

Aquinas to Whitehead: Seven Centuries of Metaphysics of Religion. Milwaukee: Marquette University Publications, 1976.

Beyond Humanism: Essays in the New Philosophy of Nature. 1937. Gloucester: Peter Smith, 1975.

Born to Sing: An Interpretation and World Survey of Bird Song. Bloomington: Indiana UP, 1973.

Creativity in American Philosophy. Albany: State U of New York P, 1984.

Creative Synthesis and Philosophic Method. 1970. Lanham: UP of America, 1983.

The Darkness and the Light. Albany: State U of New York P, 1990.

The Divine Relativity: A Social Conception of God. New Haven: Yale UP, 1983.

Insights and Oversights of Great Thinkers: An Evaluation of Western Philosophy. Albany: State U of New York P, 1983.

The Logic of Perfection and Other Essays in Neoclassical Metaphysics. La Salle: Open Court, 1962.

Man's Vision of God and the Logic of Theism. 1941. Hamden: Archon, 1964.

A Natural Theology for Our Time. La Salle: Open Court, 1967.

Omnipotence and Other Theological Mistakes. Albany: State U of New York P, 1984.

The Philosophy and Psychology of Sensation. 1934. Port Washington, N.Y.: Kennikat, 1968.

Philosophers Speak of God with William Reese 1953. Chicago: Midway Reprints, 1976.

Reality as Social Process: Studies in Metaphysics and Religion. 1953. New York: Hafner, 1971.

Whitehead and the Modern World (with Victor Lowe and A. H. Johnson) (1950). New York: Books for Libraries, 1972.

Whitehead's Philosophy: Selected Essays, 1935-1970. Lincoln: U of Nebraska P, 1972.

Wisdom as Moderation: A Philosophy of the Middle Way. Albany State U of New York P, 1987.

The Zero Fallacy and Other Essays in Neoclassical Philosophy. Ed. Mohammed Valady. La Salle: Open Court, 1997.

The Unity of Being. Doctoral Dissertation, Harvard University. 1923. Ed. Randall E. Auxier and Hyatt Carter. Forthcoming. La Salle: Open Court.

God in Three Questions

I

Is God a Principle or a Person?

To the claim that God is a principle, a primary objection would be that a *principle* is an abstraction. What seems to me one of Whitehead's most unassailable insights states that only actualities can act.[1] Abstractions simply have no agency. Can "creativity" create? Can "liberty" free anyone? Can "prosperity" put money in your pocket? Language shows its wisdom here, for there's a word for this, *reification*, that means to treat an abstraction as if it concretely exists. "Creativity" creates only when instantiated in some actuality. If this analysis is correct, we can only conclude that God, *as principle*, cannot act.

God has an abstract essence, true, but as the word *abstract* implies, this essence is abstracted from God's concrete actuality. The word "abstract" derives from two Latin roots that mean "to draw from, or separate."

David Griffin puts it this way:

"The abstract essence of God is analogous to what we call the 'character' of a human being, meaning that set of characteristics that remains virtually the same day after day, month after month, while the person lives through millions of experiences, these occasions of experience being the 'concrete states' in which the abstract essence is exemplified now in this way, now in that. The difference, which is why we have here only an analogy, is that a human being's personality can change whereas the abstract essence of God is strictly immutable. One attribute of God's abstract essence, for example, is omniscience, the characteristic of knowing everything knowable at any given time. God's concrete *knowledge* grows, insofar as new events happen which add new knowable things to the universe. But the abstract attribute of *omniscience*—the attribute of always knowing everything that is (then) knowable—is exemplified in every concrete state of the divine existence. In Hartshorne's writings, 'dipolar theism' always refers to this distinction between the abstract essence and the concrete states of God, which provides a coherent way of distinguishing that aspect of God that does not change from that which does."[2]

Hartshorne observes that the universe, thus far, has evolved no experience of wholeness, or integration on a complex level, that goes beyond that of personality[3] or, in more precise terms, what he (and Whitehead) call a "living person." Does this not suggest that person, suitably qualified, rather than principle, comes closer to the character of a God whom we feel to be loving, relational, and, above all, worshipful? What is there to worship in the icy absolute of an abstraction?

Indeed, it took *fifteen billion years* for God and the world to co-create the human "living person" so it must be of exceptional worth and precious value.

To say that God is a person does not mean that there is a point-to-point correspondence between human personhood and the personhood of God. Far from it. If we affirm that evolution really means *creative* advance, then human personhood is asymptotic to the personhood that God enjoys.[4]

Unlike pantheism, which says that God is everything, panentheism says that all things are in God and God is in all things. Following Saint Paul, who affirms that "we are members one of another,"[5] and going even farther, I affirm that "mutual immanence is the *universal* theme."[6] We live in a universe that is deeply and inwardly relational. In the process view, our *personal* relationship with God is not only deep and inward, it is inextricable.

Moreover, if we are to enjoy an I-Thou relationship with God, especially in our deeply felt prayers, and if, like Jesus, we are to enjoy a relationship of such intimacy that we address God as *Abba*, or "Papa," how can this be except in a *personal* relationship?

It would seem more accurate to say not that God *is* principle, but that God *exemplifies* principles. In a statement often quoted, Whitehead tells us that, "God is not to be treated as an exception to all metaphysical principles, invoked to save their collapse. He is their chief exemplification."[7]

A final thought:

There is a type of reality that everlastingly exists and is the locus of all power in this universe, or in any other universe that could possibly exist. God is the unsurpassable, but self-surpassing, exemplification of this reality, but there are many others, including all the natural unities such as subatomic particles, atoms, molecules, living cells, animals, and the *human soul,* which is the most complex and powerful *earthly* exemplification of this reality. The One is never without the many; that is, although it may be in a state of maximal entropic disorder, God is never without a "universe" of some sort. The story of co-creation in Genesis begins not with God creating a world out of *nothingness,* but with an evocation that begins to draw order out of an *already-existing chaos.*

II

Does God Have a Future?

This question presents an ambiguity that reveals at least two questions, at one and the same time. The least interesting has to do with Nietzsche's assertion that "God is dead,"[8] a bold claim that summarily denies God any future—period! Far more interesting are the entwined questions of whether God is, in an important sense, temporal . . . and whether God is wholly, and without qualification, immutable.

For two thousand years or more the Holy Reality has been almost exclusively defined by all those icy Absolutes attributed to Her long ago by a stubborn masculine and patriarchal bias. When the "wheels of thought" run in deep ruts, it's hard to get them going in a new direction.

In the divine cry of our time, Our Lady of Process, the new womanly God, who, through her boundless love, is as intimate with each one of us as mother with fetus, as Madonna and Child, calls out for a new name and a reattribution of all Her "yin" virtues.

After discussing how, in Oriental thought, the great Tao is often compared to water, Charles Hartshorne makes a revealing observation: that it is a typically Western idea to exalt "masculine mastery, power, stability, control, being, absoluteness, while depreciating the feminine: yielding, passive, fluid—that is, becoming and relativity."[9]

What is it to say that someone is "relative"? In a process world, it is merely to say that he or she is "rich in relations." God, then, as the great example, not the great exception, to metaphysical principles, is said to be surrelative: supremely relative and wondrously rich in relations, both giving and receiving influence to and from all actualities throughout the vast universe. This supports the perennial intuition that God is love—love in the most fundamental sense, that is, a sympathetic love that shares and feels the feelings of others: rejoicing in their joys and sorrowing with them in their sorrows. This is a rejection of the purely impassive God of medieval theology and Aristotle's so-called "Unmoved Mover," to whom the apocalyptic suffering of the Jewish Holocaust would cause not so much as a single blip on the Divine Sonar.

One of our great mystic poets suggests that, far from being unmoved by our suffering, God is the best- and the most-moved mover:

> O! he gives to us his joy
> That our grief he may destroy;
> Till our grief is fled and gone
> He doth sit by us and moan.[10]

And stop for a moment and reflect on what has been called the two most moving words in the Gospels: Jesus wept.[11]

III

Did God Create Once and for All?
During the 300-year reign of science over which the analytical spirit of Sir Isaac Newton presided, the universe was viewed as a gigantic clockwork machine, ticking away in timeless perfection, a perfection created once and for all by God, who then stepped back, according to that view, to dispassionately contemplate his handiwork for all eternity.[12]

The world the scientist looked out upon was, in essence, a fixed world, a changeless world, governed by immutable laws. It was a predictable world of force and matter, ruled by a rigid determinism, a mechanical world of billiard-ball cause and effect. And back of it all, a changeless God—Aristotle's Unmoved Mover.

With the publication in 1859 of his book *On the Origin of Species*, Charles Darwin tossed a monkey-wrench in that colossal machine, for he hypothesized the evolution of organic life on this planet.[13] And evolution presupposes not only change, but *creative* change.

On the macrocosmic level, Newton's "machine" was effectively dismantled with the appearance of Einstein's Special Theory of Relativity in 1905, and, on the microcosmic level of atoms and subatomic particles, with the later development of Quantum Theory.

But Newton's well-oiled machine did not really grind to a halt until a new cosmology was conceived. This revolutionary new cosmology sees the universe not as a clockwork machine, but as organic. The entire universe is throbbing with life, a life that expresses as continuous creative advance in the vast evolutionary saga.

Did you ever stop and wonder why God chose to create the universe by the long, long way of evolution (15 billion years and counting), rather than creating it once and for all?[14] If this could have been accomplished in a shorter period of time, or even by a simple unilateral divine fiat (Let there be!), then why didn't God take the shorter route? The process answer is that evolution, guided not by *coercion* but by *persuasive love*, is the shortest route that is metaphysically possible, even for God. This is no diminishment of God, or God's power, but rather his exaltation as "poet of the world, with tender patience leading it by his vision of truth, beauty, and goodness."[15] Whitehead sums it up in a soul-stirring epiphany: "The power of God is the worship he inspires."[16]

To create once and for all would be to create a completed product, a static universe, a clockwork universe, a mechanical universe—the very universe, in fact, that Newton described. "May God us keep from Single vision & Newton's sleep!" cried out another Englishman, the great mystic William Blake.[17]

Another reason for the long, long way is what may be called the *order of actualization*. Chimpanzees cannot evolve directly from cockroaches, or Einstein could not have suddenly showed up among the ancient Sumerians. The technology of the aerospace industry presupposes many other more basic technologies that must precede the advent of airplanes or space shuttles.[18] Far from our possibilities being unlimited or infinite, we humans are constrained within the limits of this order of actualization. What even God can accomplish in any new moment is largely, but not completely, determined by what has been accomplished in preceding moments. This does not mean that great, wonderful, and even astonishing things cannot happen; what it does mean is that a certain level of continuity seems to be the general rule. Process thought does allow for what are called "saltations" (or "big jumps") in evolutionary theory, in the history of ideas, in personal transformation, and in healing. But analysis will reveal an underlying continuity even here so as to avoid any suggestion of "supernatural" events.

And so . . . creation continues—forevermore!

Endnotes

1. This is Whitehead's Ontological Principle.

2. David Ray Griffin, _Reenchantment without Supernaturalism: A Process Philosophy of Religion_, 158-59.

3. Over his long life, philosopher Charles Hartshorne consistently presented a case for God not as impersonal or the unmoved mover but as the Personality most rich in relations. He liked to quote Rabbi Heschel that "God is the most moved mover." Even as early as his Harvard dissertation, he was saying, "Person as a legal concept is a highly abstract term, but personality in the end is the richest and most concrete of all ideas." And then in his autobiography, _The Darkness and the Light_, 67 years later: "I held that the idea of a personal God was not simply an illusion, that personality is our best sample of reality and value and could not be simply set aside in trying to conceive the cosmic, universal, and supreme form of existence."

4. In his book, _Creative Synthesis and Philosophic Method_, page 155, Hartshorne writes, "Brunner, I think, has suggested or implied that it is God who is unqualifiedly personal, and human beings are only imperfect, fragmentary pointers towards true personality."

5. Ephesians 4:25.

6. This quote is from my poem, "Process and Presence," and is the concluding sentence of this verse:

Every new moment, in a twinkling of eyes,
Numberless minds perish, and as quickly arise.
Fresh in the flow of this interweaving stream,
Mutual immanence is the universal theme.

The complete poem can be found at the end of "An Introduction to Process Thought in Five Easy Pieces."

7. Alfred North Whitehead, *Process and Reality*, Corrected Edition edited by David Ray Griffin and Donald W. Sherburne, 343.

8. The divine death sentence, "God is dead!" reverberates in two of Nietzsche's books, *The Gay Science* and *Thus Spoke Zarathustra*, and the passages wherein both occur can be found in *The Portable Nietzsche*, edited and translated by Walter Kaufmann, on pages 95 and 202.

9. Hartshorne, *Anselm's Discovery*, 147.

10. William Blake, *Songs of Innocence*.

11. John 11:35.

12. James Joyce describes it nicely: "The artist, like the God of creation, remains within or behind or beyond or above his handiwork, invisible, refined out of existence, indifferent, paring his fingernails." *A Portrait of the Artist as a Young Man*, 252.

13. One of several "decentering" episodes in our history: Before Copernicus, people *thought* the Earth was the center of the universe. Before Darwin, people *thought* that humankind was a special creation, somehow set apart from the rest of animal life. Before Freud, people *thought* that they were the conscious masters of their own personal lives.

14. A perspective on our place in the cosmic scheme of things can be gained by reflecting on how late we showed up in the evolutionary timeline. In *The Universe Story*, by Brian Swimme and Thomas Berry, the authors state that *Homo sapiens*, our species, made their first appearance a mere two hundred thousands years ago. Given that the physicists now place the age of universe at 15 billion years, the ratio that shows the proportional amount of time we've been here is:

$$200,000/15,000,000,000$$

The equivalent of this in decimal expression is:

.0000133

To scale this to the dimension of a single day, we first multiply 24 times 60 times 60 to get the number of seconds in a day, or:

86,400

And, secondly, multiplying 86,400 by .0000133 gives us the proportional amount of time, on this scale, that we, as a species, have been here, or:

1.149 seconds

Or, if you have a scientific calculator on your computer, you can do it in three remarkably swift steps and come up with a slightly more precise figure, which is: 1.152—but it still boils down to approximately one second. And is there not a wonderful, a radical humility, in knowing that, if the 15-billion-year history of the universe is scaled down to the dimension of a single day, we, *Homo sapiens*, arrived on the scene at one second before midnight? One second! On this scale, Creation has been going on for 23 hours, 59 minutes, and 59 seconds—and we show up only during the last second.

15. Whitehead, *Process and Reality*, 346.

16. Whitehead, *Science and the Modern World*, 192.

17. This exclamation is the final sentence in a poem that Blake included in a letter he wrote to Thomas Butts on November 22, 1802. One source for this letter is *Selected Poetry and Prose of Blake*, edited with an Introduction by Northrop Frye, 417-20.

18. Even great ideas have developmental steps. For example, the theory of evolution didn't suddenly appear full bloom in the mind of Darwin. The germ of the idea is present at least as early as the writings of Plotinus (205-270) with his notion of the great hierarchy of being. But Plotinus conceived this hierarchy in essentially static terms, as if given all at once. It was left for Leibniz (1646-1716)

to add a temporal dimension and to see the great hierarchy as developing over vast stretches of time. As Ken Wilber points out, "Plotinus temporalized = evolution."

The Revolution in Metaphysics: A Mandate for Rethinking Religious Science

Announcing the Revolution

One of the brightest luminaries of the twentieth century, who lived to the ripe old age of 103 years, was a philosopher who helped to overturn some of the longest-standing errors in philosophy, theology, and metaphysics. The philosopher is Charles Hartshorne, and he has been hailed as the Einstein of religious thought.

Born in 1897, Hartshorne may become the only major philosopher to have lived in three different centuries. So far as I know, he is the only philosopher to have published a new book in his hundredth year. He credits to his longevity, which he calls his secret weapon, some of his most important insights into tenaciously held errors in philosophy and religion. I have found that I held some of these errors, and you might be interested in finding out whether there are any that you may hold.

Proclaiming a brave new world in metaphysics, Charles Hartshorne wrote: "theology is now passing through its profoundest revolution since the early Christian Era. There has, in fact, been a basic revolution in metaphysics, quite as revolutionary as the revolution in physics. If classical physics has been permanently superseded, so for many of us has classical theology, or philosophy of religion." [1,2,3]

Hartshorne suggests that for a metaphysician or student of religion to ignore this revolution is on a par with a scientist choosing to ignore Relativity Theory or Quantum Mechanics. Some key aspects of the Revolution are:

1) the idea that creativity is the ultimate principle, that creative becoming is primary, that becoming is more fundamental than, and inclusive of, mere being,

2) a radical rethinking of three fundamental ideas of classical metaphysics: substance, causality, and God,

3) a new vision of God: that qualifies the medieval idea of God as the God of Negation and High Abstractions,

4) that we have been misled for centuries by the Greek ideal of the glorification of abstractions,

5) the social structure of all experience, including that of deity,

6) a new logic of theism and metaphysics, a logic of relations that reveals two crucial insights: (a) the axiom of polarity, or ultimate contrasts, and (b) a basic asymmetry in the scheme of things,

7) the disclosure of much upside-down thinking in the history of human thought, or what might be called the theme of "getting it exactly backwards,"

8) a recognition, in light of the science of our day, that the idea of immutable law is antiquated if not obsolete, and that the new idea is that laws are not exact and everlasting, but statistical and probabilistic, and that laws can evolve like anything else,

9) the necessity of taking time as seriously as the timeless,

And finally:

10) a higher synthesis of some of the scattered verities and truths long known by humankind.

Although I will not have time to cover all these, they will, perhaps, give some idea of the scope of the Revolution.

The Medieval (and Modern) Misconception of God

In Religious Science,[4] God is often identified with abstractions such as Being, the Absolute, and Pure Actuality, or with negations like non-temporal, immutable, and infinite. With help from Aristotle and his Unmoved Mover, this is the idea of God proposed by Medieval Theology, and the idea has gone relatively unchallenged for, lo, these many centuries.

That Religious Science is infatuated with abstractions is clearly shown in the tendency to further "abstractify" an already adequate abstraction. Thus, instead of the words "being" and "living," we hear talk of "beingness," "livingness," and so forth. The word "being" is already a static abstraction or concept, and to add a "-ness" only makes it more so. Are we suffering a hangover from what Hartshorne has called the Greek "intoxication with abstractions"?

Is it not interesting (and a little disturbing) that the God the atheists seem to find good reason to reject is the same God the medieval theologians would have us believe in and worship? That is, God conceived wholly and exclusively in absolute or abstract terms.

A process metaphysics holds that the God of worship is not to be found in an abstraction or in a mere negation. And Charles Hartshorne, not mincing words, claims that a negative theology is a subtle form of atheism. To exalt being over becoming, the absolute over the relative, the abstract over the concrete—when the medieval theologians first began doing this centuries ago, and when someone does it today, a process metaphysics would caution that they have it exactly backwards. More about this later when we get to the "logic of ultimate contrasts."

Omnipotence

A slogan often heard in Religious Science is "God is the only Presence and the only Power." Socrates said that the unexamined life is not worth living. Could it be, perhaps, that the unexamined slogan may not be worth believing? For does this curious idea, God is the only power, really qualify as anything more than a mere slogan?

If we human creatures have any degree of self-determination, then God cannot be the only power. If God is the only power, period, then we live, or better, we exist, or go through the vacuous motions of existing, in a preprogrammed, deterministic universe. If God is the only power, then he has power over—what? Nothing worth having power over, so far as I can see. For what value is a block universe with countless entities who themselves have zero power?

In theory, perhaps, maybe, just maybe, people may profess belief in the abstract idea that "God is the only power," or while under the hypnotic influence of this mantra, or slogan, they may profess so to believe, but I submit that in the actual practice of everyday life, and in the presuppositions that underlie that practice, nobody seriously doubts that there are many centers of power (other than God's), and that each and every human is one of those centers.

What logical sense is there in having power over creatures who are themselves completely powerless? Analysis shows that this is really a non-idea. If God is omnipotent, that is, if God is the only power, (the only power—period!), then we are faced with the interesting but inescapable conclusion that it is impossible to disobey God's will. And there can be no talk about choosing what we do, for choice implies power, and we have already stipulated that there is only one power: God's.

The omnipotence idea opens the door for one contradiction after another, not the least of which is the following: that if God is the only power, then when we are worshipping God, this becomes not the worship of God by us, but God worshipping God.

After discussing how, in Oriental thought, the great Tao is often compared to water, Hartshorne makes the revealing observation that it is a typically Western idea to exalt "'masculine' mastery, power, stability, control, being, absoluteness, while depreciating the feminine, yielding, passive, fluid—that is, becoming and relativity."[5]

In view of what seems, in Religious Science, a bias for absolute terms in defining the idea of God, this makes me wonder whether we are paying more than lip-service in all our talk about a Father-Mother God.

Can we not simply say that God's power must excel all other, that the divine power is the highest conceivable form of power, that God's power is beyond question the greatest power, exponentially greater beyond imagination than any other power—and still say that even the greatest power is still one power among many? If the creatures have no power, then: no freedom, no creativity, no world, in fact, at least no world worth talking about.

Omniscience

Are there some things that even God can't know? The process answer is a clear Yes.

God knows all there is to know, but some things are just not there to know, such as my future decisions. The possible cannot be known as actual until a concrete decision is made that makes it actual. If God knows my decisions before I make them, then it is God who is doing the deciding, not me. Just as no parent I know of would wish to make all the decisions for a beloved child, how much less would the all-loving and all-wise Father-Mother God wish to make all decisions for the creatures.

If our decisions and, hence, our freedom, count for anything more than sheer illusion, then what _is to be_ decided remains in the realm of possibility until what _is_ decided is made actual when the decision is made. How, in any coherent sense that avoids double-talk, can the fully actual be known, even by deity, before it _is_ fully actual?

This is not a new idea. The Socinians long ago proposed that "the highest conceivable from of knowledge is of the past-and-definite _as_ past-and-definite, and of the future and partly indefinite _as_ future and partly indefinite."[6]

Some of you right now may be wondering about precognition. But do accounts of precognition ever give us the fully actual, or rather dim outlines? The President will be assassinated, rather than President Lincoln will be shot in the head by John Wilkes Booth at about 10:30 at night on Good Friday, April 14, 1865 while watching the performance of a comic melodrama, _Our American Cousin_, at Ford's Theater in Washington, and will die the next morning at 7:20 AM.

Precognition may be possible because we live in an almost—but not quite—deterministic world where causal laws and the past pretty well determine what happens. Thus we have relative determinism, or relative indeterminism, whichever you care to choose, since they both amount to the same thing. This may, at times, make for things, or events, that are highly predictable, but to say that something is highly predictable is not to say that it is wholly so, even for God. In this, and in the "not quite" of the first sentence, resides the glorious word "freedom."

Another variation of this error is that God exists in a timeless realm wherein, with divine foresight, he knows all our future actions spread out before the divine gaze as one totality. Not only does this view commit the fallacy of what Bergson calls "the spatialization of time," it also does not take into account the process view that there is no such totality, but a new totality in every new moment. In a very real sense, every single time you utter the word "cosmos," you're referring to a new cosmos. Likewise with the word, "God." Meister Eckhart has a wonderful saying that God is always *novissimus*, the newest of the new. At any given moment, it is God's singular distinction that he is both the youngest *and* the oldest of all beings.

God As Immutable

If reality is productive of novelty, and how can this be denied, and if God is the all-inclusive reality, how without contradiction can we say that God is not changed by this addition of novelty? Hartshorne apparently agrees, for he says: "God is no mere whole, complete once for all. If each of us is a new whole every new moment, then much more so is God, whose increase is uniquely eminent since it is inclusive of all the increase there is."[7]

If God loves all creatures, then, with the appearance of a new creature, that love must change to include and appreciate that creature. If God is immutable, then it seems logically necessary to deny that God has experience, for is it not obvious that the notion of "immutable experience" is self-contradictory?

It is far from obvious that the so-called idea or ideal of immutability is always a positive value. The movie *Groundhog Day*, starring Bill Murray, seems to suggest that the realm of the unchanging, or ceaseless repetition, may be more hellish than heavenly. Sartre's *No Exit* is another variation on this time-honored theme.

If process is primary, then, in Paul Weiss's words: "To be is to be *in*complete."[8] And this applies to all levels of reality, from electrons, to the human, and even the divine. And who, really, would wish to have it otherwise? To be complete is to be finished. Done. Who wants that?

God in Neoclassical Metaphysics

One of the problems with the medieval idea of God is that, according to process philosophy, at best it is only a half-truth and tells only half the story. While there is an abstract essence of God that is wholly absolute, necessary, and immutable, God, as a concrete actuality, is, in a uniquely excellent way, also relative, contingent, and subject to change.

God as a concrete actuality is the living God who inspires worship, devotion, and our unstinted love, the God who loves all creatures, rejoicing in their joys, suffering in their sorrows, the inclusive God who contains and perfectly knows and appreciates all creatures, God as a loving and relational Thou in place of the medieval God of High Abstractions—the It defined as Absolute, Immutable, Infinite . . . and the long litany of abstractions that characterize the God of a negative theology.

From a process perspective, God is not wholly immutable but is, in a sense, the individual most open to change. This follows, by any logic I know, from the idea that God is all-inclusive.

The God of process is the all-surpassing God, unsurpassable by all conceivable others, but everlastingly self-surpassing in terms of endless growth and enrichment through his own inexhaustible creativity and the creative enrichment contributed by all creatures, both great and small. To some of us, this seems a far more glorious idea than the static and one-sided idea of God as wholly immutable.

Process philosophy holds that all actual entities, without exception, are dipolar, in that they have both backward-looking physical and forward-looking mental poles. If reality on all levels is essentially dipolar, is this perhaps one nuance of why we now have two physics to describe that reality? For there is indeed not one, but two physics—a macrophysics called Relativity Theory that deals with very large systems such as galaxies and the universe itself, and a microphysics called Quantum Mechanics whose domain is the very small world of atoms and sub-atomic particles.

In this science the smallest entities—such as photons and electrons—are described as both particle and wave, showing that the least entity mirrors the dipolar nature of the greatest, or God, and vice versa. As above, so below. And in Taoism there is not one primordial force, but two: yin and yang.

Yet another variation on the theme of dipolarity is a dipolar rhythm that is pervasive throughout all nature. This two-phase universal rhythm reveals itself everywhere: in the beating of our hearts, in our breath, the action and rest of neurons and sensory organs, waking and sleeping, day and night caused by the rotation of the Earth in orbit round the sun, which brings us back to light seen as both particle and wave, and thus high and low tides . . .

A Logic of Ultimate Contrasts

Consider for a moment pairs of contrasting terms such as absolute and relative, cause and effect, object and subject, being and becoming— Charles Hartshorne calls these ultimate contrasts, or contraries. For many centuries it has been customary in theology to exalt one side of these contraries at the expense of the other—to such an extent that one side has been used exclusively as names or designations of deity. Thus we have God as Absolute, Universal, Cause, Infinite . . .

In thus exalting the absolute over the relative, being over becoming, Hartshorne argues that the medieval theologians did not get it right once and for all, but, on the contrary, they got it exactly backwards. And we, as inheritors of this tradition, when we do likewise, we repeat the same old, centuries-old, mistake.

When talking or reasoning about these metaphysical contraries or ultimate contrasts, Hartshorne holds that a certain logic must be kept in mind if we are to avoid error. He calls this a logic of ultimate contrasts and he has constructed a table that reveals the structure and implications of this logic. One feature of this logic is that all the relative terms are inclusive of the absolute terms. The relation of concrete to abstract perhaps shows this most clearly, for, by definition, the abstract is abstracted *from* the concrete.

An abstraction such as the number "two," for example, can be abstracted from the concrete reality of two elephants. From two elephants you can infer the idea of the number "two," but not vice versa. Does this not show that through mere analysis of the concrete the abstract can be discovered? But no amount of analysis of the abstract will ever lead from the number "two" to two elephants.

If Hartshorne's table is accurate, then to exalt the abstract over the concrete implies that we should value objects over subjects, the possible more than the actual, and that the movement from cause through effect is a descent from better to worse, from more to less. As Hartshorne says, if this is indeed the case, then "pessimism is a metaphysical axiom."[9]

It is of the nature, and the logic, of these contraries that the meaning of each term logically requires the contrast of its polar opposite. They are so related that neither, by itself, has any meaning. Collapse the contrast and you collapse the meaning.

In one aspect of what Hartshorne calls the "higher synthesis," the unity of these contraries is the inclusion of one in the other, as of whole to part, a unity that does not dissolve but preserves the polar distinctions. The unity is a unity of contrast, not a mere unity, for a mere unity is a mere abstraction. And what can the unity of God be but the unity of an evolving and ever-increasing reality, or actuality, and thus no mere unity but the unity of a maximal, ever-more-complex, and ever-growing diversity?

Another feature of this logic is that a basic asymmetry defines the relation between any pair of contrasting terms. Whereas the step from an a-term to an r-term is a creative step, the step in the reverse direction is merely a matter of logical entailment or analysis.

To quote Hartshorne: "Since r-terms are inclusive and express the overall truth, the entire table tells us that we can find the absolute only in the relative, objects . . . only in subjects, causes only in effects . . . earlier events only in later, being only in becoming, the eternal only in the temporal, the abstract only in the concrete, the potential only in the actual, the necessary only in the contingent . . . the infinite only in the finite . . . the specific only in the individual, the generic only in the specific . . . the metaphysical only in the generic, God in the necessary, and eternal essence only in divine contingent, temporal states. . . . If one wants to understand an a-term, one should locate it in its r-correlate. There are not subjects *and* objects but only objects in subjects, not causes and effects but only causes in effects, not earlier and later but earlier in later, not necessary things and contingent things but necessary constituents of contingent wholes . . . not God and the world but the world in God."[10]

If Hartshorne is correct about this, then the vast majority of humanity has had it exactly backwards for many centuries. Such upside-down thinking and the possibility that so many for so long have believed this suggests a collective blindness that gives one pause.

The following Table of Metaphysical Contraries, along with the Rules of Interpretation, is from Hartshorne's book, *The Zero Fallacy*, pp. 110-11:

Metaphysical Contraries

R-Terms	A-Terms
1r relative, dependent, internally related	1a absolute, independent, externally related
2r experience, subject	2a things experienced, objects
3r whole, inclusive	3a constituents, included
4r effect, conditioned	4a cause, condition (sine qua non)
5r later, successor	5a earlier, predecessor
6r becoming, nascent, being created	6a in being, already created
7r temporal, succeeding some, preceding others	7a nontemporal as (i) primordial and (ii) everlasting*
8r concrete, definite, particular	8a abstract, indefinite, universal
9r actual	9a potential
10r contingent	10a necessary
11r a portion, P, of process as past	11a earlier futuristic outline of P
12r finite	12a infinite
13r discrete	13a continuous
14r complex, with constituents	14a simple, without (or with fewer) constituents
15r singular, member ("mind")	15a composite, group, mass ("matter")
16r singular event, so and so now, individual state or actuality	16a so and so through change, individual being or existent
17r individual	17a specific character
18r specific character	18a generic character
19r generic character	19a metaphysical category
20r God now, divine state or actuality	20a God as primordial and everlasting, divine essence and existence
21r God now	21a God and the world as they just have been

* i. preceding every occasion, ii. succeeding every occasion

Rules of Interpretation

I. Proportionality: as an r-item in a specified context is to its a-correlate (say, 1r to 1a), so (*mutatis mutandis*) is any other r-item to its a-correlate (say, 2r to 2a). Thus (no. 2) an experience depends upon the things experienced, a subject upon things given to it, but these latter are independent of the subject.

II. Two-way, yet asymmetrical necessity: an r-item necessitates (10a) its particular contextual a-correlates; an a-item necessitates only that a class of suitable r-correlates be nonempty, the particular members of the class being (10r) contingent (others might have existed in their place). (In the case—19a—of metaphysical categories, the class of suitable r-correlates is the widest class of particular actualities; in the case of generic or specific characters, the r-correlate may be merely that the idea of the character is imagined in some actual experience.)

According to Hartshorne, it takes the entire table to describe God, not just the absolute column alone. And Whitehead says that "God is not to be treated as an exception to all metaphysical principles, invoked to save their collapse. He is their chief exemplification."[11] And indeed the divine dipolarity, as mentioned earlier, elegantly exemplifies the general principle of polar contrast.

Dual Transcendence

As an alternative to conceiving God in wholly absolute terms, Hartshorne offers his idea of "dual transcendence," or of God as "uniquely excellent in two really distinguishable aspects, the one infinite, absolute, immutable, eternal, and necessary as nothing else is, and the other finite, relative, mutable, temporal, and contingent, also as nothing else is. The divine preeminence is not to be captured by asserting one side of these ultimate contrasts and negating the other. Rather there is a divine form of finitude, relativity, mutability, temporality, and contingency that in principle surpasses all other conceivable forms."[12] He thus distinguishes the abstract essence from the concrete actuality of God's dipolar nature.

Alfred North Whitehead used a different terminology for essentially the same idea in distinguishing between God's abstract primordial nature and concrete consequent nature.

Hartshorne makes the excellent point that consequent "nature" should really be "natures," making it plural, for there is a new consequent nature each moment.

Cause and Effect

A metaphysical axiom long unchallenged is the notion that cause equals effect, that a cause cannot impart what it lacks. This is an error at least as old as Aristotle, and one that is still going strong. Ernest Holmes, in the Science of Mind textbook, on page 144, writes, "Cause and effect are really one . . . the effect equal[s] the cause." Process philosophy so opposes such a view that Hartshorne has even coined a term: "etiolatry"—meaning, "the idolatrous worship of causes."

If cause imparts to effect precisely no more and no less than what it in itself contains, then what we have is indeed an identity: cause = effect. Therefore, no longer is there any need to distinguish them as two different terms. Also, if this is indeed the case, then, in the cause-effect transaction, nothing has truly happened in any clear and meaningful sense except a mechanical duplication of one form by itself. Does not logical analysis show that if cause = effect then we have only the illusion of new events, and is not time itself reduced to an absurdity?

The basic misconception here is that an effect has a single cause whereas, in reality, there are innumerable strands of influence. The causes molding an experience are always many, but the effect is one: a unity of creative synthesis. In Whitehead's famous phrase, "The many become one, and are increased by one."[13]

From a process perspective, the causal factors *plus* creativity make it possible to produce an effect that somehow surpasses the causal factors themselves, and, indeed, if this is not the whole point in producing an effect, what is it? If effects cannot be a creative enrichment of reality, why bother?

In the notion that cause = effect, once again, as in so many other cases, the missing ingredient is creativity.

Perhaps, instead of the Law of Cause and Effect, we should think more in terms of the logic of cause and effect, or the modality of cause and effect. In such a logic or modality, there is a basic asymmetry in the relation between the two terms.

For Hartshorne, the asymmetry inherent in relations is a primordial principle. That asymmetry is primary, and more basic than symmetry, seems obvious from a process standpoint, for process itself, like time, is uni-directional and everlastingly exemplifies the asymmetry of change.

If the cause-and-effect transaction is not process, not change of some sort, what is it?

It Is No Accident That There Are Accidents

In Religious Science the claim is often heard that "There are no accidents," or, what amounts to the same thing, that God never makes a mistake. Quite to the contrary, I submit that not only are there accidents, but accidents, risks, and even danger are pervasive, and, if the words "freedom" and "creativity" mean anything at all, are integral to the very structure of reality. In other words, it is no accident that there are accidents.

The crux of all this has to do with the implications of multiple freedom, for even in the simple case of two such freedoms, husband and wife, things start to get chancy. For example: early on a cold winter morning, the husband, after freely choosing to do so, is enjoying a hot shower. Unaware of this, his wife decides to do a load of laundry, sets the water temperature to hot, and turns on the washer, thereby reducing the flow of hot water to the shower. A sudden howl from another part of the house startles the morning calm and alerts her that something is amiss. Two decisions, freely made by hubby and wife, have interfaced, or concurred, to form a third situation that was decided by neither. Accidents such as these are decided by no one, not even God, nor are they somehow fully determined by antecedent conditions—they just happen.

If there is multiple freedom on all levels, if there is free will, how can it not be the case that at times these free wills are on a collision course that results in an accident? With this in mind, given a vast variety of agents and forces within a vast universe where, at each and every successive moment, there are innumerable decisions and vectors of action, the complexity of which boggles the mind—how could all this avoid disorder, chaos, and even ultimate destruction, except . . . except thanks to some principle of order, something to coordinate, to limit, though not to eliminate, the play of chance, and to secure a ratio of risk and opportunity such that it all adds up to a coherent world, a world sufficiently good that the opportunities justify the risks?

A key word is "ratio." Too much freedom would result in chaos, too little, in a world of tedium and monotony. How can one ponder the complexity involved in determining this ratio and not be radically amazed at the awesome grandeur of the divine consciousness, a consciousness "whose datum is the universe."[14] This principle of order is, of course, God, who, as Whitehead so beautifully puts it, is "the poet of the world, with tender patience leading it by his vision of truth, beauty, and goodness."[15] Note that Whitehead says "leading" and not "coercing" or "fully determining."

There must be order and stability, true enough, but not the pervasive tedium and monotony implied by predeterminism. For relief from this, process celebrates and sings the creative spring of life, overflowing with the spice of unexpected variety, the zest of novelty and surprise, the dialectic of risk and opportunity, the dance of choice and chance.

Hartshorne argues that the universe is not "the expression of a single will only . . . it is a community of countless wills, whose supreme Will is not a tyrant, however benevolent or otherwise, nor yet the contriver of an all-inclusive machine, but the supreme inspiring genius of the Great Community of partly self-determining creatures. How this could be without risk of incompatibility and hence suffering in the innumerable decisions out of which existence is woven I at least cannot see. But I can see, I think, how sublime beauty and pervasive zest can and do result."[16]

Chance and indeterminacy are at the heart of quantum mechanics and evolutionary theory. In regard to his "uncertainty principle," Heisenberg held that this was no matter of our mere ignorance, but has to do with the very nature of reality itself.[17] Even the so-called laws of nature are no longer thought of as immutable, fixed, or even exact—but as statistical or probabilistic.

Concepts of probability are so central to Quantum theory that working physicists today have been compared to high-level actuaries. Nor are these laws causal—physical laws do not cause or create the behaviors they describe, they presuppose them. The vast number of eggs that some animals lay—is this not a cushion against accidents. In the world of nature, if ample provision were not made for accidents, the species would rapidly disappear. We see the prodigal waste of seed and life so that a few may survive. Surely we must concede some intuitive wisdom to our language, a language, like all other languages, one would suppose, overflowing with many variations on the theme of chance or accident. And consider this true story:

Three days after Hiroshima, on August 9, 1945, a B-29 was headed for the Japanese city of Kokura to drop the second atomic bomb, a plutonium-based device named "Fat Man." However, since there was heavy cloud cover over Kokura, the pilot changed course for Nagasaki, the secondary target, where the bomb was dropped, producing an explosion described as twenty times brighter than the sun. How can this be understood except in terms of chance or luck: astonishing good luck for the people of Kokura and catastrophic bad luck for the unfortunate folk of Nagasaki?

"There are no accidents." Is this not another slogan that, upon careful examination, proves unworthy of belief? The whole gist of what I have said can be put in four words: No risks, no opportunities. Or: _If_ freedom, _then_ contingency (or chance, accidents, risks, danger, randomness, and even at times catastrophe).

God Cannot See Disease

We are told, in Religious Science, that God cannot see disease. This is implied by the medieval doctrine that God is impassive and does not know and is not moved by the moving, contingent world. And this, in turn, stems from the notion that God is wholly immutable. We are back to Aristotle's Unmoved Mover.

Again, process philosophy would propose just the opposite—that, in Rabbi Abraham Heschel's words, "God is the most [and best] moved mover."

Process holds that the most fundamental relation of all is the "feeling _of_ feeling," and for this most basic transaction Whitehead has a technical term: prehension. God _feels_ our feelings, but _as ours_, and this is a distinction that makes all the difference. For Whitehead, "God is the great companion—the fellow-sufferer who understands."[18] Berdyaev concurs that God suffers and even says that there is tragedy in God.

And Hartshorne says, "Even the great message of the cross, that the divine suffers, is a truism for metaphysics as I conceive it. It _could not_ be that an inclusive mind excluded the suffering of the world from itself. Nothing is more irrational than the notion of an all-knowing mind that does not know suffering, in the only conceivable way in which suffering can be known—by feeling it."[19]

In a creative and an ever-evolving universe, with continual additions of novelty and beauty, that is, with new things to know, I can see no clear way that an intelligible idea of omniscience can ever be reconciled with the notion of a wholly immutable God.

It seems strange that God would not know the contingent truths that science comes to know. If this is correct, then where do we draw the line as to the contingent truths that God knows and those he doesn't? If one contingent truth, how not all?

Does God know the elementary particles referred to in physics? The atoms and molecules constituted by those particles? The molecules that constitute a blind eye, an arthritic joint, a decayed tooth? Can a dental X-ray "see" what God cannot see? Can a biopsy performed in a medical lab detect what God cannot know? I presume that God knows that there are diagnostic tools such as CAT scans. How, then, can he know that there are such tools and not know what they diagnose?

We have fossils of hominids in an early stage of human evolution. One of these fossils, as reported in the LA Times not long ago, has what scientists say is an obviously diseased organ. Is God not able to see or have knowledge of this fossil record of a diseased organ?

Can God know, or see, the basic building blocks of the universe? Well, the building blocks of the universe are not blocks at all, but events, occasions, processes, experiences. And if diseases are not experiences, what are they?

Perfection and Perfect Pattern

Religious Science teaches that healing is not a process, but a revelation of an already-existing perfection.

The idea of perfection is an abstraction, a universal, an ideal. An ideal, as ideal, cannot be fully determinate in the actual, or the particular. Perfection *exemplified* cannot itself be perfect. Ideals reside in the abstract realm of possibility, and, by definition, are not allowed full ingression into the here-and-now of actuality. This is to confuse the determinable with the determinate. Whether determined by the past, or determined by an ideal, this is still determinism.

Rather than the idea of an eternal, already-existing perfection, the process view would suggest an everlasting creative advance into novelty, with God, in every new moment, always there in the midst of our becoming—leading, luring, inviting, but never coercing—always offering a perfect plan, the perfect possibility, but one that changes from one moment to the next, adjusting to what the many experiences (both human and nonhuman, as there is some freedom at all levels) choose to do.

Instead of predetermining us to the dead past, even a past perfection, God, with his vision of truth and beauty, leads us into the ever more abundant life of an open future. Is this not made crystal clear by the 15-billion-year pageant of evolution, including the glory and the grandeur of biological evolution that produced our own species, the human animal. The human animal did not somehow float into existence "perfect, whole, and complete."

Instead of an already-existing model or pattern of the world, the process alternative is a general abstract principle, a principle of order and diversity, that can be realized in all kinds of creative and divergent ways. Moreover, rather than _conforming_ to a static pattern, a process approach would hold that healing is a dynamic process that produces the creative _breaking_ of a pattern: the pattern of the past. Perfection, such as perfect health, is not an already-established fact, but is the ideal aim of our co-creative efforts.

What is missing in the "perfect pattern" idea is the _creative_ particularization that occurs in the _creative_ synthesis in the _creative_ advance into novelty. Creativity, as self-surpassing process, is the very essence of reality. And God is no exception to this, but its chief exemplification. The idea of a perfect pattern also implies that being, a static abstraction, is more basic and fundamental than the dynamic process we call becoming. If Hartshorne's logic is correct, we have yet another example of upside-down thinking, or getting it exactly backwards.

In one of his most famous remarks, Ernest Holmes spoke about "perfect God, perfect man, perfect being." In times of challenge or trouble, this is the ideal we are always to turn to. But is it really a worthy ideal? If God, once and for all, created the universe perfect, whole, and complete—then a little reflection will show that we have not a paradise but a nightmare, for we then inhabit a world of iron determinism. If God has already done it all, what is there left for us to do?

In such a "world"—no world, really, worth that name—there's no useful work to be done, our decisions count for nothing, the evolution of the cosmos is a mere charade . . . what dignity is there in never doing more than merely revealing what is already there? If healing is a revelation of an already-existing perfection, and not a process, then, in a very real sense, the future is not before us, but—paradoxically— somehow behind us.

As to the idea of some sort of cosmic blueprint back of everything, Hartshorne says: "One form of teleology that we are, I think, well rid of is the notion of a single absolute world-plan, complete in every detail from all eternity, and executed with inexorable power. The objection is not solely that God would be made responsible for the imperfect adaptations and discords in nature. There is the further objection that the world process would be the idle duplicate of something in eternity. A God who eternally knew all that the fulfillment of his purpose would bring could have no need of that fulfillment or of purpose. Complete knowledge is complete possession: it is just because a man does not know in detail what 'knowing his friends better' would be like that he has the purpose to come to know them better. As Bergson and Peirce were among the first to see, even a world-purpose must be indeterminate as to details. For one thing, an absolute and inexorable purpose, supposing this meant anything, would deny individuality, self-activity, hence reality, to the lesser individuals, the creatures."[20]

Universal Subjective

It seems to me that Holmes made a major mistake in borrowing the idea and the term "Universal Subjective" from Thomas Troward. To read Troward is to immediately sense the presence of a brilliant mind, but one somehow limited by Newtonian horizons. Various aspects of Religious Science seem limited by these same horizons, and a metaphysical system that remains essentially Newtonian in some of its metaphysical foundations, and does not incorporate the radically new, even topsy-turvy insights of Relativity Theory and Quantum physics, some of which are a direct affront to common sense—how could this not eventuate in serious problems?

When Holmes describes the workings of the Universal Subjective as "mechanical" and "automatic," which he often does, this makes it sound like some kind of Holographic Replicating Machine—you have only to pop in a thought and it, since "it knows only to obey," will mechanically and automatically churn out an equivalent thing. Both terms, "mechanical" and "automatic" are the very opposite of "creative."

It also implies that the creative process is a power somehow unto itself that does not include, or seem to take into account, the causal influence of the past. This is in violation of Whitehead's Ontological Principle, which says that, apart from actual entities, there is no creativity.

If it knows _only_ to obey, than how does it know _what_ to create? For "to obey" is the antithesis of "to create." If it can create nothing that surpasses the "imprint of our thought," then it adds nothing to our thought and is thus superfluous. Whose impress of thought did the Universal Subjective receive before there were thinking animals to think those thoughts?

With freedom and creativity as ultimate principles, process philosophy suggests that there is no experience whatever—not even the "experience" of an electron—that "knows only to obey." Although it may be so small as to be statistically negligible, still there is always some trace of "self-determination" on even the lowest levels of actual entities. To attribute no freedom to that eminent and inexhaustible fountain of everlasting creativity, the creative process of God—this is sharply self-contradictory to a process understanding wherein freedom and creativity are, if not virtually equated, at least one the _sine qua non_ of the other.

That there must be some sort of "mechanism" to do the actual work of creativity, and to use the words "mechanical" and "automatic" to describe its operations—this betrays the limitations of a Newtonian horizon. Process thought holds that all creation is co-creation, understandable in terms of the unmediated interaction of Creator and creatures, with no need, so to speak, of a "middle man," or mechanism to do the work somewhere off in the background.

Hartshorne speaks of one aspect of our creativity that, for me at least, almost takes the breath away: "The question of the legendary bright child, 'Who made God'? has an answer. God in his concrete de facto state is in one sense simply self-made, like every creature spontaneously springing into being as something more than any causal antecedents could definitely imply. In another sense, or causally speaking, God, in his latest concrete state, is jointly 'made' or produced by God and the world in the prior states of each. We are not simply co-creators, with God, of the world, but in last analysis co-creators, with him, of himself. As the Socinians, Fechner, Lequier, Varisco, Berdyaev, and a few others saw, while the proud scholarly world in general as yet could not see, to do anything at all is to do something to God, to decide anything is to decide something divine."[21]

Prehension

No discussion of the revolution would be complete without some mention of Alfred North Whitehead's revolutionary concept of prehension. Therefore . . . consider, if you will, the nature of time as an emergent process of creative synthesis, time not as mere or pure succession, the succession of one moment or event by another, but as the objective modality of experience itself—as one experience derives from, must largely conform to, and yet is capable of surpassing, that prior experience which is its own immediate past.

Every becoming occasion of experience is inclusive of, and is shaped by, the ineluctable presence of the past. Such an occasion begins by feeling not just one, but the many influences that make up its immediate past, and thus it includes the spatial dimension as well as the temporal. The process by which the immediate past is included— Whitehead calls this "prehension." It is, as he says, "the most concrete form of relatedness."

A prehension is constituted by three parts:

1) the subject who experiences
2) the object or datum that is experienced
3) the subjective form of the experience, i.e., *how* the datum is experienced

That the past, or datum, must be included is a necessary and a "stubborn fact," but, as there is some measure of freedom in deciding *how* to include the immediate past, we thereby escape a strict determinism by antecedent conditions. To decide is to create.

Due to how evanescent they are and how deeply embedded in experience, prehensions occur largely in the background of consciousness, and indeed their momentary evanescings may, like a motion picture, flicker by unnoticed at ten frames a second or more.

Prehensions, or the "feeling of feeling," are the most basic transactions in reality. It is through prehension that an actual entity, as subject, both inherits from, and transcends, the past, and the key to all concrete relationships is this subject-object structure. This relational structure is temporal in that an earlier object is always prehended by a later subject, and asymmetrical in terms of influence: though Plato can affect me, I cannot affect him. Prehension, as the general principle of causality, explains the solidarity of the universe. To be is to be related.

Prehensions are ubiquitous throughout the universe and operative on all levels, ranging from the excitation of the "incredibly lively careers of . . . rhythmic adventures"[22] enjoyed by electrons, to the primitive advance-and-retreat gropings of unicellular beings such as the amoeba, all the way up to the infallible prehensions of deity, God, whose prehensions in every fraction of a second must number far beyond the reach of even our wildest imagination.

How is God inclusive of all things, and how is it that we can say that all things include God? (panentheism) Is it a merely simple or static inclusion—the way a package includes its contents? Surely not. God includes all by prehending all. If this is so, then we, as living creatures, are not in God, once and for all, as a final and accomplished fact; rather, at each new tick of the clock, because of increments of at least a modicum of change, we are prehended by God as a new entity.

Prehension is the way whereby God is immanent *in* the world, and also open to, and receptive of, influence *from* the world. In opposition to Aristotle and his Unmoved Mover, a moment's reflection on this may suggest that not only is God far busier than you may have thought, but that also: *so are you.* A Zen koan asks, "Who is the Artist who makes the grass green?"

Hartshorne on Whitehead's theory of prehension: "No more magnificent metaphysical generalization has ever been made.[23] Of all Whitehead's conceptions, perhaps the most original is prehension. No standard philosophical term current before his work is even roughly equivalent to it.[24] With the one three-word phrase, 'feeling *of* feeling,' as he used it for his single term prehension, Whitehead inaugurated a new epoch in the intellectual history of mankind.[25] In sum, prehension is one of the most original, central, lucid proposals ever offered in metaphysics."[26]

Conclusion

In exploring the revolution in metaphysics, this essay has primarily been a variation on one theme: that the errors I see in Religious Science are those ideas that deny creativity or somehow misconstrue the creative process itself.

Thus, with Omnipotence, the idea that God is the only power: this is the denial that God is only one power among others.

With Omniscience, we have the denial that there can be new things for God to know.

And Immutability: the denial that God can be self-surpassing.

A Logic of Ultimate Contrasts shows that to exalt being over becoming, is to exalt the static over the dynamic, and to indulge in upside-down thinking.

The Law of Cause and Effect: the denial that an effect can surpass a cause.

There Are No Accidents: by affirming a subtle determinism, denies that chance is integral to the creative process.

In affirming that God Cannot See Disease, but only perfection, we are placing God exclusively in the realm of abstract essence, and excluding him from creative and concrete actuality.

With the idea of a Perfect Pattern, we have the denial of creative particularization.

And finally, in regard to the Universal Subjective, analysis seems to show that this Newtonian apparatus, in its mechanical and automatic workings is, paradoxically, not creativity but, rather, its very antithesis.

I offer the above criticism in the spirit of Ernest Holmes' explicit stand that Religious Science is "open at the top."[27]

Although my contention is that Religious Science is fundamentally flawed in its metaphysical foundations, it is alive and well in its purpose, attitude, and practice. It's not so much the case that Holmes got it all wrong, but that he sometimes unknowingly presented only half the story, or a half-truth, and this is rather easily made consistent by simply telling the other half. The spirit of Religious Science is wonderful, invigorating, and refreshing. I know of no better practical approach to the challenges of everyday life. But in any metaphysical system there is always the danger that doctrine may ossify into dogma. To guard against this, may we be ever vigilant lest we lapse into dogmatic slumbers.

With the revolution wrought by Bill Gates and others in the computer industry, the idea of upgrades, and even frequent upgrades, should be familiar and even welcome. Who doesn't look forward to a new and exciting upgrade to a favorite software program?

Should we not be open to the idea of upgrading our spiritual operating systems? Did not Holmes himself say that if he came back in a hundred years and found Religious Science unchanged, he'd be surprised and disappointed?

There is a tradition in Zen Buddhism that if the student does not surpass the Master, the Master is thereby dishonored. Therefore, as we take Religious Science into the new millennium, let us honor Holmes, and the other pioneers of this movement, by recognizing and applauding their wonderful accomplishments—but let us honor them even more by glimpsing brave new horizons, and by accomplishing our own creative breakthroughs and self-surpassing innovations as we climb ever upward on that spiral of life that Ernest Holmes himself often spoke about.

Addenda

For those of a logical persuasion, Hartshorne provides a formal proof that there is contingency in God: "The following propositions form, I hold, an inconsistent triad. One of them must be false.

P. God has infallible knowledge that the world exists contingently.
Q. The world exists contingently.
R. There is in God nothing contingent.
1. P entails Q.
2. R entails that either P is necessary or God's knowledge is not in God (which is absurd).
3. Hence, Q is necessary (what a necessary proposition entails is necessary).

"The non-thomistic solution is to say with Socinus, Whitehead, and many others, that R *is false, God has contingent aspects* (*and* is *not wholly* immutable, impassable, and the other Thomistic attributes). A Thomist must either admit contingency in God, or deny that what P asserts is anything in God. But then what is it, something outside God? I am reminded that [Mortimer] Adler once wrote me that he had used a quotation from me similar, if I recall correctly, to the preceding on an examination and had been disappointed in his students' comments. I have wondered if I did not have some part in Adler's partial loss of confidence in the Thomistic form of theism."[28]

And one final quote:

"The almost complete overlooking of the second* of the three main types of doctrine has some title to be called **the greatest intellectual error mankind has ever made**, since it affects the most basic of all ideas, and since it escaped widespread detection for nearly the whole period of recorded philosophico-scientific development, at any rate for well over two thousand years. The only error perhaps surpassing it is indeed closely connected with it. This is the misconception of the nature and function of mathematics, the notion that mathematical knowledge is the model of all knowledge instead of merely the model of one aspect of knowledge, radically incomplete in itself, that therefore what mathematics knows is independent of everything else, pure 'being' above 'becoming,' and that therefore all thought about high matters should follow the mathematical pattern of deduction from easily established axioms, settled once for all, and should see as its ideal object some timeless essence, or sheer perfection, devoid, in Plato's memorable words, of motion and life and power. These words are all the more memorable because Plato is partly responsible, as he is usually interpreted, for the error. It is a great mathematico-philosophical mind, perhaps the nearest to Plato in combination of interests that our time has produced, Alfred North Whitehead, who has most effectively criticized this mistake. The whole modern era has seen the increasing emancipation of natural science from false mathematicism or deductivism; it is not surprising that theology has also been learning the lesson, though more quietly and with inferior publicity."[29]

* The "second" doctrine is the process, or neoclassical, idea of God as presented in this essay.

Endnotes

1. Charles Hartshorne, *The Philosophy and Psychology of Sensation* (1934), (Port Washington, New York: Kennikat Press, 1968), 271.

2. Charles Hartshorne, *Reality as Social Process: Studies in Metaphysics and Religion* (Glencoe, Ill.: The Free Press, 1953), 167.

3. Charles Hartshorne, *The Zero Fallacy and Other Essays in Neoclassical Philosophy*, ed. Mohammad Valady, (La Salle, Ill.: Open Court Publishing Company, 1997), 73.

4. Founded by Ernest Holmes, Religious Science, or the Science of Mind, is a branch of the New Thought movement, a movement that William James called "the religion of healthy-mindedness." Whether you call it religion, philosophy, faith, or simply a way of life, Science of Mind is optimistic: a positive spirituality that includes in its eclectic canon important truths from all the great religions of the world.

   A basic *practical* teaching is the power of thought to co-create, with God, the conditions of our lives, and a primary way to accomplish this is through a form of affirmative prayer that is structured in five steps: recognition, unification, realization, thanksgiving, and release. This power of thought is reflected in a popular slogan— Change your thinking, change your life.

   It is important to note that Science of Mind has no relation or connection whatsoever to Scientology, the movement founded by science-fiction writer L. Ron Hubbard.

   For William James' discussion of "the religion of healthy-mindedness," see Lectures IV and V in *The Varieties of Religious Experience*.

5. Charles Hartshorne, *Anselm's Discovery* (La Salle, Ill.: Open Court Publishing Company, 1965), 147.

6. Charles Hartshorne, *Omnipotence and Other Theological Mistakes* (Albany: State University of New York Press, 1984) 26-27.

7. Charles Hartshorne, *Creativity in American Philosophy* (Albany: State University of New York Press, 1984), 279.

8. Lewis Hahn, ed., *The Philosophy of Charles Hartshorne* (La Salle, Ill.: Open Court Publishing Company, 1991), 708.

9. Hartshorne, *The Zero Fallacy*, 116.

10. Hartshorne, *The Zero Fallacy*, 124.

11. Alfred North Whitehead, *Process and Reality* (1929), Corrected Edition, Edited by David Ray Griffin and Donald W. Sherburne (New York: The Free Press, 1978), 143.

12. Hartshorne, *Insights and Oversights of Great Thinkers: An Evaluation of Western Philosophy* (Albany: State University of New York Press, 1983), 376.

13. Whitehead, *Process and Reality*, 21.

14. Charles Hartshorne, *The Divine Relativity: A Social Conception of God* (New Haven: Yale University Press, 1983), 76.

15. Whitehead, *Process and Reality*, 346.

16. Charles Hartshorne, *The Logic of Perfection and Other Essays in Neoclassical Metaphysics*, (La Salle, Ill.: Open Court Publishing Company, 1962), 316.

17. Hartshorne, *Creativity in American Philosophy*, 139.

18. Whitehead, *Process and Reality*, 351.

19. Hartshorne, *Reality as Social Process*, 172.

20. Hartshorne, *The Logic of Perfection*, 205-06.

21. Charles Hartshorne, *A Natural Theology for Our Time* (La Salle, Ill.: Open Court Publishing Company, 1967), 113-14.

22. Charles Hartshorne, *Beyond Humanism: Essays in the New Philosophy of Nature* (1937), (Gloucester, Mass.: Peter Smith, 1975), 202.

23. Charles Hartshorne, *Aquinas to Whitehead: Seven Centuries of Metaphysics of Religion* (Milwaukee: Marquette University Publications, 1976), 41-42.

24. Hartshorne, *Creativity in American Philosophy*, 104.

25. Charles Hartshorne, *Wisdom as Moderation: A Philosophy of the Middle Way* (Albany: State University of New York Press, 1987), 25.

26. Hartshorne, *Creativity in American Philosophy*, 109.

27. As to just how open, consider the following: in his later years, as a guest speaker at a Fort Lauderdale church, Ernest Holmes began his talk with a thought that may surprise or even startle some of you. His opening statement was: "Someday, not too many years from now, *The Science of Mind* book will be filed away on a dusty old bookshelf and forgotten because so much new knowledge and information will be available that the book will become archaic."

28. Charles Hartshorne, *The Darkness and the Light* (Albany: State University of New York Press, 1990), 232-33.

29. Charles Hartshorne, *Man's Vision of God and the Logic of Theism* (Hamden, Conn.: Archon Books, 1964), 28.

About the Author

Hyatt Carter is a licensed counselor, a writer/editor, and a lifelong scholar with a wide spectrum of interests. He is a longtime member of Founder's Center for Positive Spirituality and served for four years on the Board of Trustees there. He is assistant editor of *The Word*, a publication now in its 54th year, and co-editor, along with philosopher Randall Auxier, of Charles Hartshorne's *The Unity of Being*, a new book that will be published soon by Open Court.

His fields of expertise include process philosophy, Zen Buddhism, positive psychology, and contemplative spirituality. Three of the essays in this volume are longer versions of papers he presented at national conventions. In the spirit of serious play, or maybe *four-play*, he continues to add to his ever-growing collection of what he calls Meta-Fours—significant and sometimes amusing ways in which the archetypal number four seems to turn up all over the place, such as in his personal slogan: May the *fours* be with you!

For the last twenty years he and his wife Linda have lived in the seaside community of Marina del Rey, California.

Website:
http://hyattcarter.com